THE THREE WORLDS OF WELFARE
CAPITALISM

The Three Worlds of Welfare Capitalism

Gøsta Esping-Andersen

Princeton University Press

Princeton, New Jersey

Copyright 1990 © Gøsta Esping-Andersen

Published by Princeton University Press,
41 William Street, Princeton, New Jersey 08540

Reprinted 1991, 1993, 1998

Library of Congress Cataloging-in-Publication Data
Esping-Andersen, Gøsta, 1947–
The three worlds of welfare capitalism.
Includes bibliographical references.
1. Welfare economics.   I. Title.   II. Title: 3 worlds
of welfare capitalism.
HB846.E78   1990   330.15'56   89–24254
ISBN 0–691–09457–8 (alk. paper)
ISBN 0–691–02857–5 (pbk.: alk. paper)

Printed in Great Britain

10   9   8   7   6   5

Contents

Tables

Preface

It may not show, but this is a book that stands on a veritable mountain of data and years of endless statistical manipulation. It uses three large data bases that have been constructed over the past eight years. In my analyses of the institutional characteristics of welfare-state programs, the data derive from the comparative welfare-state project begun by Walter Korpi and myself in 1981 at the Swedish Institute for Social Research. Joakim Palme contributed enormously in collecting, assembling, and now analyzing, the data. Here I must also acknowledge my gratitude to the Bank of Sweden Tercentenniary Fund and the Swedish Delegation for Social Research for research funding. Several tables in the following chapters are constructed on the basis of these data; the reference used is '*SSIB data files*' (Svensk Socialpolitik i International Belysning).

Many of the analyses on welfare-state and labor-market interactions are based on our WEEP data base (Welfare State Entry and Exit Project); again, the reader will find a number of table references to '*WEEP data files*'. This is a multi-national project (covering ten nations over 25 years) that, begun in 1985, was directed by Jon Eivind Kolberg in Scandinavia and Lee Rainwater, Martin Rein, and myself at the Science Center in Berlin. It would fill at least a whole chapter to list all the underlying sources. In the main, however, the WEEP data derive from national labor-force surveys and census data. The WEEP data base would not have come into existence without the help of Kaare Hagen, Tom Cusack, and Frieder Nashold. Much gratitude is also owed to the Nordic Council and the Science Center in Berlin for research financing.

The third data set has been constructed here at the European

University Institute in Florence with the help of Gianna Giannelli and Joyce Reese, and financed with the generous help of the Research Council of the EUI. It contains both time-series and cross-sectional data on employment structure and change in European countries and the United States. Here, we have relied principally on raw tables from censuses and unpublished data provided to us directly by the national statistical authorities. When we employ these data in our tables, we refer directly to the underlying source. It is disgraceful that we usually forget the people who, in the first place, furnished us with the data. We depend heavily on their services, and they often devote substantial efforts to what, to them, may appear as rather absurd requests.

In building our data sets, we have approached countless government departments and statistical offices in 18 nations over the past eight years. In its own right, this is a valuable research experience that can be transmitted to others. If I am permitted the prerogative of international ranking, this is one case in which the United States is an unchallenged number one. There is no other country that I know of which even comes near the quantity, quality, helpfulness, and generosity of the United States Department of Labor, Bureau of the Census, or Social Security Administration. With some distance to travel, Sweden, Norway, and Great Britain follow suit in the rankings. Denmark and Italy are helpful, but burdened with really second-rate statistical systems. In my experience with social security and labor-force data, the lowest ranking must go to Germany (where you hardly ever get anything) and the Netherlands (where you have to pay for everything). In Switzerland, the banks and insurance companies often constitute the principal sources of data.

In terms of its substance, this book probably began when Martin Rein persuaded me that social policy can be an extraordinarily exciting field of research. Half of the ideas that generated this volume have sprung from my fortune of collaborating with Martin Rein and Lee Rainwater; the other half from my work with Walter Korpi, Jon Eivind Kolberg, and John Myles. Indeed, these five people could have just sat down together and written a better version of this book. Attentive readers will surely recognize the presence of Martin Rein, especially in chapters 6 and 8; of John Myles in chapter 4; and of Jon Eivind Kolberg in chapter 6.

It would deflate their real importance were I to list all the other many persons who have helped me along the way. I shall thank them all in person, tomorrow.

Chapter 1 is a modified version of an article first published in the *Canadian Review of Sociology and Anthropology* (Spring, 1989). Likewise, a somewhat different version of chapter 7 was first published in H. Keman, H. Paloheimo, and P. F. Whiteley (eds), *Coping With The Crisis* (London: Sage Publications (1987)). I am very grateful to both publishers for their permission to include these two publications in the present book.

Introduction

The welfare state has been a favored topic of research for many years now. This is not very surprising when we consider its fantastic pace of growth in most countries during the 1960s and 1970s. What once were night-watchman states, law-and-order states, militarist states, or even repressive organs of totalitarian rule, are now institutions predominantly preoccupied with the production and distribution of social well-being. To study the welfare state is therefore a means to understand a novel phenomenon in the history of capitalist societies.

In the league of advanced capitalist democracies, states clearly vary considerably with regard to their accent on welfare. Even if the lion's share of expenditures or personnel serves welfare aims, the kind of welfare provided will be qualitatively different, as will its prioritization relative to competing activities, be they warfare, law and order, or the promotion of profits and trade.

The historical characteristics of states have played a determinant role in forging the emergence of their welfare-statism. In his recent book, Giddens (1985) highlights the causal influence of wars, a factor which has been almost wholly neglected in the large literature on welfare-state origins. In our account, this argument cannot be confronted directly. Yet, it is given some indirect support in our emphasis on the relative strength of absolutist and authoritarian rule. The leading theme in our account, however, is that the history of political class coalitions is the most decisive cause of welfare-state variations.

The welfare state has been approached both narrowly and broadly. Those who take the narrower view see it in terms of the traditional terrain of social amelioration: income transfers and social services, with perhaps some token mention of the housing question. The broader view often frames its questions in terms of political economy, its interests focused on the state's larger role in managing and organizing the economy. In the broader view, therefore, issues of employment, wages, and overall macro-economic steering are considered integral components in the welfare-state complex. In a sense, this approach identifies its subject matter as the 'Keynesian welfare state' or, if you like, 'welfare capitalism'.

In this book, we follow the broad approach; this is why we begin with the issues of classical and modern political economy, and why we devote the last third of the book to issues of employment and general macro-economic steering. This is also why we prefer to employ terms such as 'welfare capitalism' and 'welfare-state regimes'.

'Welfare-state regimes' is, in a way, the organizing concept of the book. The reasons are several. First, as it is commonly used, the concept of the welfare state is too narrowly associated with the conventional social-amelioration policies. Second, what we will show is that contemporary advanced nations cluster not only in terms of how their traditional social-welfare policies are constructed, but also in terms of how these influence employment and general social structure. To talk of 'a regime' is to denote the fact that in the relation between state and economy a complex of legal and organizational features are systematically interwoven.

The broader approach implies a trade-off. Since our intention is to understand the 'big picture', we shall not be able to dwell on the detailed characteristics of the various social programs. So, when we study pensions, for example, our concern is not pensions *per se*, but the ways in which they elucidate how different nations arrive at their peculiar public–private sector mix. A related trade-off is that large-scale comparisons, such as ours, prohibit detailed treatments of individual countries. I am convinced that readers knowledgeable about any of the 18 nations included in the study will feel that my treatment of 'their' country is superficial, if not outright misrepresentative. This is unfortunately the price to be paid for making grand comparisons, given the intellectual limitations of the author and the page limitations set by the publisher.

This book has been written with two beliefs in mind. The first is that existing theoretical models of the welfare state are inadequate. The ambition is to offer a reconceptualization and re-theorization on the basis of what we consider important about the welfare state. The existence of a social program and the amount of money spent on it may be less important than what it does. We shall devote many pages to arguing that issues of de-commodification, social stratification, and employment are keys to a welfare state's identity. The second belief is that only comparative empirical research will adequately disclose the fundamental properties that unite or divide modern welfare states. The distant dream of social science is to formulate laws of societal motion. Whether formulated in terms of the logic of capitalism, industrialism, modernization, or nation-building, they nearly always posit similar and convergent evolutionary paths. Obviously, laws are not supposed to have deviant cases.

The comparative approach is meant to (and will) show that welfare states are not all of one type. Indeed, the study presented here identifies three highly diverse regime-types, each organized around its own discrete logic of organization, stratification, and societal integration. They owe their origins to different historical forces, and they follow qualitatively different developmental trajectories.

In the first chapter, our task is to reintegrate the welfare-state debate into the intellectual tradition of political economy. This serves to bring into sharper focus the principal theoretical questions involved. On this basis we will be in a better position to specify the salient characteristics of welfare states. The convention of conceptualizing welfare states in terms of their expenditures will no longer do. In a sense, our ultimate goal is to 'sociologize' the study of welfare states. Most studies have assumed a world of linearity: of more or less power, industrialization, or spending. We will in this book understand welfare states as clustering into three different types of regime that we have labeled conservative, liberal, and 'social democratic'. Their crystallization and subsequent development can hardly be explained with analytical parsimony.

In chapters 2, 3, and 4 we offer a reconceptualization of what we believe to be the salient characteristics of welfare states. The extension of social rights has always been regarded as the essence of social policy. Inspired by the contributions of Karl Polanyi, we choose to view social rights in terms of their capacity for 'de-commodification'. The outstanding criterion for social rights must be the degree to which they permit people to make their living standards independent of pure market forces. It is in this sense that social rights diminish citizens' status as 'commodities'.

Social stratification is part and parcel of welfare states. Social policy is supposed to address problems of stratification, but it also produces it. Equality has always been what welfare states were supposed to produce, yet the image of equality has always remained rather vague. In some analyses it is simply taken for granted that social benefits diminish inequalities. In others, the focus is on the eradication of poverty or the overall distribution of income. The really neglected issue is the welfare state as a stratification system in its own right. Does it enhance or diminish existing status or class differences; does it create dualisms, individualism, or broad social solidarity? These are the issues of chapter 3.

Both social rights and social stratification are shaped by the nexus of state and market in the distribution system. To a social democrat, reliance on the market for the basic means of welfare is problematic because it fails to provide inalienable rights and because it is inequitable. To a laissez-faire liberal, reliance on the welfare state is dangerous because it cripples freedom and efficiency. In chapter 4, we examine how the interplay of public and private sector has contributed to the crystallization of the pension-mix in different welfare-state regimes. The point is two-fold. First, we cannot grasp the welfare state without locating its activities in relation to the private sector. Second, it is a myth to think that either markets or the state are more naturally equipped to develop welfare. Instead, markets are often politically created and form an integral part of the overall welfare-state regime.

Part I of the book develops the dimensions of comparative welfare states, and demonstrates the clustering of advanced capitalist democracies into three distinct regimes. Part II examines how this came to be. In this analysis we can obviously not limit ourselves to why some welfare states score more or less than others on some attribute. We have to account for why the world is composed of three qualitatively different welfare-state logics. In chapter 5, we adopt the standard comparative correlational approach to identify the relative importance of political forces in the creation of welfare states. In line with the prevailing academic consensus today, we must conclude that politics not only matters, but is decisive. In contrast to most studies, however, it is not necessarily the political mobilization of the working classes that matters here. For some regimes, their role has been marginal and we must instead understand the evolution of welfare states here as the result of the state's history of nation-building and/or the influence of conservatism and Catholicism. We have tried to embed our explanations in the political histories of nations.

The second part of the book broadens the field of investigation considerably. Here the focus is not so much on what created welfare states as on what their effects are on our economies. Specifically, we examine three facets of welfare-state–employment interactions. To begin with, in chapter 6 we lay out an argument for why labor-market structures are closely tied to welfare-state regimes. We show that the coincidence of the two is striking, and that the behavioral characteristics of labor markets cross-nationally depend on how the welfare state is constructed.

In chapters 7 and 8, we examine in greater detail how welfare states affect employment by selecting a representative country from each of our three types of regime. In chapter 7, the focus is on nations' capacities to maintain full employment; in chapter 8, it is on the post-industrial transformation of employment structures. In the former chapter, we analyze how welfare states have become key institutions in managing the dilemmas and tensions that emerge with a full-employment commitment. In the latter, we argue that it is false to believe in the emergence of a general post-industrial employment path. We identify three qualitatively diverse trajectories, each of which owes its dynamic to the structuring of the welfare state. We conclude that each trajectory produces its own stratification outcome, and results, therefore, in very different conflict scenarios.

The book, then, sees the welfare state as a principal institution in the construction of different models of post-war capitalism. Hence, the choice of its title, *The Three Worlds of Welfare Capitalism*.

PART 1

The Three Welfare-State Regimes

1

The Three Political Economies of the Welfare State*

The Legacy of Classical Political Economy

Most debates on the welfare state have been guided by two questions. First, will the salience of class diminish with the extension of social citizenship? In other words, can the welfare state fundamentally transform capitalist society? Second, what are the causal forces behind welfare-state development?

These questions are not recent. Indeed, they were formulated by the nineteenth-century political economists 100 years before any welfare state can rightly be said to have come into existence. The classical political economists – whether of liberal, conservative, or Marxist persuasion – were preoccupied with the relationship between capitalism and welfare. They certainly gave different (and usually normative) answers, but their analyses converged around the relationship between market (and property), and the state (democracy).

Contemporary neo-liberalism is very much an echo of classical liberal political economy. For Adam Smith, the market was the superior means for the abolition of class, inequality, and privilege. Aside from a necessary minimum, state intervention would only stifle the equalizing process of competitive exchange and create monopolies, protectionism, and inefficiency: the state upholds class; the market can potentially undo class society (Smith, 1961, II, esp. pp. 232–6).[1]

Liberal political economists were hardly of one mind when it came

* This chapter is adapted from an article which previously appeared in the *Canadian Review of Sociology and Anthropology*, Vol. 26:2 (1989) under the title 'The three political economies of the welfare state'.

to policy advocacy. Nassau Senior and later Manchester liberals emphasized the laissez-faire element in Smith, rejecting any form of social protection outside the cash nexus. J. S. Mill and the 'reformed liberals', in turn, were proponents of a modicum of political regulation. Yet they all were agreed that the road to equality and prosperity should be paved with a maximum of free markets and a minimum of state interference.

Their enthusiastic embrace of market capitalism may now appear unjustified. But we must not forget that the reality they spoke of was a state upholding absolutist privileges, mercantilist protectionism, and pervasive corruption. What they attacked was a system of government that repressed their ideals of both freedom and enterprise. Hence, theirs was revolutionary theory, and from this vantage point, we can understand why Adam Smith sometimes reads like Karl Marx.[2]

Democracy became an Achilles' heel to many liberals. As long as capitalism remained a world of small property owners, property itself would have little to fear from democracy. But with industrialization, the proletarian masses emerged, for whom democracy was a means to curtail the privileges of property. The liberals rightly feared universal suffrage, for it would be likely to politicize the distributional struggle, pervert the market, and fuel inefficiencies. Many liberals discovered that democracy would usurp or destroy the market.

Both conservative and Marxist political economists understood this contradiction, but proposed, of course, opposite solutions. The most coherent conservative critique of laissez-faire came from the German historical school, in particular from Friedrich List, Adolph Wagner, and Gustav Schmoller. They refused to believe that the raw cash-nexus of the market was the only or the best guaranteee of economic efficiency. Their ideal was the perpetuation of patriarchy and absolutism as the best possible legal, political, and social shell for a capitalism without class struggle.

One prominent conservative school promoted the 'monarchical welfare state', which would guarantee social welfare, class harmony, loyalty, and productivity. In this model, an efficient production system comes not from competition, but from discipline. An authoritarian state would be far superior to the chaos of markets in harmonizing the good of the state, community, and individual.[3]

Conservative political economy emerged in reaction to the French Revolution and the Paris Commune. It was avowedly nationalistic and anti-revolutionary, and sought to arrest the democratic impulse. It feared social leveling, and favored a society that retained both hierarchy and class. Status, rank, and class were natural and given; class conflicts, however, were not. If we permit democratic mass participation, and allow authority and status boundaries to dissolve, the result is a collapse of the social order.

Marxist political economy not only abhorred the market's atomizing effects, but also attacked the liberal claim that markets guarantee equality. Since, as Dobb (1946) puts it, capital accumulation disowns people of property, the end result will be ever-deeper class divisions. And as these generate sharpened conflicts, the liberal state will be forced to shed its ideals of freedom and neutrality, and come to the defence of the propertied classes. For Marxism this is the foundation of class dominance.

The central question, not only for Marxism but for the entire contemporary debate on the welfare state, is whether, and under what conditions, the class divisions and social inequalities produced by capitalism can be undone by parliamentary democracy.

Fearing that democracy might produce socialism, the liberals were hardly eager to extend it. The socialists, in contrast, suspected that parliamentarism would be little more than an empty shell or, as Lenin suggested, a mere 'talking shop' (Jessop, 1982). This line of analysis, echoed in much of contemporary Marxism, produced the belief that social reforms were little more than a dike in a steadily leaking capitalist order. By definition, they could not be a response to the desire of the working classes for emancipation.[4]

It took major extensions of political rights before the socialists could wholeheartedly embrace a more optimistic analysis of parliamentarism. The theoretically most sophisticated contributions came from the Austro-German Marxists such as Adler, Bauer, and Eduard Heimann. According to Heimann (1929), it may have been the case that conservative reforms were motivated by little else than a desire to repress labor mobilization. But once introduced, they become contradictory: the balance of class power is fundamentally altered when workers enjoy social rights, for the social wage lessens the worker's dependence on the market and employers, and thus turns into a potential power resource. To Heimann, social policy introduces an alien element into the capitalist political economy. It is a Trojan horse that can penetrate the frontier between capitalism and socialism. This intellectual position has enjoyed quite a renaissance in recent Marxism (Offe, 1985; Bowles and Gintis, 1986).

The social democratic model, as outlined above, did not necessarily abandon the orthodoxy that, ultimately, fundamental equality requires economic socialization. Yet historical experience soon demonstrated that socialization was a goal that could not be pursued realistically through parliamentarism.[5]

Social democracy's embrace of parliamentary reformism as its dominant strategy for equality and socialism was premised on two arguments. The first was that workers require social resources, health, and education to participate effectively as socialist citizens. The second argument was that social policy is not only emancipatory, but is also a precondition for economic efficiency (Myrdal and Myrdal, 1936). Following Marx, in this argument the strategic value of welfare policies is that they help promote the onward march of the productive forces in capitalism. But the beauty of the social democratic strategy was that social policy would also result in power mobilization. By eradicating poverty, unemployment, and complete wage dependency, the welfare state increases political capacities and diminishes the social divisions that are barriers to political unity among workers.

The social democratic model, then, is father to one of the leading hypotheses of contemporary welfare-state debate: parliamentary class-mobilization is a means for the realization of the socialist ideals of equality, justice, freedom, and solidarity.

The Political Economy of the Welfare State

Our forebears in political economy defined the analytic basis of much recent scholarship. They isolated the key variables of class, state, market, and democracy, and they formulated the basic propositions about citizenship and class, efficiency and equality, capitalism and socialism. Contemporary social science distinguishes itself from classical political economy on two scientifically vital fronts. First, it defines itself as a positive science and shies away from normative prescription (Robbins, 1976). Second, classical political economists had little interest in historical variability: they saw their efforts as leading towards a system of universal laws. Although contemporary political economy sometimes still clings to the belief in absolute truths, the comparative and historical method that today underpins almost all good political economy is one that reveals variation and permeability.

Despite these differences, most recent scholarship has as its focal point the state–economy relationship defined by nineteenth-century political economists. And, given the enormous growth of the welfare state, it is understandable that it has become a major test case for contending theories of political economy.

We shall review below the contributions of comparative research on the development of welfare states in advanced capitalist countries. It will be argued that most scholarship has been misdirected, mainly because it became detached from its theoretical foundations. We must therefore recast both the methodology and the concepts of political economy in order to adequately study the welfare state. This will constitute the focus of the final section of this chapter.

Two types of approach have dominated in explanations of welfare states; one stresses structures and whole systems, the other, institutions and actors.

THE SYSTEMS/STRUCTURALIST APPROACH

Systems or structuralist theory seeks to capture the logic of development holistically. It is the system that 'wills', and what happens is therefore easily interpreted as a functional requisite for the reproduction of society and economy. Because its attention is concentrated on the laws of motion of systems, this approach is inclined to emphasize cross-national similarities rather than differences; being industrialized or capitalist over-determines cultural variations or differences in power relations.

One variant begins with a theory of industrial society, and argues that industrialization makes social policy both necessary and possible — necessary because pre-industrial modes of social reproduction, such as the family, the church, *noblesse oblige*, and guild solidarity are destroyed by the forces attached to modernization, such as social mobility, urbanization, individualism, and market dependence. The crux of the matter is that the market is no adequate substitute because it caters only to those who are able to perform in it. Hence, the 'welfare function' is appropriated by the nation-state.

The welfare state is also made possible by the rise of modern bureaucracy as a rational, universalist, and efficient form of organization. It is a means for managing collective goods, but also a center of power in its own right, and it will thus be inclined to promote its own growth. This kind of reasoning has informed the so-called 'logic of industrialism' perspective, according to which the welfare state will emerge as the modern industrial economy destroys traditional social institutions (Flora and Alber, 1981; Pryor, 1969). But the thesis has difficulties explaining why government social policy only emerged 50 and sometimes even 100 years after traditional community was effectively destroyed. The basic response draws on Wagner's Law of 1883 (Wagner, 1962) and on Alfred Marshall (1920) – namely that a certain level of economic development, and thus surplus, is needed in order to permit the diversion of scarce resources from productive use (investment) to welfare (Wilensky and Lebeaux, 1958). In this sense, this perspective follows in the footsteps of the old liberals. Social redistribution endangers efficiency, and only at a certain economic level will a negative-sum trade-off be avoidable (Okun, 1975).

The new structuralist Marxism is strikingly parallel. Abandoning its classical forebears' strongly action-centered theory, its analytical starting-point is that the welfare state is an inevitable product of the capitalist mode of production. Capital accumulation creates contradictions that compel social reform (O'Connor, 1973). In this tradition of Marxism, as in its 'logic of industrialism' counterpart, welfare states hardly need to be promoted by political actors, whether they be unions, socialist parties, humanitarians, or enlightened reformers. The point is that the state, as such, is positioned in such a way that the collective needs of capital are served, regardless. The theory is thus premised on two crucial assumptions: first, that power is structural, and second, that the state is 'relatively' autonomous from class directives (Poulantzas, 1973; Block, 1977; for a recent critical assessment of this literature, see Therborn, 1986a; and Skocpol and Amenta, 1986).

The 'logic of capitalism' perspective invites difficult questions. If, as Przeworski (1980) has argued, working-class consent is assured on the basis of material hegemony, that is, self-willed subordination to the system, it is difficult to see why up to 40 percent of the national product must be allocated to the legitimation activities of a welfare state. A second problem is to derive state activities from a 'mode of production' analysis. Eastern Europe may perhaps not qualify as socialist, but neither is it capitalist. Yet there we find 'welfare states', too. Perhaps accumulation has functional requirements no matter how it proceeds? (Skocpol and Amenta, 1986; Bell, 1978).

THE INSTITUTIONAL APPROACH

The classical political economists made it clear why democratic institutions should influence welfare-state development. The liberals feared that full democracy might jeopardize markets and inaugurate socialism. Freedom, in their view, necessitated a defence of markets against political intrusion. In practice, this is what the laissez-faire state sought to accomplish. But it was this divorce of politics and economy which fuelled much institutionalist analysis. Represented best by Polanyi (1944), but also by a number of anti-democratic exponents of the historical school, the institutional approach insists that any effort to isolate the economy from social and political institutions will destroy human society. The economy must be embedded in social communities in order for it to survive. Thus, Polanyi sees social policy as one necessary precondition for the reintegration of the social economy.

An interesting recent variant of institutional alignment theory is the argument that welfare states emerge more readily in small, open economies that are particularly vulnerable to international markets. As Katzenstein (1985) and Cameron (1978) show, there is a greater inclination to regulate class-distributional conflicts through government and interest concertation when both business and labor are captive to forces beyond domestic control.

The impact of democracy on welfare states has been argued ever since J. S. Mill and Alexis de Tocqueville. The argument is typically phrased without reference to any particular social agent or class. It is in this sense that it is institutional. In its classical formulation, the thesis was simply that majorities will favor social distribution to compensate for market weakness or market risks. If wage-earners are likely to demand a social wage, so are capitalists (or farmers) apt to demand protection in the form of tariffs, monopoly, or subsidies. Democracy is an institution that cannot resist majority demands.

In its modern formulations, the democracy thesis has many variants. One identifies stages of nation-building in which the extension of full citizenship must also include social rights (Marshall, 1950; Bendix, 1964; Rokkan, 1970). A second variant, developed by both pluralist and public-choice theory, argues that democracy will nurture intense party competition around the median voter which, in turn, will fuel rising public expenditure. Tufte (1978), for example, argues that major extensions of public intervention occur around elections as a means of voter mobilization.

This approach also faces considerable empirical problems (Skocpol and Amenta, 1986). When it holds that welfare states are more likely to develop the more democratic rights are extended, the thesis confronts the historical oddity that the first major welfare-state initiatives occurred prior to democracy and were powerfully motivated by the desire to arrest its realization. This was certainly the case in France under Napoleon III, in Germany under Bismarck, and in Austria under von Taaffe. Conversely, welfare-state development was most retarded where democracy arrived early, such as in the United States, Australia, and Switzerland. This apparent contradiction can be explained, but only with reference to social classes and social structure: nations with early democracy were overwhelmingly agrarian and dominated by small property owners who used their electoral powers to reduce, not raise, taxes (Dich, 1973). In contrast, ruling classes in authoritarian polities were better positioned to impose high taxes on an unwilling populace.

Social Class as a Political Agent

We have noted that the case for a class-mobilization thesis flows from social democratic political economy. It differs from structuralist and institutional analyses in its emphasis on the social classes as the main agents of change, and in its argument that the balance of class power determines distributional outcomes. To emphasize active class-mobilization does not necessarily deny the importance of structured or hegemonic power (Korpi, 1983). But it is held that parliaments are, in principle, effective institutions for the translation of mobilized power into desired policies and reforms. Accordingly, parliamentary politics is capable of overriding hegemony, and can be made to serve interests that are antagonistic to capital. Further, the class-mobilization theory assumes that welfare states do more than simply alleviate the current ills of the system: a 'social democratic' welfare state will, in its own right, establish critical power resources for wage-earners, and thus strengthen labor movements. As Heimann (1929) originally held, social rights push back the frontiers of capitalist power.

The question of why the welfare state itself is a power resource is vital for the theory's applicability. The answer is that wage-earners in the market are inherently atomized and stratified – compelled to compete, insecure, and dependent on decisions and forces beyond their control. This limits their capacity for collective solidarity and mobilization. The social rights, income security, equalization, and eradication of poverty that a universalistic welfare state pursues are necessary preconditions for the strength and unity that collective power mobilization demands (Esping-Andersen, 1985a).

The single most difficult problem for this thesis is to specify the conditions for power mobilization. Power depends on the resources that flow from electoral numbers and from collective bargaining. Power mobilization, in turn, depends on levels of trade-union organization, share of votes, and parliamentary and cabinet seats held by left or labor parties. But the power of one agent cannot simply be indicated by its own resources: it will depend on the resources of contending forces, on the historical durability of its mobilization, and on patterns of power alliances.

There are several valid objections to the class-mobilization thesis. Three in particular are quite fundamental. One is that the locus of decision-making and power may shift from parliaments to neo-corporatist institutions of interest intermediation (Shonfield, 1965; Schmitter and Lembruch, 1979). A second criticism is that the capacity of labor parties to influence welfare-state development is circumscribed by the structure of right-wing party power. Castles (1978; 1982) has argued that the degree of unity among the conservative parties is more important than is the activated power of the left. Other authors have emphasized the fact that denominational (usually social Catholic) parties in countries such as Holland, Italy, and Germany mobilize large sections of the working classes and pursue welfare-state programs not drastically at variance with their socialist competitors (Schmidt, 1982; Wilensky, 1981). The class-mobilization thesis has, rightly, been criticized for its Swedocentrism, i.e. its inclination to define the process of power mobilization too much on the basis of the rather extraordinary Swedish experience (Shalev, 1984).

These objections hint at a basic fallacy in the theory's assumptions about the class formation: we cannot assume that socialism is the natural basis for wage-earner mobilization. Indeed, the conditions under which workers become socialists are still not adequately documented. Historically, the natural organizational bases of worker mobilization were pre-capitalist communities, especially the guilds, but also the Church, ethnicity, or language. A ready-made reference to false consciousness will not do to explain why Dutch, Italian, or American workers continue to mobilize around non-socialist principles. The dominance of socialism among the Swedish working class is as much a puzzle as is the dominance of confessionalism among the Dutch.

The third and perhaps most fundamental objection has to do with the model's linear view of power. It is problematic to hold that a numerical increase in votes, unionization, or seats will translate into more welfare-statism. First, for socialist as for other parties, the magical '50 percent' threshold for parliamentary majorities seems practically insurmountable (Przeworski, 1985). Second, if socialist parties represent working classes in the traditional sense, it is clear that they will never succeed in their project. In very few cases has the traditional working class been numerically a majority; and its role is rapidly becoming marginal.[6]

Probably the most promising way to resolve the combined linearity and working-class minority problem lies in recent applications of Barrington Moore's path-breaking class-coalition thesis to the transformation of the modern state (Weir and Skocpol, 1985; Gourevitch, 1986; Esping-Andersen, 1985a; Esping-Andersen and Friedland,

1982). Thus, the origins of the Keynesian full-employment commitment and the social democratic welfare-state edifice have been traced to the capacity of (variably) strong working-class movements to forge a political alliance with farmer organizations; additionally, it is arguable that sustained social democracy has come to depend on the formation of a new-working-class–white-collar coalition.

The class-coalitional approach has additional virtues. Two nations, such as Austria and Sweden, may score similarly on working-class mobilization variables, and yet produce highly unequal policy results. This can be explained by differences in the history of coalition formation in two countries: the breakthrough of Swedish social democratic hegemony stems from its capacity to forge the famous 'red–green' alliance with the farmers; the comparative disadvantage of the Austrian socialists rests in the 'ghetto' status assigned to them by virtue of the rural classes being captured by a conservative coalition (Esping-Andersen and Korpi, 1984).

In summary, we have to think in terms of social relations, not just social categories. Whereas structural functionalist explanations identify convergent welfare-state outcomes, and class-mobilization paradigms see large, but linearly distributed, differences, an interactive model such as the coalition approach directs attention to distinct welfare-state regimes.

What is the Welfare State?

Every theoretical paradigm must somehow define the welfare state. How do we know when and if a welfare state responds functionally to the needs of industrialism, or to capitalist reproduction and legitimacy? And how do we identify a welfare state that corresponds to the demands that a mobilized working class might have? We cannot test contending arguments unless we have a commonly shared conception of the phenomenon to be explained.

A remarkable attribute of the entire literature is its lack of much genuine interest in the welfare state as such. Welfare-state studies have been motivated by theoretical concerns with other phenomena, such as power, industrialization, or capitalist contradictions; the welfare state itself has generally received scant conceptual attention. If welfare states differ, how do they differ? And when, indeed, is a state a welfare state? This turns attention straight back to the original question: what is the welfare state?

A common textbook definition is that it involves state responsibility for securing some basic modicum of welfare for its citizens. Such a definition skirts the issue of whether social policies are emancipatory or not; whether they help system legitimation or not; whether they contradict or aid the market process; and what, indeed, is meant by 'basic'? Would it not be more appropriate to require of a welfare state that it satisfies more than our basic or minimal welfare needs?

The first generation of comparative studies started with this type of conceptualization. They assumed, without much reflection, that the level of social expenditure adequately reflects a state's commitment to welfare. The theoretical intent was not really to arrive at an understanding of the welfare state, but rather to test the validity of contending theoretical models in political economy. By scoring nations with respect to urbanization, level of economic growth, and the proportion of aged in the demographic structure, it was believed that the essential features of industrial modernization were properly considered. Alternatively, power-oriented theories compared nations on left-party strength or working-class power mobilization.

The findings of the first-generation comparativists are difficult to evaluate, since there is no convincing case for any particular theory. The shortage of nations for comparisons statistically restricts the number of variables that can be tested simultaneously. Thus, when Cutright (1965) or Wilensky (1975) find that economic level, with its demographic and bureaucratic correlates, explains most welfare-state variations in 'rich countries', relevant measures of working-class mobilization or economic openness are not included. Their conclusions in favor of a 'logic of industrialism' view are therefore in doubt. And, when Hewitt (1977), Stephens (1979), Korpi (1983), Myles (1984a), and Esping-Andersen (1985b) find strong evidence in favor of a working-class mobilization thesis, or when Schmidt (1982; 1983) finds support for a neo-corporatist, and Cameron (1978) for an economic openness argument, it is without fully testing against plausible alternative explanations.[7]

Most of these studies claim to explain the welfare state. Yet their focus on spending may be misleading. Expenditures are epiphenomenal to the theoretical substance of welfare states. Moreover, the linear scoring approach (more or less power, democracy, or spending) contradicts the sociological notion that power, democracy, or welfare are relational and structured phenomena. By scoring welfare states on spending, we assume that all spending counts equally. But some welfare states, the Austrian one, for example, spend a large share on benefits to privileged civil servants. This is normally not what we would consider a commitment to social citizenship and solidarity. Others spend disproportionately on means-tested social assistance. Few contemporary analysts would agree that a reformed poor-relief tradition qualifies as a welfare-state commitment. Some nations spend enormous sums on fiscal welfare in the form of tax privileges to private insurance plans that mainly benefit the middle classes. But these tax expenditures do not show up on expenditure accounts. In Britain, total social expenditure has grown during the Thatcher period, yet this is almost exclusively a function of very high unemployment. Low expenditure on some programs may signifiy a welfare state more seriously committed to full employment.

Therborn (1983) is right when he holds that we must begin with a conception of state structure. What are the criteria with which we should judge whether, and when, a state is a welfare state? There are three approaches to this question. Therborn's proposal is to begin with the historical transformation of state activities. Minimally, in a genuine welfare state the majority of its daily routine activities must be devoted to servicing the welfare needs of households. This criterion has far-reaching consequences. If we simply measure routine activity in terms of spending and personnel, the result is that no state can be regarded as a real welfare state until the 1970s, and some that we normally label as welfare states will not qualify because the majority of their routine activities concern defence, law and order, administration, and the like (Therborn, 1983). Social scientists have been too quick to accept nations' self-proclaimed welfare-state status. They have also been too quick to conclude that if the standard social programs have been introduced, the welfare state has been born.

The second conceptual approach derives from Richard Titmuss's (1958) classical distinction between residual and institutional welfare states. In the former, the state assumes responsibility only when the family or the market fails; it seeks to limit its commitments to marginal and deserving social groups. The latter model addresses the entire population, is universalistic, and embodies an institutionalized commitment to welfare. It will, in principle, extend welfare commitments to all areas of distribution vital for societal welfare.

The Titmuss approach has fertilized a variety of new developments in comparative welfare-state research (Myles, 1984a; Korpi, 1980; Esping-Andersen and Korpi, 1984; 1986; Esping-Andersen, 1985b; 1987b). It is an approach that forces researchers to move from the black box of expenditures to the content of welfare states: targeted versus universalistic programs, the conditions of eligibility, the quality of benefits and services, and, perhaps most importantly, the extent to which employment and working life are encompassed in the state's extension of citizen rights. The shift to welfare-state typologies makes simple linear welfare-state rankings difficult to sustain. Conceptually, we are comparing categorically different types of states.

The third approach is to theoretically select the criteria on which to judge types of welfare states. This can be done by measuring actual welfare states against some abstract model and then scoring programs, or entire welfare states, accordingly (Day 1978; Myles, 1984a). But this is ahistorical, and does not necessarily capture the ideals or designs that historical actors sought to realize in the struggles over the welfare state. If our aim is to test causal theories that involve actors, we should begin with the demands that were actually promoted by those actors that we deem critical in the history of welfare-state development. It is difficult to imagine that anyone struggled for spending *per se*.

A Re-Specification of the Welfare State

Few can disagree with T. H. Marshall's (1950) proposition that social citizenship constitutes the core idea of a welfare state. But the concept must be fleshed out. Above all, it must involve the granting of social rights. If social rights are given the legal and practical status of property rights, if they are inviolable, and if they are granted on the basis of citizenship rather than performance, they will entail a de-commodification of the status of individuals *vis-à-vis* the market. But the concept of social citizenship also involves social stratification: one's status as a citizen will compete with, or even replace, one's class position.

The welfare state cannot be understood just in terms of the rights it grants. We must also take into account how state activities are interlocked with the market's and the family's role in social provision. These are the three main principles that need to be fleshed out prior to any theoretical specification of the welfare state.

RIGHTS AND DE-COMMODIFICATION

In pre-capitalist societies, few workers were properly commodities in the sense that their survival was contingent upon the sale of their labor power. It is as markets become universal and hegemonic that the welfare of individuals comes to depend entirely on the cash nexus. Stripping society of the institutional layers that guaranteed social reproduction outside the labor contract meant that people were commodified. In turn, the introduction of modern social rights implies a loosening of the pure commodity status. De-commodification occurs when a service is rendered as a matter of right, and when a person can maintain a livelihood without reliance on the market.

The mere presence of social assistance or insurance may not necessarily bring about significant de-commodification if they do not substantially emancipate individuals from market dependence. Means-tested poor relief will possibly offer a safety net of last resort. But if benefits are low and associated with social stigma, the relief system will compel all but the most desperate to participate in the market. This was precisely the intent of the nineteenth-century poor laws in most countries. Similarly, most of the early social-insurance programs were deliberately designed to maximize labor-market performance (Ogus, 1979).

There is no doubt that de-commodification has been a hugely contested issue in welfare state development. For labor, it has always been a priority. When workers are completely market-dependent, they are difficult to mobilize for solidaristic action. Since their resources mirror market inequalities, divisions emerge between the 'ins' and the 'outs', making labor-movement formation difficult. De-commodification strengthens the worker and weakens the absolute authority of the employer. It is for exactly this reason that employers have always opposed de-commodification.

De-commodified rights are differentially developed in contemporary welfare states. In social-assistance dominated welfare states, rights are not so much attached to work performance as to demonstrable need. Needs-tests and typically meager benefits, however, service to curtail the de-commodifying effect. Thus, in nations where this model is dominant (mainly in the Anglo-Saxon countries), the result is actually to strengthen the market since all but those who fail in the market will be encouraged to contract private-sector welfare.

A second dominant model espouses compulsory state social insurance with fairly strong entitlements. But again, this may not automatically secure substantial de-commodification, since this hinges very much on the fabric of eligibility and benefit rules. Germany was the pioneer of social insurance, but over most of the century can hardly be said to have brought about much in the way of de-commodification through its social programs. Benefits have depended almost entirely on contributions, and thus on work and employment. In other words, it is not the mere presence of a social right, but the corresponding rules and preconditions, which dictate the extent to which welfare programs offer genuine alternatives to market dependence.

The third dominant model of welfare, namely the Beveridge-type citizens' benefit, may, at first glance, appear the most de-commodifying.

It offers a basic, equal benefit to all, irrespective of prior earnings, contributions, or performance. It may indeed be a more solidaristic system, but not necessarily de-commodifying, since only rarely have such schemes been able to offer benefits of such a standard that they provide recipients with a genuine option to working.

De-commodifying welfare states are, in practice, of very recent date. A minimal definition must entail that citizens can freely, and without potential loss of job, income, or general welfare, opt out of work when they themselves consider it necessary. With this definition in mind, we would, for example, require of a sickness insurance that individuals be guaranteed benefits equal to normal earnings, and the right to absence with minimal proof of medical impairment and for the duration that the individual deems necessary. These conditions, it is worth noting, are those usually enjoyed by academics, civil servants, and higher-echelon white-collar employees. Similar requirements would be made of pensions, maternity leave, parental leave, educational leave, and unemployment insurance.

Some nations have moved towards this level of de-commodification, but only recently, and, in many cases, with significant exemptions. In almost all nations, benefits were upgraded to nearly equal normal wages in the late 1960s and early 1970s. But in some countries, for example, prompt medical certification in case of illness is still required; in others, entitlements depend on long waiting periods of up to two weeks; and in still others, the duration of entitlements is very short. As we shall see in chapter 2, the Scandinavian welfare states tend to be the most de-commodifying; the Anglo-Saxon the least.

The Welfare State as a System of Stratification

Despite the emphasis given to it in both classical political economy and in T. H. Marshall's pioneering work, the relationship between citizenship and social class has been neglected both theoretically and empirically. Generally speaking, the issue has either been assumed away (it has been taken for granted that the welfare state creates a more egalitarian society), or it has been approached narrowly in terms of income distribution or in terms of whether education promotes upward social mobility. A more basic question, it seems, is what kind of stratification system is promoted by social policy. The welfare state is not just a mechanism that intervenes in, and possibly corrects, the structure of inequality; it is, in its own right, a system of stratification. It is an active force in the ordering of social relations.

Comparatively and historically, we can easily identify alternative systems of stratification embedded in welfare states. The poor-relief tradition, and its contemporary means-tested social-assistance offshoot, was conspicuously designed for purposes of stratification. By punishing and stigmatizing recipients, it promotes social dualisms and has therefore been a chief target of labor-movement attacks.

The social-insurance model promoted by conservative reformers such as Bismarck and von Taffe, was also explicitly a form of class politics. It sought, in fact, to achieve two simultaneous results in terms of stratification. The first was to consolidate divisions among wage-earners by legislating distinct programs for different class and status groups, each with its own conspicuously unique set of rights and privileges which was designed to accentuate the individual's appropriate station in life. The second objective was to tie the loyalties of the individual directly to the monarchy or the central state authority. This was Bismarck's motive when he promoted a direct state supplement to the pension benefit. This state-corporatist model was pursued mainly in nations such as Germany, Austria, Italy, and France, and often resulted in a labyrinth of status-specific insurance funds.

Of special importance in this corporatist tradition was the establishment of particularly privileged welfare provisions for the civil service (*Beamten*). In part, this was a means of rewarding loyalty to the state, and in part it was a way of demarcating this group's uniquely exalted social status. The corporatist status-differentiated model springs mainly from the old guild tradition. The neo-absolutist autocrats, such as Bismarck, saw in this tradition a means to combat the rising labor movements.

The labor movements were as hostile to the corporatist model as they were to poor relief – in both cases for obvious reasons. Yet the alternatives first espoused by labor were no less problematic from the point of view of uniting the workers as one solidaristic class. Almost invariably, the model that labor first pursued was that of self-organized friendly societies or equivalent union- or party-sponsored fraternal welfare plans. This is not surprising. Workers were obviously suspicious of reforms sponsored by a hostile state, and saw their own organizations not only as bases of class mobilization, but also as embryos of an alternative world of solidarity and justice; as a microcosm of the socialist haven to come. Nonetheless, these micro-socialist societies often became problematic class ghettos that divided rather than united workers. Membership was typically restricted to the strongest strata of the working class, and the weakest – who most needed protection – were most likely excluded. In brief, the fraternal society model frustrated the goal of working-class mobilization.

The socialist 'ghetto approach' was an additional obstacle when socialist parties found themselves forming governments and having to pass the social reforms they had so long demanded. For political reasons of coalition-building and broader solidarity, their welfare model had to be recast as welfare for 'the people'. Hence, the socialists came to espouse the principle of universalism; borrowing from the liberals, their program was, typically, designed along the lines of the democratic flat-rate, general revenue-financed Beveridge model.

As an alternative to means-tested assistance and corporatist social insurance, the universalistic system promotes equality of status. All citizens are endowed with similar rights, irrespective of class or market position. In this sense, the system is meant to cultivate cross-class solidarity, a solidarity of the nation. But the solidarity of flat-rate universalism presumes a historically peculiar class structure, one in which the vast majority of the population are the 'little people' for whom a modest, albeit egalitarian, benefit may be considered adequate. Where this no longer obtains, as occurs with growing working-class prosperity and the rise of the new middle classes, flat-rate universalism inadvertently promotes dualism because the better-off turn to private insurance and to fringe-benefit bargaining to supplement modest equality with what they have decided are accustomed standards of welfare. Where this process unfolds (as in Canada or Great Britain), the result is that the wonderfully egalitarian spirit of universalism turns into a dualism similar to that of the social-assistance state: the poor rely on the state, and the remainder on the market.

It is not only the universalist but, in fact, all historical welfare-state models which have faced the dilemma of changes in class structure. But the response to prosperity and middle-class growth has been varied, and so, therefore, has been the outcome in terms of stratification. The corporatist insurance tradition was, in a sense, best equipped to manage new and loftier welfare-state expectations since the existing system could technically be upgraded quite easily to distribute more adequate benefits. Adenauer's 1957 pension-reform in Germany was a pioneer in this respect. Its avowed purpose was to restore status differences that had been eroded because of the old insurance system's incapacity to provide benefits tailored to expectations. This it did simply by moving from contribution- to earnings-graduated benefits without altering the framework of status-distinctiveness.

In nations with either a social-assistance or a universalistic Beveridge-type system, the option was whether to allow the market or the state to furnish adequacy and satisfy middle-class aspirations. Two alternative models emerged from this political choice. The one typical of Great Britain and most of the Anglo-Saxon world was to preserve an essentially modest universalism in the state, and allow the market to reign for the growing social strata demanding superior welfare. Due to the political power of such groups, the dualism that emerges is not merely one between state and market, but also between forms of welfare-state transfers: in these nations, one of the fastest growing components of public expenditure is tax subsidies for so-called 'private' welfare plans. And the typical political effect is the erosion of middle-class support for what is less and less a universalistic public-sector transfer system.

Yet another alternative has been to seek a synthesis of universalism and adequacy outside of the market. This road has been followed in countries where, by mandating or legislation, the state incorporates the new middle classes within a luxurious second-tier, universally inclusive, earnings-related insurance scheme on top of the flat-rate egalitarian one. Notable examples are Sweden and Norway. By guaranteeing benefits tailored to expectations, this solution reintroduces benefit inequalities, but effectively blocks off the market. It thus succeeds in retaining universalism and also, therefore, the degree of political consensus required to preserve broad and solidaristic support for the high taxes that such a welfare-state model demands.

Welfare-State Regimes

As we survey international variations in social rights and welfare-state stratification, we will find qualitatively different arrangements between state, market, and the family. The welfare-state variations we find are therefore not linearly distributed, but clustered by regime-types.

In one cluster we find the 'liberal' welfare state, in which means-tested assistance, modest universal transfers, or modest social-insurance plans predominate. Benefits cater mainly to a clientele of low-income, usually working-class, state dependents. In this model, the progress of social reform has been severely circumscribed by traditional, liberal work-ethic norms: it is one where the limits of welfare equal the marginal propensity to opt for welfare instead of work. Entitlement rules are therefore strict and often associated with stigma; benefits are typically modest. In turn, the state encourages the market, either passively – by guaranteeing only a minimum – or actively – by subsidizing private welfare schemes.

The consequence is that this type of regime minimizes de-commodification-effects, effectively contains the realm of social rights, and erects an order of stratification that is a blend of a relative equality of poverty among state-welfare recipients, market-differentiated welfare among the majorities, and a class-political dualism between the two. The archetypical examples of this model are the United States, Canada and Australia.

A second regime-type clusters nations such as Austria, France, Germany, and Italy. Here, the historical corporatist-statist legacy was upgraded to cater to the new 'post-industrial' class structure. In these conservative and strongly 'corporatist' welfare states, the liberal obsession with market efficiency and commodification was never preeminent and, as such, the granting of social rights was hardly ever a seriously contested issue. What predominated was the preservation of status differentials; rights, therefore, were attached to class and status. This corporatism was subsumed under a state edifice perfectly ready to displace the market as a provider of welfare; hence, private insurance and occupational fringe benefits play a truly marginal role. On the other hand, the state's emphasis on upholding status differences means that its redistributive impact is negligible.

But the corporatist regimes are also typically shaped by the Church, and hence strongly committed to the preservation of traditional family-hood. Social insurance typically excludes non-working wives, and family benefits encourage motherhood. Day care, and similar family services, are conspicuously underdeveloped; the principle of 'subsidiarity' serves to emphasize that the state will only interfere when the family's capacity to service its members is exhausted.

The third, and clearly smallest, regime-cluster is composed of those countries in which the principles of universalism and de-commodification of social rights were extended also to the new middle classes. We may call it the 'social democratic' regime-type since, in these nations, social democracy was clearly the dominant force behind social reform. Rather than tolerate a dualism between state and market, between working class and middle class, the social democrats pursued a welfare state that would promote an equality of the highest standards, not an equality of minimal needs as was pursued elsewhere. This implied, first, that services and benefits be upgraded to levels commensurate with even the most discriminating tastes of the new middle classes; and, second, that equality be furnished by guaranteeing workers full participation in the quality of rights enjoyed by the better-off.

This formula translates into a mix of highly de-commodifying and universalistic programs that, nonetheless, are tailored to differentiated expectations. Thus, manual workers come to enjoy rights identical to those of salaried white-collar employees or civil servants; all strata are incorporated under one universal insurance system, yet benefits are graduated according to accustomed earnings. This model crowds out the market, and consequently constructs an essentially universal solidarity in favor of the welfare state. All benefit; all are dependent; and all will presumably feel obliged to pay.

The social democratic regime's policy of emancipation addresses both the market and the traditional family. In contrast to the corporatist-subsidiarity model, the principle is not to wait until the family's capacity to aid is exhausted, but to preemptively socialize the costs of family-hood. The ideal is not to maximize dependence on the family, but capacities for individual independence. In this sense, the model is a peculiar fusion of liberalism and socialism. The result is a welfare state that grants transfers directly to children, and takes direct responsibility of caring for children, the aged, and the helpless. It is, accordingly, committed to a heavy social-service burden, not only to service family needs but also to allow women to choose work rather than the household.

Perhaps the most salient characteristic of the social democratic regime is its fusion of welfare and work. It is at once genuinely committed to a full-employment guarantee, and entirely dependent on its attainment. On the one side, the right to work has equal status to the right of income protection. On the other side, the enormous costs of maintaining a solidaristic, universalistic, and de-commodifying welfare system means that it must minimize social problems and maximize revenue income. This is obviously best done with most people working, and the fewest possible living off of social transfers.

Neither of the two alternative regime-types espouse full employment as an integral part of their welfare-state commitment. In the conservative tradition, of course, women are discouraged from working; in the liberal ideal, concerns of gender matter less than the sanctity of the market.

In the chapters to follow, we show that welfare states cluster, but we must recognize that there is no single pure case. The Scandinavian countries may be predominantly social democratic, but they are not free of crucial liberal elements. Neither are the liberal regimes pure types. The American social-security system is redistributive, compulsory, and far from actuarial. At least in its early formulation, the New Deal was as social democratic as was contemporary Scandinavian social democracy.

And European conservative regimes have incorporated both liberal and social democratic impulses. Over the decades, they have become less corporativist and less authoritarian.

Notwithstanding the lack of purity, if our essential criteria for defining welfare states have to do with the quality of social rights, social stratification, and the relationship between state, market, and family, the world is obviously composed of distinct regime-clusters. Comparing welfare states on scales of more or less or, indeed, of better or worse, will yield highly misleading results.

The Causes of Welfare-State Regimes

If welfare states cluster into three distinct regime-types, we face a substantially more complex task of identifying the causes of welfare-state differences. What is the explanatory power of industrialization, economic growth, capitalism, or working-class political power in accounting for regime-types? A first superficial answer would be: very little. The nations we study are all more or less similar with regard to all but the variable of working-class mobilization. And we find very powerful labor movements and parties in each of the three clusters.

A theory of welfare-state developments must clearly reconsider its causal assumptions if it wishes to explain clusters. The hope of finding one single powerful causal force must be abandoned; the task is to identify salient interaction-effects. Based on the preceding arguments, three factors in particular should be of importance: the nature of class mobilization (especially of the working class); class-political coalition structures; and the historical legacy of regime institutionalization.

As we have noted, there is absolutely no compelling reason to believe that workers will automatically and naturally forge a socialist class identity; nor is it plausible that their mobilization will look especially Swedish. The actual historical formation of working-class collectivities will diverge, and so also will their aims, ideology, and political capacities. Fundamental differences appear both in trade-unionism and party development. Unions may be sectional or in pursuit of more universal objectives; they may be denominational or secular; and they may be ideological or devoted to business-unionism. Whichever they are, it will decisively affect the articulation of political demands, class cohesion, and the scope for labor-party action. It is clear that a working-class mobilization thesis must pay attention to union structure.

The structure of trade-unionism may or may not be reflected in labor-party formation. But under what conditions are we likely to expect certain welfare-state outcomes from specific party configurations? There are many factors that conspire to make it virtually impossible to assume that any labor, or left-wing, party will ever be capable, single-handedly, of structuring a welfare state. Denominational or other divisions aside, it will be only under extraordinary historical circumstances that a labor party alone will command a parliamentary majority long enough to impose its will. We have noted that the traditional working class has hardly ever constituted an electoral majority. It follows that a theory of class mobilization must look beyond the major leftist parties. It is a historical fact that welfare-state construction has depended on political coalition-building. The structure of class coalitions is much more decisive than are the power resources of any single class.

The emergence of alternative class coalitions is, in part, determined by class formation. In the earlier phases of industrialization, the rural classes usually constituted the largest single group in the electorate. If social democrats wanted political majorities, it was here that they were forced to look for allies. One of history's many paradoxes is that the rural classes were decisive for the future of socialism. Where the rural economy was dominated by small, capital-intensive family farmers, the potential for an alliance was greater than where it rested on large pools of cheap labor. And where farmers were politically articulate and well-organized (as in Scandinavia), the capacity to negotiate political deals was vastly superior.

The role of the farmers in coalition formation and hence in welfare-state development is clear. In the Nordic countries, the necessary conditions obtained for a broad red–green alliance for a full-employment welfare state in return for farm-price subsidies. This was especially true in Norway and Sweden, where farming was highly precarious and dependent on state aid. In the United States, the New Deal was premised on a similar coalition (forged by the Democratic Party), but with the important difference that the labor-intensive South blocked a truly universalistic social security system and opposed further welfare-state developments. In contrast, the rural economy of continental Europe was very inhospitable to red–green coalitions. Often, as in Germany and Italy, much of agriculture was labor-intensive; hence the unions and left-wing parties were seen as a threat. In addition, the conservative forces on the continent had succeeded in incorporating farmers into 'reactionary' alliances, helping to consolidate the political isolation of labor.

Political dominance was, until after World War II, largely a question of rural class politics. The construction of welfare states in this period was, therefore, dictated by whichever force captured the farmers. The absence of a red–green alliance does not necessarily imply that no welfare-state reforms were possible. On the contrary, it implies which political force came to dominate their design. Great Britain is an exception to this general rule, because the political significance of the rural classes eroded before the turn of the century. In this way, Britain's coalition-logic showed at an early date the dilemma that faced most other nations later; namely, that the rising white-collar strata constitute the linchpin for political majorities. The consolidation of welfare states after World War II came to depend fundamentally on the political alliances of the new middle classes. For social democracy, the challenge was to synthesize working-class and white-collar demands without sacrificing the commitment to solidarity.

Since the new middle classes have, historically, enjoyed a relatively privileged position in the market, they have also been quite successful in meeting their welfare demands outside the state, or, as civil servants, by privileged state welfare. Their employment security has traditionally been such that full employment has been a peripheral concern. Finally, any program for drastic income-equalization is likely to be met with great hostility among a middle-class clientele. On these grounds, it would appear that the rise of the new middle classes would abort the social democratic project and strengthen a liberal welfare-state formula.

The political leanings of the new middle classes have, indeed, been decisive for welfare-state consolidation. Their role in shaping the three welfare-state regimes described earlier is clear. The Scandinavian model relied almost entirely on social democracy's capacity to incorporate them into a new kind of welfare state: one that provided benefits tailored to the tastes and expectations of the middle classes, but nonetheless retained universalism of rights. Indeed, by expanding social services and public employment, the welfare state participated directly in manufacturing a middle class instrumentally devoted to social democracy.

In contrast, the Anglo-Saxon nations retained the residual welfare-state model precisely because the new middle classes were not wooed from the market to the state. In class terms, the consequence is dualism. The welfare state caters essentially to the working class and the poor. Private insurance and occupational fringe benefits cater to the middle classes. Given the electoral importance of the latter, it is quite logical that further extensions of welfare-state activities are resisted.

The third, continental European, welfare-state regime has also been patterned by the new middle classes, but in a different way. The cause is historical. Developed by conservative political forces, these regimes institutionalized a middle-class loyalty to the preservation of both occupationally segregated social-insurance programs and, ultimately, to the political forces that brought them into being. Adenauer's great pension-reform in 1957 was explicitly designed to resurrect middle-class loyalties.

Conclusion

We have here presented an alternative to a simple class-mobilization theory of welfare-state development. It is motivated by the analytical necessity of shifting from a linear to an interactive approach with regard to both welfare states and their causes. If we wish to study welfare states, we must begin with a set of criteria that define their role in society. This role is certainly not to spend or tax; nor is it necessarily that of creating equality. We have presented a framework for comparing welfare states that takes into consideration the principles for which the historical actors have willingly united and struggled. When we focus on the principles embedded in welfare states, we discover distinct regime-clusters, not merely variations of 'more' or 'less' around a common denominator.

The historical forces behind the regime differences are interactive. They involve, first, the pattern of working-class political formation and, second, political coalition-building in the transition from a rural economy to a middle-class society. The question of political coalition-formation is decisive. Third, past reforms have contributed decisively to the institutionalization of class preferences and political behavior. In the corporatist regimes, hierarchical status-distinctive social insurance cemented middle-class loyalty to a peculiar type of welfare state. In liberal regimes, the middle classes became institutionally wedded to the market. And in Scandinavia, the fortunes of social democracy over the past decades were closely tied to the establishment of a middle-class welfare state that benefits both its traditional working-class clientele and the new white-collar strata. The Scandinavian social democrats were able to achieve this in part because the private welfare market was relatively undeveloped and in part because they were capable of building a welfare state with features of sufficient luxury to satisfy the wants of a more discriminating public. This also explains the extraordinarily high cost of Scandinavian welfare states.

But a theory that seeks to explain welfare-state growth should also be able to understand its retrenchment or decline. It is generally believed that welfare-state backlash movements, tax revolts, and roll-backs are ignited when social expenditure burdens become too heavy. Paradoxically, the opposite is true. Anti-welfare-state sentiments over the past decade have generally been weakest where welfare spending has been heaviest, and vice versa. Why?

The risks of welfare-state backlash depend not on spending, but on the class character of welfare states. Middle-class welfare states, be they social democratic (as in Scandinavia) or corporatist (as in Germany), forge middle-class loyalties. In contrast, the liberal, residualist welfare states found in the United States, Canada and, increasingly, Britain, depend on the loyalties of a numerically weak, and often politically residual, social stratum. In this sense, the class coalitions in which the three welfare-state regime-types were founded, explain not only their past evolution but also their future prospects.

Notes

1 Adam Smith is often cited but rarely read. A closer inspection of his writings reveals a degree of nuance and a battery of reservations that substantially qualify a delirious enthusiasm for the blessings of capitalism.

2 In *The Wealth of Nations* (1961, II, p. 236), Smith comments on states that uphold the privilege and security of the propertied as follows: 'civil government, so far as it is instituted for the security of property, is in reality instituted for the defence of the rich against the poor, or of those who have some property against those who have none at all.'

3 This tradition is virtually unknown to Anglo-Saxon readers since so little has been translated into English. A key text which greatly influenced public debate and later social legislation was Adolph Wagner's *Rede Ueber die Soziale Frage* (1872). For an English language overview of this tradition of political economy, see Schumpeter (1954), and especially Bower (1947).

From the Catholic tradition, the fundamental texts are the two Papal Encyclicals, *Rerum Novarum* (1891) and *Quadrogesimo Anno* (1931). The social Catholic political economy's main advocacy is a social organization where a strong family is integrated in cross-class corporations, aided by the state in terms of the subsidiarity principle. For a recent discussion, see Richter (1987).

Like the liberals, the conservative political economists also have their contemporary echoes, although substantially fewer in number. A revival occurred with Fascism's concept of the corporative (*Standische*) state of Ottmar Spann in Germany. The subsidiarity principle still guides much of German Christian Democratic politics (see Richter, 1987).

4 Chief proponents of this analysis are the German 'state derivation' school (Muller and Neususs, 1973); Offe (1972); O'Connor (1973); Gough (1979); and also the work of Poulantzas (1973). As Skocpol and Amenta (1986) note

in their excellent overview, the approach is far from one-dimensional. Thus, Offe, O'Connor and Gough identify the function of social reforms as also being concessions to mass demands and as potentially contradictory.

Historically, socialist opposition to parliamentary reforms was motivated less by theory than by reality. August Bebel, the great leader of German social democracy, rejected Bismarck's pioneering social legislation not because he did not favor social protection, but because of the blatantly anti-socialist and divisionary motives behind Bismarck's reforms.

5 This realization came from two types of experiences. One, typified by Swedish socialism in the 1920s, was the discovery that not even the working-class base showed much enthusiasm for socialization. In fact, when the Swedish socialists established a special commission to prepare plans for socialization, it concluded after ten years of exploration that it would be quite impossible to undertake practically. A second kind of experience, typified by the Norwegian socialists and Blum's Popular Front government in 1936, was the discovery that radical proposals could easily be sabotaged by the capitalists' capacity to withhold investments and export their capital abroad.

6 This is obviously not a problem for the parliamentary class hypothesis alone; structural Marxism faces the same problem of specifying the class character of the new middle classes. If such a specification fails to demonstrate that it constitutes a new working class, both varieties of Marxist theory face severe (although not identical) problems.

7 This literature has been reviewed in great detail by a number of authors. See, for example, Wilensky et al. (1985). For excellent and more critical evaluations, see Uusitalo (1984), Shalev (1983), and Skocpol and Amenta (1986).

2

De-Commodification in Social Policy

The mainsprings of modern social policy lie in the process by which both human needs and labor power became commodities and, hence, our well-being came to depend on our relation to the cash nexus. This is not to say that social policy was unknown prior to the onslaught of modern capitalism, only that its nature and organization became transformed. Traditional social welfare spoke to a world that was only very imperfectly commodified. Thus, in the Middle Ages it was not the labor contract, but the family, the church, or the lord that decided a person's capacity for survival.

The blossoming of capitalism came with the withering away of 'pre-commodified' social protection. When the satisfaction of human wants came to imply the purchase of commodities, the issue of purchasing-power and income distribution became salient. When, however, labor power also became a commodity, peoples' rights to survive outside the market are at stake. It is this which constitutes the single most conflictual issue in social policy. The problem of commodification lay at the heart of Marx's analysis of class development in the accumulation process: the transformation of independent producers into propertyless wage-earners. The commodification of labor power implied, for Marx, alienation.

Labor's commodity form has been a central concern of modern philosophy, ideology, and social theory. The classical laissez-faire liberals opposed alternatives to the pure cash-nexus because they would disturb and even thwart the sacred equilibrium of supply and demand. They held, like their contemporary followers, that a minimum social wage would not eradicate poverty but, indeed, actively contribute to its perpetuation. Marxism, in turn, was always ambivalent, in some cases arguing that genuine human welfare could only occur with the complete abolition of wage labor, in other cases believing that social amelioration would bring about decisive change. The latter view was not merely an invention of reformist social democrats, but was voiced in the *Communist Manifesto* and in Marx's analyses of the English Factory Acts. T. H. Marshall's (1950) view was that the rights of social citizenship essentially resolved the problem of commodification and that they therefore helped erode the salience of class. Finally, traditional conservatism opposed outright the principle of commodifying humanity because it would jeopardize authority and social integration; conservatives feared that it would lend a fatal blow to the perpetuation of the old order.

In *The Great Transformation*, Polanyi (1944) identifies a fundamental contradiction in laissez-faire capitalism's drive to commodify labor power completely. While the system itself can only evolve by commodifying labor, by doing so it also sows the seeds of its own self-destruction: if labor power is nothing more than a commodity, it will likely destruct.

With reference to Britain, Polanyi held that the pre-industrial Speenhamland system of income security prohibited the transformation of labor power into a pure commodity. Since the system guaranteed a *de facto* social wage, it alleviated the kind of dire need that would have forced the landless workers to move to the new mill towns. Hence, until replaced by the new Poor Laws in 1834, Speenhamland was a fetter on British capitalism.

They may not have appeared as such, but the new Poor Laws were an active social policy designed to make wage employment and the cash nexus the linchpin of a person's very existence. Welfare, if not survival, came to depend on the willingness of someone to hire one's labor power. We might say that Speenhamland espoused principles of pre-commodification since it adhered to traditional guarantees of feudal society. The Poor Laws of laissez-faire appear at first as an extreme case of government passivity. Yet behind this facade we must recognize the heavy hand of an active social policy designed to establish market hegemony in the distribution of welfare. With no recourse to property, and no state to which human needs can be directed, the market becomes to the worker a prison within which it is imperative to behave as a commodity in order to survive.

The commodification of both wants and people may strengthen the engine of capitalist accumulation, but it weakens the individual worker. Within the market the liberal dogma of freedom appears justified: the worker can freely choose between alternative utilities, jobs, employers, and leisure trade-offs. But Marx and Polanyi and, more recently, Lindblom (1977) are correct in arguing that it is a freedom behind prison walls, and hence fictitious. Workers are not commodities like others because they must survive and reproduce both themselves and the society they live in. It is possible to withhold washing-machines from the market until the price is agreeable; but labor is unable to withhold itself for long without recourse to alternative means of subsistence.

The politics of commodifying workers was bound to breed its opposite. As commodities, people are captive to powers beyond their control; the commodity is easily destroyed by even minor social contingencies, such as illness, and by macro-events, such as the business cycle. If workers actually do behave as discrete commodities, they will by definition compete; and the fiercer the competition, the cheaper the price. As commodities, workers are replacable, easily redundant, and atomized. De-commodification is therefore a process with multiple roots. It is, as Polanyi argued, necessary for system survival. It is also a precondition for a tolerable level of individual welfare and security. Finally, without de-commodification, workers are incapable of collective action; it is, accordingly, the alpha and omega of the unity and solidarity required for labor-movement development.

The variability of welfare-state evolution reflects competing responses to pressures for de-commodification. To understand the concept, de-commodification should not be confused with the complete eradication of labor as a commodity; it is not an issue of all or nothing. Rather, the concept refers to the degree to which individuals, or families, can uphold a socially acceptable standard of living independently of market participation. In the history of social policy, conflicts have mainly revolved around what degree of market immunity would be permissible; i.e. the strength, scope, and quality of social rights. When work approaches free choice rather than necessity, de-commodification may amount to de-proletarianization.

It was the commodity status of labor that lay at the heart of the nineteenth-century debates and conflicts over the 'social question' or, as it was most commonly termed in Germany, the *Arbeiterfrage*. It is, of course, unlikely that the pure commodity-status of the worker ever really existed. Even at the apex of laissez-faire, pre-capitalist residues of communalism persisted, and novel mechanisms of protection emerged. For analytical purposes, however, it is fruitful to treat the pure case of laissez-faire as an ideal type from which we can more clearly identify the main deviations. Since, in the nineteenth century, traditional conservatism, by upholding pre-capitalist norms, constituted the single major force against commodification, and since this significantly influenced social-policy development, we should properly begin our treatment with the legacy of 'pre-commodification'.

Pre-Commodification and the Legacy of Conservatism

We should not confuse pre-capitalist society with the absence of the commodity form. Feudal agriculture typically produced cash crops, and the medieval towns were heavily engaged in the production and exchange of commodities. The manorial or absolutist economy required taxation which, in turn, required the sale of commodities. It was the commodity form of labor which was undeveloped.

It was certainly not the case that the pre-capitalist producers, peasants, serfs, or journeymen could count on a lot of welfare irrespective of their work performance. One could not make many claims to subsistence independently of one's labors. Yet, the commodity form was absent in the sense that the majority of people were not dependent entirely on wage-type income for their survival. Households often remained fairly self-sufficient; feudal servitude also assumed a degree of reciprocity and paternal aid on the part of the lord; the urban producer was generally a compulsory member of a guild or fraternal association; and the destitute could normally approach the Church. Thus, in contrast to the naked commodity-logic of capitalism, the majority could count on prevailing norms and communal organizations for subsistence. And, in comparison to laissez-faire poor relief, 'pre-capitalist' social aid was generous and benign.

A hallmark of conservative ideology is its view that the commodification of individuals is morally degrading, socially corrupting, atomizing, and anomic. Individuals are not meant to compete or struggle, but to subordinate self-interest to recognized authority and prevailing institutions. How, in practice, has conservatism addressed the problem of commodification? We can distinguish several models: the first is largely feudal; the second, corporativist; and the third is etatist.

Feudal ideals are strongly antagonistic to the commodity status; markets do not matter and wage labor is only marginally important for human well-being. A (true) story illustrates the logic well: a typical American corporation (textiles) decided in the 1970s to start production in Haiti, attracted by the prospects of extraordinarily low wage-costs. Upon completion of the plant, the firm's managers, all Americans, decided to lure the island's best workers by offering a marginally higher wage. Of course, on the opening day, the unemployed came by the thousands to offer their services, and management had no difficulty in selecting a choice workforce. Yet, after only a few months, the plant was closed down. Why? The reason was simply that American management had failed to reckon with feudal welfare arrangements which provide that when a worker's mother's house burnt down, it was the boss's (in Haiti, workers call him Papa) obligation to repair it, or when a child needed medical attention or a brother was getting married, again it was Papa's obligation to help. Obviously, the Americans assumed wrongly when they accepted the market wage as the real wage. Where workers are genuinely commodified, the manager is no Papa.

We should not dismiss the feudal paternalism of Haiti as a relic of our own distant past. Patronage and clientelism are modern versions of the same phenomenon, and have been extraordinarily influential in taming the brutal world of commodification. In the United States, the urban machine became the mechanism through which ethnic immigrants could integrate wage-work and welfare; in Italy, Christian Democracy's post-war power owes much to its welfare-clientelism, especially in the distribution of jobs and invalid pensions. Even more relevant are the early employer occupational fringe-benefit schemes that emerged in Europe and the United States. They were typically discretionary and awarded benefits to especially favored employees. In the United States, the American Express Company (then a shipping firm) was the forerunner, but this style of paternal, clientelistic largesse remained a typical feature of private corporations well into the post-war era (Weaver, 1982).

Corporate societies are a second variant of pre-capitalist and pre-commodified arrangements. They emerged in the towns among artisans and craftsmen as a means to close ranks and monopolize entry, membership, prices, and production. The guilds and fraternal associations also integrated pay and social welfare, taking care of disabled members, widows, and orphans. Their members were not commodities, and not in the market, but were defined by their corporate status. Significantly, the guilds merged masters and journeymen, and accepted rank and hierarchy but not class. When the guilds were abolished, they were often transformed into mutual societies. In Germany, the mutual societies and the subsequent social-insurance laws were endowed with much of the old feudal spirit, as was seen in their ideas of compulsory membership for certain groups, and in the principle of corporative self-administration (Neumann and Schapter, 1982).

The corporate model was one of the early and most prevalent responses to commodification. It clearly penetrated the infant working-class friendly societies, offering a closed world of services and protection for members; not surprisingly, the friendly societies predominantly addressed privileged craft-workers.

But the corporate model was mainly favored by the conservative ruling circles in continental Europe. They perceived it as a way to uphold traditional society in the unfolding capitalist economy; as a means to integrate the individual into an organic entity, protected from the individualization and competitiveness of the market, and removed from the logic of class opposition. Corporatist welfare became the dogma of the Catholic Church and was actively espoused in the two major Papal Encyclicals on the social question: *Rerum Novarum* (1891) and *Quadrogesimo Anno* (1931) (Messner, 1964). The corporatist element was especially strong in the latter, and was in line with current Fascist ideology. In Germany, as in Italy, Fascism was not particularly keen on nurturing a workforce of atomized commodities, but wanted to reinstall the principle of moral desert. Thus, its social policy was positively in favor of granting an array of social rights. These rights, nonetheless, were conditional upon appropriate loyalty and morality; they were seen as part and parcel of the new Fascist man (Rimlinger, 1987; Guillebaud, 1941; Preusser, 1982).

The readiness of conservatism to grant social rights, albeit conditional upon morals, loyalties, or convention, is also evident in the etatist tradition, historically perhaps best exemplified in the regimes of Germany under Bismarck, and von Taaffe''s Austria. As in the case of corporativism, the ulterior motives were social integration, the preservation of authority, and the battle against socialism. It was also motivated by an equally strong opposition to individualism and liberalism. Intellectually guided by conservative academicians such as Gustav Schmoller and Adolph Wagner, and the Catholic teachings, such as Bishop Ketteler's, there emerged the principle of 'monarchical socialism', an absolutist model of paternal-authoritarian obligation for the welfare of its subjects.

Etatist conservatism saw in social rights the solution to the 'social question'. When Bismarck and von Taaffe pioneered modern social insurance, they were in fact following the lead of Napoleon III in France. But Bismarck wanted to go further, and even contemplated legislating the right (or obligation, if you wish) to employment as part and parcel of his larger vision of *Sodaten der Arbeit*: workers as soldiers in an economy functioning like the army (Preller, 1949; 1970; Briggs, 1961). In the 1930s, the Nazis actually began implementing Bismarck's old notion of militarized labor, through work conscription, a policy against women's employment, and compulsory membership in Robert Ley's hyper-corporativist Labor Front (Rimlinger, 1987). In conservative social policy, the boundary between duties and rights is often very blurred.

Our lengthy excursion into the conservative foundations of social rights was necessary because they are, indeed, the historical origins of modern social policy. In almost every country, be it in Scandinavia, Britain, or on the European continent, it was the conservative tradition that gave rise to the first systematic and deliberate attacks on the commodification of labor. The reasons are not especially difficult to discern. First, these conservative forces feared, quite correctly, that the onward march of liberalism, democracy, and capitalism would destroy the institutions upon which their power and privileges were based. Labor as a commodity clearly would tear asunder feudal and absolutist systems of labor control.

Second, the pre-commodified status of workers was a model that was already available and typically also present in the heyday of laissez-faire; it was a response that came naturally, and which could claim considerable legitimacy. The guilds may have been abolished, but lingered on as mutual benefit societies; the capitalist company (as well as the state) offered a menu of social benefits outside of the work contract; and paternalism was not something that seemed especially contradictory to the entrepreneurial spirit. As Schumpeter (1970) argued so eloquently, the capitalist order worked because it was ruled and organized by the protective strata of an earlier era. The social policy of 'pre-commodification' was, so to speak, one of the 'flying buttresses that prevented capitalism's collapse' (Schumpeter, 1970, p. 139). It was also one of the cornerstones of what we today consider the modern welfare state.

The Liberal Response to the Dilemmas of Commodification

The pure and undiluted labor commodity that we associate with laissez-faire probably never existed in real life. Neither did it, in fact, in any serious theory of laissez-faire. Theorists like Adam Smith or Nassau Senior were not advocating a political economy in which the state withholds any form of social protection. But this does not imply that the problem is reduced to a historical phantom. Some labor markets do resemble the pure case, as is illustrated by the street-corner labor auctions that take place in Texas. And in respectable theory, the state was meant to be absolutely minimalist, to be called upon only in situations of genuine human crisis.

It was among the laissez-faire popularizers, such as Smiley or

Martineau, that the pure commodity-form was sanctified. From a welfare perspective, their argument was a double one. First, they held that a guaranteed social minimum would cause poverty and unemployment, not eradicate it – an argument that has found new life in recent neo-liberalism. Second, to them, social protection caused moral corruption, thriftlessness, idleness, and drunkenness. The morals of liberalism and conservatism were clearly at odds.

The general assumption in liberalism is that the market is emancipatory, the best possible shell for self-reliance and industriousness. If not interfered with, its self-regulatory mechanisms will ensure that all who want to work will be employed, and thus be able to secure their own welfare. Private life may be wrought with insecurity, danger, and pitfalls; and poverty or helplessness is in principle not unlikely to occur. Yet, this is not a fault of the system, but solely a consequence of an individual's lack of foresight and thrift.

This raw model of the liberal 'good society' contains a number of obvious and well-known weaknesses. It assumes that all individuals are indeed capable of market participation, something which of course they are not. The old, the infirm, the blind, and the crippled are forced into family dependency which, in turn, constrains the family's capacity to supply its labor in the market. Saving for future social catastrophies may not be possible when wages approximate the minimum for survival. And almost no individual can safeguard himself against a prolonged crisis.

In all such cases, the liberal dogma is forced to seek recourse in pre-capitalist institutions of social aid, such as the family, the church, and the community. And in doing so, it contradicts itself, because these institutions cannot play the game of the market if they are saddled with social responsibilities.

Liberalism recognized in the principle of public good a rationale for social intervention. Merchant ships would run aground without lighthouses, and the population similarly would die out without public sanitation. It was mainly in the force of circumstance that liberalism came to accept the must of social rights. As the British discovered in the Boer War, an empire is difficult to sustain without an army of healthy and educated soldiers. Likewise, the performance of a poverty-stricken and destitute English working class seemed to compare unfavorably on efficiency terms with the industrial parvenues, such as Germany. How, then, did liberalism come to terms with the dilemmas of labor commodification?

Liberalism found two acceptable answers. One was to transfer a modified version of the 'less eligibility' principle from the old poor laws into a framework of means-tested social assistance. In this way, the extension of unconditional social rights was avoided, and government largesse was limited to the certifiably needy and would not induce workers to choose welfare instead of work. A means-tested assistance system is, in a sense, a way of ensuring that non-market income is reserved for those who are unable to participate in the market anyhow. Titmuss's (1974) concept of the residual, or marginal, welfare state tries to capture exactly this property of the liberal paradigm; namely, that public obligation enters only where the market fails: the commodity-logic is supreme.

The social-assistance model mainly found its way into the more liberally dominated Anglo-Saxon and early Scandinavian social policies. Well into this century, and sometimes even after World War II, it was often strictly conditional upon proper 'commodified' (and sometimes also moral) behavior. In Denmark, for example, the means-tested assistance pension was denied persons who had failed to repay to the state previously received poor relief. In New Zealand, social assistance has been refused to persons of 'amoral' marital conduct, i.e. divorce.

It is the same philosophy which informs the second approach. Even the purest form of liberalism never objected to charity or insurance *per se*. What matters is that charity, or any kind of insurance, be based on voluntarism and that, moreover, insurance arrangements be soundly contractual and actuarial. Since there is no such thing as a free lunch, rights and benefits must reflect contributions. Once liberalism came to accept the principle of unionism, it was also perfectly capable of extending the idea of individual insurance to collectively bargained social benefits. Indeed, the latter came to inspire the whole ideology of welfare capitalism that so enthused American liberalism between the wars (Brandes, 1976). The idea here was that the United States could be spared the 'socialistic' flavor of state social insurance by encouraging company-based welfare schemes.

Liberalism's preference is obviously for privately organized insurance in the market. But, as Ogus (1979) has noted, the idea of public social insurance was not as difficult to reconcile with the commodity-logic of labor as purist ideology assumed. Social insurance, like its private-sector kin, pegs entitlements and benefits to employment, work performance, and contributions. It should therefore strengthen the work incentive and productivity. If built on an actuarial basis, it also retains the pure exchange nexus of welfare. And, as Graebner (1980) has argued, old-age pensions even came to be regarded by the business community as a means to make the labor market more flexible: with pensions, employers could – at others' expense – rid themselves more easily of the older, less efficient workers. Even the idea of compulsory social insurance could be accommodated to liberal dogma. For, if some groups were to be covered and others not, the result would be unfair competition. It was clearly this, and not ideals of social solidarity, which motivated a universally compulsory unemployment insurance in the United States. The tendency in liberalism to favor universal solutions once social insurance becomes inescapable is therefore not an accident.

In summary, liberalism's accommodation of social protection is in practice much more elastic than is normally thought, precisely because under certain conditions it promises to actually strengthen the commodity status of labor without adverse social effects.

De-Commodification as the Politics of Socialism

Socialism, whether as a theory, an ideology, or a political strategy, emerged very much in response to capitalism's commodification of labor power. To socialism the commodification of labor is an integral element in the process of alienation and class; it is the condition under which workers abandon control over their work in return for wages; the condition under which their dependence on the market is affirmed, and, therefore, also a key source of employer control. It is, moreover, a cause of class division and an obstacle to collective unity. Simply by definition, commodities compete, and the fiercer the competition, the cheaper the price. It is therefore natural that the workers' desire for de-commodification became the guiding principle of labor-movement policy. Be it the worker's welfare or the movement's power, both depend on lessening the individual's enslavement in the cash nexus.

Classical socialist theory is often depicted as advocating an all-out destruction of the commodity-logic of labor. Certainly this is true in terms of the end-goal, but not with regard to practical analysis. In *Capital*, Marx hailed the British Factory Acts because they helped lessen the powerlessness of workers. In the *Communist Manifesto*, the concluding chapter propagates a series of ameliorative social reforms that would augment the workers' resources and strengthen their position *vis-à-vis* the market. And both Karl Kautsky and Rosa Luxemburg actively promoted the social wage. In general, revolutionary and reformist theories both agreed on the necessity and desirability of struggling for the right to a social income outside of wage labor. What divided the reformist and revolutionary wings of socialism was mainly the issue of strategy.

The embryonic policies of de-commodification had a close kinship with the corporative conservative tradition. This comes as no surprise, since the early labor movements were largely built around restrictive crafts unions, mutual-aid societies, and sometimes a political party. One weakness of these schemes was, of course, their modest benefits and limited reach among the most vulnerable members of the working classes. It was the unorganized, the 'slum proletariat', that posed the greatest threat to labor unity. These were the workers that needed to be empowered, but micro-socialist welfare societies had difficulty reaching them. Thus evolved the debate on whether to support the extension of social rights in the bourgeois state.

This was a dilemma that severely stifled socialists' capacity to act. Until after World War I, the state in virtually all nations was controlled by conservative or liberal forces, and the socialists saw few alternatives but to oppose what they perceived as harmful social pacification. This certainly was the dominant response in German social democracy until well into the twentieth century. Nonetheless, the schism between socialists and conservatives was not necessarily that deep on the question of social rights. This was gradually realized by important socialist figures, such as Branting in Sweden and Heiman and Kalecki in Germany, and it fell neatly in place with the emerging paradigm of the 'slow revolution' espoused in Austrian and German social democracy.

These socialists, then, reconciled conservative reformism with socialist objectives. For Lederer and Marshack (1926), two prominent German social democrats, worker protection advanced the cause of labor because it would inevitably restrict the employers' scope of control. To Eduard Heiman (1929), one of the foremost theoreticians among his contemporaries, social policy was Janus-faced: it may very well be a means to prop up and save the capitalist system, but at the same time it is also a foreign body, threatening to emasculate the rule of capital. Armed with this kind of analysis, socialism could also defend the gradualist strategy against the more apocalyptic scenario presented in revolutionary communist dogma. Where the latter believed that the roots of revolution lay in crisis and collapse, the reformists realized that the human misery that crises bred would only weaken the socialist project. Hence, a gradual augmentation of the scope and quality of social rights was seen as the precondition for the larger struggle, not merely the fruits of its final success. It was through this strategic realignment that socialism eventually embraced the welfare state as the focus for its long-term project. It is in this sense that social democracy becomes synonymous with welfare-statism.

It would be absolutely wrong to believe that the socialists had a blueprint for de-commodification. Even the illustrious Swedish socialists fumbled between a variety of policies, many of which were objectively on unsound socialist footing. The source of confusion was twofold. One source had to do with an interpretation of the 'ability–needs' nexus, so central to classical Marxism. If social amelioration was to be a function of need, the socialists easily found themselves operating in the largely liberal mold of means-tests and benefit standards tailored to the living conditions of the poor. In many cases, such as Australia and Denmark, the social-assistance model was embraced by the labor movements on such grounds. The socialists struggled, perhaps, to upgrade benefits and minimize social stigma, but they saw the assistance type of scheme as clearly the most egalitarian: helping the really needy.

Another source of confusion had to do with the clientele for de-commodification. Until World War II, labor parties were strongly 'workerist', seeing themselves as the defenders of the industrial working class. Under such conditions, it was natural to espouse class-exclusive schemes. But, where the socialists moved towards the broader image of embracing 'all the little people', they were politically compelled to approach rights in terms of universal coverage. This, as we discuss in chapter 3, was the root of universalist solidarity in socialist social policy.

What characterizes almost all early socialist social policy is the notion of basic, or minimal, social rights: the idea was to install strong entitlements, but at fairly modest benefit levels, and typically limited to the core areas of human need (old-age pensions, accident insurance, unemployment and sickness benefits). Financial constraints surely played a role, but the modesty in their approach can also be seen as a reflection of how early socialists defined the problem – they saw the issue in workerist terms, in terms of providing a basic floor beneath which no one would be allowed to fall. Indeed, until the 1950s and 1960s, the social programs of the labor parties were almost universally of modest scope and quality, although providing for very generous eligibility criteria. The goal was to stave off poverty, not really to emancipate workers from market dependency. To do so would have required a major realignment of social policy, including two basic changes: first, the extension of rights beyond the narrow terrain of absolute need; and second, the upgrading of benefits to match normal earnings and average living standards in the nation. In reference to the former, what mattered especially was the introduction of a variety of schemes that permit employees to be paid while pursuing activities other than working, be they child-bearing, family responsibilities, re-education, organizational activities, or even leisure. Such programs are, in spirit, truly de-commodifying. With respect to the latter, the crucial issue was that the status of welfare client should impose no decline in living standards, even over an extended time.

In sum, the gist of de-commodification in the socialist paradigm is the emancipation from market dependency. It is in the quality and arrangement of social rights, not in their existence *per se*, that we can identify a distinct socialist approach. In contrast to the conservative models, dependence on family, morality, or authority is not the substitute for market dependence; the notion is rather that of individual independence. And, in contrast to liberalism, socialism's aim is to maximize and institutionalize rights. Where the fully developed socialist paradigm is pursued, it should, in principle, facilitate a de-proletarianization of the worker's status: the worker's relationship to work will begin to approximate what privileged strata (such as the civil service) had enjoyed for decades and even centuries.

Welfare States and De-Commodification in the Real World

Variations in the de-commodifying potential of social policies should be empirically identifiable across time and nations. This potential can clearly not be captured solely by social expenditure levels, but requires analysis of the rules and standards that pertain to actual welfare programs. The question is how we adequately operationalize the crucial dimensions.

One set of dimensions must speak to the rules that govern peoples' access to benefits: eligibility rules and restrictions on entitlements. A program can be seen to harbor greater de-commodification potential if access is easy, and if rights to an adequate standard of living are guaranteed regardless of previous employment record, performance, needs-test, or financial contribution. The other side of the coin of 'entry' is exit. If programs provide benefits for only limited duration, clearly their capacity to de-commodify is diminished.

A second set of dimensions has to do with income replacement, for if benefit levels fall substantially below normal earnings or the standard of living considered adequate and acceptable in the society, the likely result is to drive the recipient back to work as soon as possible. We will therefore have to consider the levels of income replacement.

Thirdly, the range of entitlements provided for is of utmost importance. Almost all advanced capitalist countries recognize some form of social right to protection against the basic social risks: unemployment, disability, sickness, and old age. A highly advanced case would be where a social wage is paid to citizens regardless of cause. The idea of a *de facto* guaranteed citizens' wage, as has been under discussion in Scandinavia and the Netherlands, and with more modest aspirations in the case of the American negative income-tax proposal, comes close to this scenario.

Social rights are hardly ever unconditional. Claimants will at least have to satisfy the condition of being ill, old, or unemployed to receive the benefits. Beyond the mere presence of a problem, however, conditions are usually linked to type of social security arrangement.

We may in general distinguish three kinds of arrangements, each one with its own peculiar effect on de-commodification. One type of system, historically most pronounced in the Anglo-Saxon nations, builds entitlements around demonstrable and abject need. With its mainsprings in the poor-law tradition, the social-assistance tradition is characterized by the application of a means- or income-test with varying degrees of stringency. These systems do not properly extend citizen rights. The main examples of this tradition are the early pension schemes in Scandinavia, the British scheme of supplementary benefits, the American SSI, and virtually the entire Australian welfare system. Every nation has some type of means-tested social assistance or poor-relief arrangement. What counts most heavily in this type of regime are the restrictiveness of means/incomes tests and the generosity of benefits.

A second type of system extends entitlements on the basis of work performance. This variant has its roots in the insurance tradition that was most consistently developed first in Germany, and then across the European continent. Rights here are clearly conditional upon a blend of labor-market attachment and financial contributions, and have usually been subjected to a logic of actuarialism; i.e. the idea that the individual has a personal entitlement of a contractual nature. The degree to which this kind of regime offers opportunities for de-commodification depends largely on how much it relaxes the actuarial principle: how much a person will have to have worked or contributed to qualify, and how strict is the relationship between prior performance and benefits.

The third type of system springs from the Beveridge principle of universal rights of citizenship, regardless of degree of need or extent of work performance. Eligibility rests instead on being a citizen or long-time resident of the country. Invariably, these types of programs are built on the flat-rate benefit principle. In principle, this 'people's welfare' approach has a strong de-commodifying potential, but obviously circumscribed by the largesse of the benefits. The people's-welfare system has taken strongest hold in the Scandinavian nations, and has been a long-standing principle in the socialist tradition of social policy.

Although never implemented, it has been a perennial ideal in German social democracy.

To an extent the three system-types mirror Titmuss's well-known trichotomy of residual, industrial-achievement, and institutional welfare states (Titmuss, 1958). In reality, however, there are no one-dimensional nations in the sense of a pure case. In the Anglo-Saxon countries, such as Australia, Canada, and the United States, the social-assistance system may be dominant, but is complemented by alternative programs. In the United States, the social security system falls into the social-insurance category; Canada has a blend of a people's pension and a social-insurance based pension, and even Australia is approaching the principle of a people's pension. In the continental European nations, where the social-insurance tradition is strongest, a host of alternatives has emerged over the years: in Italy, the social pension; in France, the 'solidarity funds'. And, finally, almost all countries dominated by a people's-welfare approach have developed earnings- and work-related schemes to complement the usually modest benefits awarded by the flat-rate universal plans. In short, every country today presents a system mix.

Despite the complexity this involves, it is possible to empirically distinguish welfare states' variable capacity to de-commodify. We will here present combined scores of de-commodification for the three most important social-welfare programs: pensions, sickness, and unemployment cash benefits. The scores summarize an array of variables that illustrate the ease with which an average person can opt out of the market: first, the prohibitiveness of conditions for eligibility, such as work experience, contributions, or means-tests; second, the strength of in-built disincentives (such as waiting days for cash benefits) and maximum duration of entitlements; and third, the degree to which benefits approximate normal expected earnings-levels. The overall de-commodification scores are weighted by the percent of the relevant population covered by the social security program. This reflects the probability that any given person will possess the right to a transfer. A program may very well offer luxurious benefits and liberal conditions, but if it addresses solely a small clientele, it has obviously a limited capacity to de-commodify.

Table 2.1 presents de-commodification indices for the leading 18 industrial democracies in terms of old-age pensions. We have used five variables to construct the index for pensions: 1) the minimum pension as a percent of a normal worker earnings (replacement rate net of taxes) for a single person; 2) the standard pension replacement rate (net) for a single person; 3) number of years of contributions required to qualify;

TABLE 2.1   The degree of de-commodification in old-age pensions, sickness benefits, and unemployment insurance, 1980

	Pensions	Sickness	Unemployment
Australia	5.0	4.0	4.0
Austria	11.9	12.5	6.7
Belgium	15.0	8.8	8.6
Canada	7.7	6.3	8.0
Denmark	15.0	15.0	8.1
Finland	14.0	10.0	5.2
France	12.0	9.2	6.3
Germany	8.5	11.3	7.9
Ireland	6.7	8.3	8.3
Italy	9.6	9.4	5.1
Japan	10.5	6.8	5.0
Netherlands	10.8	10.5	11.1
New Zealand	9.1	4.0	4.0
Norway	14.9	14.0	9.4
Sweden	17.0	15.0	7.1
Switzerland	9.0	12.0	8.8
United Kingdom	8.5	7.7	7.2
United States	7.0	0.0[a]	7.2
Mean	10.7	9.2	7.1
S. D.	3.4	4.0	1.9

The higher the score the greater is the degree of de-commodification. For scoring procedure, see appendix to this chapter.
[a] Program non-existent and therefore scored 0.
Source: SSIB data files

4) the share of total pension finance paid by individuals. The scores for these four variables are added, and then weighted by 5) the percent of persons above pension age actually receiving a pension (the take-up rate). For sickness and unemployment benefits, the procedure is almost identical, with the following exceptions: here we include only the replacement rate (net) for standard benefits, omit share of individual financing, and include data on number of waiting days to receive benefits and number of weeks of benefit duration. For all three programs, we have scored the benefits double, since for any given person's work/welfare decision, expected income-levels will be absolutely decisive.

To prevent any misunderstanding, it must be clear that we are trying to measure a program's potential for de-commodification, and not its general qualities. We are capturing the degree of market-independence for an average worker. Thus, it is possible for a country normally regarded as having a first-rate pension system (like Germany) to score low. Indeed, in this case, Germany scores low because it requires long periods of contribution and a large individual financial contribution, and because its pension benefits are relatively modest. Australia and New Zealand score exceedingly low on both sickness and unemployment because they offer only means-tested benefits.

In table 2.1 we see that the three programs differ considerably in their degree of de-commodification potential. Invariably, unemployment insurance is associated with greater disincentive effects. Table 2.1 also indicates that there is a substantial variation among the advanced welfare states with regard to de-commodification. Some nations score consistently low on all programs, while others are strongly de-commodifying across the board. Thus, we confront a situation in which national welfare systems appear to harbor systematic traits. The Nordic countries are, in particular, consistently de-commodifying, while the Anglo-Saxon countries tend to be consistently least so. This is precisely what we would have expected in terms of our typology of welfare-state regimes.

The idea that welfare states cluster into distinct groups becomes more evident when we examine table 2.2. Here we present the total combined de-commodification score for the three programs in the same 18 nations. Based roughly on how nations cluster around the mean, we can distinguish three groups of countries: the Anglo-Saxon 'new' nations are all concentrated at the bottom of our index; the Scandinavian countries at the top. In between these two extremes, we find the continental European countries, some of which (especially Belgium and the Netherlands) fall close to the Nordic cluster.

Even if table 2.2 shows a number of borderline cases, the clustering remains strong. And the clusters bring together the countries which, *a priori*, we expected would look similar in terms of our welfare-state regime arguments. We would anticipate a very low level of de-commodification in the nations with a history dominated by liberalism. And this we find in the first cluster. And in the 'high de-commodification' cluster we find the social democratically dominated welfare states, exactly as we would have expected. Finally, the continental European countries, with their powerful Catholic and etatist influence, tend to occupy the middle group – prepared to extend a considerable modicum of rights outside the market, but nonetheless with a stronger accent on social control than is the case within social democracy.

How do we account for cross-national differences in de-commodifying capabilities of welfare states? As we have already discussed, a simple explanation in terms of economic development or working-class power

TABLE 2.2 The rank-order of welfare states in terms of combined de-commodification, 1980

De-commodification score	
Australia	13.0
United States	13.8
New Zealand	17.1
Canada	22.0
Ireland	23.3
United Kingdom	23.4
Italy	24.1
Japan	27.1
France	27.5
Germany	27.7
Finland	29.2
Switzerland	29.8
Austria	31.1
Belgium	32.4
Netherlands	32.4
Denmark	38.1
Norway	38.3
Sweden	39.1
Mean	27.2
S. D.	7.7

For scoring procedure, see appendix to this chapter.
Source: SSIB data files

mobilization will hardly suffice. As we shall examine more closely in chapter 5, level of economic development is negatively correlated with de-commodification, and has no explanatory power.

As we will see, the degree of left power has a fairly strong and positive influence on de-commodification, explaining about 40 percent of the variance. Yet, the non-explained residual is large and must be uncovered in order fully to understand how and why welfare-state variations have evolved to the point they have. This issue will be taken up in chapter 5; at this point it will suffice to say that the explanation will be found in the interaction between political-power variables and nations' historical legacy. The relatively high de-commodification scores found in the continental European countries are not solely the product of left political mobilization, but also of a long tradition of conservative and Catholic reformism. In converse, the exceedingly low de-commodification scores found in countries with comparatively powerful labor movements, like Australia and New Zealand, can find an explanation in the historically dominant legacy of institutionalized liberalism.

The fruitfulness of a more historically grounded account of welfare-state clusters is evident when we examine how the different countries clustered in earlier epochs, in particular prior to the advent of left or labor-party influence, on social-policy legislation. In this way, we can hold constant the 'social democracy' effect. In both 1930 and 1950, the low de-commodification group included most of the countries included in 1980: Canada, the United States, New Zealand, and (in 1950) Australia. It also included Italy and Japan, both nations under pro-longed Fascist rule, and Finland. Finland's post-war rise in de-commodification can be seen as a case of social democratization; that of the two others cannot. In turn, the Scandinavian high de-commodification cluster of 1980 is nowhere to be found prior to 1950, again a case in favor of the influence of post-war social democratic power. Most significant, however, is the consistent historical position of the 'conservative-Catholic', or etatist, regimes of continental Europe like Germany, Austria, and France, all of which consistently score medium to high in the 1930s, in 1950, and in 1980. We may, on this basis, offer the following guiding hypotheses, to be further explored in later chapters.

1 Nations with a long historical legacy of conservative and/or Catholic reformism are likely to develop a fair degree of de-commodified social policy at an early date. Their welfare states, nonetheless, circumscribe the loosening of the market's bonds with powerful social-control devices, such as a proven record of strong employment attachment or strong familial obligations. The superior performance on de-commodification that we find in countries such as Austria, Belgium, and the Netherlands after 1950 can probably best be ascribed to the strong political position of the social democratic labor movements.

2 Nations with a powerful liberalist legacy will bifurcate, depending on the structuration of political power. Where social democracy comes to political dominance, as in Denmark, Norway, and Sweden, the liberal mold is broken and replaced with a highly de-commodifying social democratic welfare-state regime. Where, on the other hand, labor fails to realign the nation's political economy and assert dominance, the result is continuously low or, at most, moderate de-commodification. This is exemplified by Great Britain at one end, and by Canada and the United States at the other end. The Labour Party's breakthrough in Britain is evidenced by the fact that Britain scored in the top de-commodification group in 1950: the universalist social citizenship

of the Beveridge model that was launched after the war placed Britain as the highest scoring nation internationally. The system certainly was not undone by the 1980s, but it failed to progress further; Labour's record of post-war power was too weak and interrupted to match the accomplishments in Scandinavia. The United States and Canada, in turn, are the 'pure' cases of liberal hegemony, virtually unchallenged by the paradigmatic alternatives of socialism or, for that matter, conservative reformism.

Appendix   Scoring procedure for indices of de-commodification

PENSIONS

De-commodification in old-age pensions is measured in terms of the additive qualities of 1) minimum pension benefits for a standard production worker earning average wages. The replacement rate here (as elsewhere) is the ratio of the benefit to normal worker earnings in that year, both benefits and earnings net of taxes; 2) standard pension benefits for a normal worker, calculated as above; 3) contribution period, measured as number of years of contributions (or employment) required to qualify for a standard pension (scored inversely); 4) individual's share of pension financing. On the basis of the values on each of these four indicators for the 18 nations, we have given a score of 1 for low de-commodification; 2 for medium; and 3 for high de-commodification. The classification into the three scores has been done on the basis of one standard deviation from the mean, in a few cases adjusted for extreme outliers. Finally, the scores have been weighted by the percent of the (relevant) population covered by the program (for pensions, the take-up rate). Where, as in Australia, the pensions are based on a means-test, we have scored 0 for contribution period, and have given the weight of 0.5 for population covered. This 'negative' scoring reflects the fact that means-tested programs are highly conditional in terms of offering rights. To take into account the singular importance of replacement rates for people's welfare–work choices, we have given extra weight to these variables (multiplied by the factor of 2).

SICKNESS AND UNEMPLOYMENT CASH BENEFITS

In sickness and unemployment programs, we have measured de-commodification in terms of 1) benefit replacement rates (net) for a standard worker during the first 26 weeks of illness/unemployment; 2) number of weeks of employment required prior to qualification; 3) number of waiting days before benefits are paid; 4) number of weeks in which a benefit can be maintained. As with pensions, we have given scores of 1, 2, or 3 on the basis of the standard deviation to develop a summary de-commodification index. This, subsequently, has been weighted by the (relevant) population covered as a percent of the labor force. Means-tested programs have been dealt with as described under pensions. As with pensions, replacement rates have been multiplied by a factor of 2.

3

The Welfare State as a System of Stratification

The welfare state may provide services and income security, but it is also, and always has been, a system of social stratification. Welfare states are key institutions in the structuring of class and the social order. The organizational features of the welfare state help determine the articulation of social solidarity, divisions of class, and status differentiation.

That the welfare state is an agent of stratification is well recognized, but, unfortunately, usually in a narrow and often mis-specified way. It is an aspect that has remained severely neglected, both theoretically and empirically. At the theoretical level, two views have dominated; one, common to a good deal of neo-Marxism, typically argues that even the advanced welfare state merely reproduces (and perhaps even nurtures) existing class society (Offe, 1972; O'Connor, 1973; Muller and Neussuss, 1973). Thus, O'Connor's argument is that welfare policies provide the legitimacy and social calm required by monopoly capitalism. In Piven and Cloward's (1971) study, government's willingness to provide relief to the poor depends less on acute need than on perceived threats to social stability.

The second view follows in the footsteps of T. H. Marshall and, to a degree, his pre-war forebears like Heimann. It sees welfare reforms as a major contribution to the declining salience of class (Lipset, 1960; Crosland, 1967; Parkin, 1979). Here, the argument is that welfare eliminates the essential causes of class struggle, incorporates the working classes, and democratizes popular access to the state; or, as Parkin argues, it transforms class conflict into status competition.

Empirically, the literature has almost exclusively focused on income redistribution. The issue is of course not whether overall inequality of income has declined – a fairly indisputable fact – but to what extent the tax/expenditure nexus of the welfare state plays a decisive role. As Kraus (1981) has shown, the empirical and methodological problems of answering such a question are severe, if not prohibitive, and so both cross-sectional and longitudinal research findings remain little more than speculative. Nonetheless, most studies come to rather similar conclusions. When studied cross-sectionally, we find tremendous national variation in the welfare state's equalizing capacity. In some countries, like Germany and France, the welfare state's redistributive effect appears quite miniscule; in contrast, its effect in Scandinavia is substantial (Sawyer, 1976; Hewitt, 1977; Stephens, 1979; Cameron, 1987; O'Higgins, 1985; Ringen, 1987; Ringen and Uusitalo, forthcoming, 1990).

These studies have been less concerned with the welfare state's impact as such than with theories of power and equality. Hence, why welfare-state structures have such different distributional consequences is left largely unexplained. And when the welfare state is brought into the analysis, as in Cameron's study, it is identified in a vague manner as levels of social expenditure. O'Higgins' and Ringen's studies are two of the few in which distribution outcomes are related more directly to the programmatic components of welfare states.

When the question is studied longitudinally over many years, the conclusions tend to be very different. Several studies conclude that the welfare state's redistributive capacity has increased only slightly, notwithstanding its phenomenal growth (Sawyer, 1982; Kenneth Hansen, 1987). It appears that the role of tax systems is gradually replaced by social transfers as the major weapon for redistribution. This is a trend clearly evident in the Scandinavian welfare states (Esping-Andersen, 1985a; Kenneth Hansen, 1987). The reasons for this shift are fairly straightforward: as welfare states get large, their financial requirements are such that they need to impose heavy taxes, even on modest-income households. As a result, the net redistributive impact of welfare states comes to depend mostly on the structuration of their social transfers. Paradoxically, one explanation is that the large welfare state therefore loses its tax-redistributive capability. And with reference to transfers, the egalitarian impulse may be blocked by the probability that the middle classes profit disproportionately (Le Grand, 1982). The middle-class bias is something that is likely to vary across nations but, as yet, we lack comparative evidence. The direct impact of welfare-state structures on equality is an issue that we shall explore in more detail below.

Instead of focusing on aggregate income distribution, a number of recent comparative studies have begun to rephrase the question in more fruitful ways. The Luxembourg Income Study, which hosts the world's only truly comparable income-distribution data at the micro-level, has produced a series of analyses on welfare states' ability to reduce or eliminate poverty, among key social groups. Hedstrom and Ringen (1985) and Smeeding, Torrey, and Rein (1988) find startling cross-national differences: the percentage of the aged in poverty ranges from 29 percent in the UK, and 24 percent in the United States, to 11 percent in Germany and less than 1 percent in Sweden. Parallel discrepancies were found with respect to families with children. Since the aged and families with children are particularly dependent on transfer incomes, these studies are able to directly identify different welfare systems' impact on stratification.

A second pathbreaking deviation from the standard income-distribution approach are the 'level of living' studies, so far limited to the Scandinavian countries. The idea here is that incomes alone provide too narrow a basis for portraying the structure of opportunities and inequality. Instead, the concept of resources is widened to include health, housing, working life, education, social and political efficacy, and other components vital to human reproduction. National surveys are used to measure the distribution-of-resource command among the population. Begun in Sweden in 1968, and subsequently carried out in Denmark and Norway, the studies have been replicated in later years, making it possible to monitor changes over time in the distribution of resources. The Swedish and Danish data offer the most interesting basis for evaluating the welfare state's distributive effects because they have surveyed the same people over many years, and because the studies span the long era of rising unemployment and economic stagnation. What they find is that, despite worsening economic conditions (particularly in Denmark), living conditions have improved overall, hard-core resource poverty has declined, and the trend towards greater equality continues (Erikson and Aaberg, 1984; Hansen, 1988). It is therefore quite evident that, for Scandinavia at least, the welfare state is a mighty opponent to the economy's inegalitarian thrust.

In any case, poverty and income distribution constitute only one (albeit important) aspect of welfare-state stratification. Even if inequalities in living standards decline, it may still be the case that essential class or status cleavages persist. What conerns us here is not so much incomes as how nations differ in the structuring of social citizenship.

What, then, constitute salient dimensions of welfare-state stratification? Apart from its purely income-distributive role, the welfare state shapes class and status in a variety of ways. The education system is an obvious and much-studied instance, in which individuals' mobility chances not only are affected, but from which entire class structures evolve. As we will see in Part II of this book, the organization of social services, particularly for women, is decisive for a nation's employment structure. At this point, we will confine our attention to the stratification impact of the welfare state's traditional, and still dominant, activity: income maintenance.

Lord Beveridge and T. H. Marshall have exhorted to the world the peculiar and essentially ethnocentric assumption that universalism is the hallmark of an advanced welfare state. It was the implied universalism of post-war British reforms that informed the theory of the declining significance of class. Yet, one does not have to travel far to discover completely different organizational features of social security. In some countries, coverage may be quite comprehensive; yet, from pensions to sick-pay, the system is built around a myriad of occupationally distinct schemes, explicitly designed so as to recognize and uphold old status distinctions. In some nations, key social groups are given special privileged status – the civil service, for example. In yet other countries, social insurance is organized so as to nurture individualism and self-reliance rather than collective solidarity. And, in still others, social programs are primarily targeted at the really needy, thus cultivating a dualism between the poor (who depend on the welfare state) and the middle classes (who mainly insure themselves in the market).

In other words, welfare states may be equally large or comprehensive, but with entirely different effects on social structure. One may cultivate hierarchy and status, another dualisms, and a third universalism. Each case will produce its own unique fabric of social solidarity. We can identify three models, or ideal types, of stratification and solidarity that closely parallel the regime-types we identified with respect to de-commodification.

Stratification in Conservative Social Policy

Traditional conservatism, as we have seen, embodies a number of divergent models of the ideal social order. What unites them, as in the case of social rights, is a loathing of the combined social leveling and class antagonisms brought about by capitalism. Be it in favor of strict hierarchy, corporatism, or of familialism, the unifying theme is that traditional status relations must be retained for the sake of social integration.

Authoritarian paternalist conservatism has been historically important in the development of welfare-state structures. With its origins in feudal manorial society and in the absolutist monarchical regimes of Europe and Russia, the guiding principles are hierarchy, authority, and direct subordination of the individual (or family) to the patriarch or state. Inspired by Hegel's theory of the state, these organizational notions were enthusiastically promoted by nineteenth-century academicians, social reformers, and politicians, especially in countries like Germany and Austria (Bower, 1947). Adolph Wagner's idea of a *Staatswirtschaftlische Oekonomie* was that the state should directly guide and organize all economic activity. Bismarck's notion of the *Soldaten der Arbeit* was borrowed from the military, the idea being to organize workers (as footsoldiers) on a company basis under the direct authority of the manager (as captain) who, in turn, was answerable to the state (as general) (Guillebaud, 1941).

When Bismarck promoted his first social-insurance schemes, he had to battle on two fronts: on one side against the liberals, who preferred market solutions, and on the other side against conservatives who sponsored the guild-model or familialism. Bismarck desired the primacy of etatism. By insisting on direct state financing and distribution of social benefits, Bismarck's aim was to chain the workers directly to the paternal authority of the monarchy rather than to either the occupational funds, or the cash nexus. In reality, his project was strongly compromised, and Bismarck's pension-legislation of 1891 retained only a fraction of the state largesse he had sought (Rimlinger, 1971). Indeed, the subsequent pension-system, as with most of the Wilhelmine social programs, can be interpreted as an etatism with partial concessions to liberalism (actuarialism), and to conservative corporativism (compulsory occupationally distinct schemes).

Etatist paternalism has left an especially strong mark on two areas of social policy. One is the tradition in some nations, such as Austria, Germany, and France, of endowing civil servants with extraordinarily lavish welfare provisions. The motive may have been to reward, or perhaps guarantee, proper loyalties and subservience, but there is also evidence that regimes deliberately wished to mold the class structure with their social-policy initiatives. Kocka (1981) shows how pension policy in Imperial Germany served to create, as special classes, both the civil servants (*Beamten*) and the private-sector salaried employees (*Privatbeamten*). Parallel policies were pursued in Austria (Otruba, 1981). The result is an especially recognizable status-barrier between the servants of the state and its subjects, and between workers and the more elevated 'estates'. We can here recognize a close affinity between etatism and the legacy of corporatism.

The second chief legacy of paternalism is found in the evolution of social assistance. As many authors recognize, poor relief was considerably more humane and generous under aristocratic regimes such as Disraeli's in Britain, Bismarck's in Germany, and Estrup's in Denmark than under liberal regimes (Briggs, 1961; Rimlinger, 1971; Evans, 1978; Viby Morgensen, 1973). Akin to their inclination to extend basic guarantees of income protection, the conservatives' readiness to grant relief was informed by the age-old principle of *noblesse oblige*.

Corporatism has always been a major conservative alternative to etatism. It springs from the tradition of the estates, guilds, monopolies, and corporations that organized social and economic life in the medieval city economy. While the guilds were being dismantled in the eighteenth and nineteenth centuries, their underlying principles were incorporated into the ideologies of corporate associationalism and mutualism. Corporatism evolved as a major conservative response to the social fragmentation and individualization brought forth by markets and industry. It was a central theme in Durkheim's analyses of how to combat anomie; it emerged as a cornerstone of Papal and Catholic social policy; and it found its greatest expression in Fascist ideology.

The unifying principles of corporatism are a fraternity based on status identity, obligatory and exclusive membership, mutualism, and monopoly of representation. Carried over into modern capitalism, corporatism was typically built around occupational groupings seeking to uphold traditionally recognized status distinctions and used these as the organizational nexus for society and economy. Often modelled directly on the old guilds, such corporate entities as mutual associations and friendly societies emerged among the more privileged workers, such as plumbers or carpenters. In other cases, corporative social welfare was erected with state participation, as occurred often among miners and seamen. As the pace of social legislation quickened in the latter part of the nineteenth century, the proliferation of corporatism often did also.

Either because of state recognition of particular status privileges, or because organized groups refused to be part of a more status-inclusive legislation, there emerged the tradition of constructing a myriad of status-differentiated social-insurance schemes – each with its peculiar rules, finances, and benefit structure; each tailored to exhibit its clientele's relative status position. Hence, Bismarck's pension for workers was not to be blended with that for miners and certainly not with the social policy for civil servants or for white-collar employees (Kocka, 1981). In Austria, the corporative principle was carried somewhat further with the official recognition that notarians enjoyed a status privilege that had to be matched by their own pension plan. A similar evolution occurred in French pension-legislation after World War II as a variety of salaried groups ('cadres') successfully claimed status uniqueness in social protection. Italy's labyrinth of pensions can probably make claim to be an international corporative leader, with its more than 120 occupationally distinct pension funds (Fausto, 1978).

Corporatism took strongest hold in the continental European nations. The reasons for this are not difficult to trace. First, these were late-industrializing nations, in which traditional guild-traditions were preserved until quite late. During the embryonic era of social protection, therefore, a viable model for programmatic development already existed. Second, and partially as a consequence of the former, the force of status distinction, hierarchy, and privilege has been unusually strong. And, third, it was in these nations that the Catholic Church succeeded in playing an instrumental role in social reform. In the late nineteenth century, the Papal Encyclical, *Rerum Novarum*, advocated a blend of etatism and corporatism; in the 1931 Encyclical, *Quadrogesimo Anno*, the corporatist element is even stronger.

For the Catholic Church, corporatism was a natural response to its preoccupation with preserving the traditional family, its search for viable alternatives to both socialism and capitalism, and its belief in the possibility of organizing harmonious relations between the social classes. Corporatism inserted itself easily into Catholicism's 'subsidiarity' principle, the idea that higher and larger levels of social collectivity should only intervene when the family's capacity for mutual protection was rendered impossible. The collective solidarity of a guild, fraternity, or mutuality was clearly closer to the family unit, and hence more capable of serving its needs, than was the more remote central state (Messner, 1964; Richter, 1987).

Corporatism became quasi-official ideology among the Fascist regimes of Europe in the 1920s and 1930s, not so much for the sake of subsidiarity as to build alternatives to large encompassing class organizations which were more amenable to central political control (Guillebaud, 1941; Rimlinger, 1987).

Stratification in Liberal Social Policy

The goals of liberalism can best be understood as opposition to the vestiges of conservative stratification. It was in the abolition of estates, guilds, monopolies, and central monarchical absolutism that liberalism saw the conditions for individual emancipation, freedom, equal opportunities, and healthy competitiveness. Clearly, both the heavy-handed state and the gluey mantle of corporatism were fetters on the free market, on voluntarism, and on the spirit of entrepreneurialism.

Liberalism's resistance to an active state is often interpreted as passivity with regard to social policy. This is, as Polanyi (1944) showed, a myth. By withholding aid, or helping eliminate traditional systems of social protection, and by refusing to place nothing but the market in their place, the classical liberal state attempted to grant the cash nexus a hegemonic role in the organization of social and economic life; the bottom line of liberal dogma was that the state had no proper reason for altering the stratification outcomes produced in the marketplace. They were just, because they mirrored effort, motivation, adeptness, and self-reliance.

In classical liberal thought, universalism and equality figure as prominent principles, certain to materialize if organized power is prevented from interfering with the market's automatic 'clearing mechanisms'. Thus, the minimalist social policy of laissez-faire was in harmony with its ideals. Social policy was equated with undesirable stratification outcomes: paternalism and elitism; dependency on the state; the perpetuation of pauperism. With no state, and no monopolies (like working-class unions), there would be no classes, just a web of freely acting individuals, atomized perhaps, but equal before the law, the contract, and the cash nexus.

Liberalism's universalist ideals were contradicted by the dualism and social stigma it promoted in practice. While the market was left unfettered to stratify its participants along the cash nexus, the liberal state established an extraordinarily punitive and stigmatizing poor relief for the market failures. Disraeli's *Sybil* remains probably the best textbook on how, in Britain, liberalism helped create a society of two nations.

The social humiliation of poor relief remained when liberalism, under pressure, moved towards modern income-tested social assistance. Denmark illustrates well the model's inadvertent dualism. The old-age assistance plan that was introduced in 1891 was little more than an upgraded system of poor relief. When it was reformed into a *de facto* universal citizens' pension after World War II, large numbers of middle-class pensioners nonetheless reneged on their pension-right because of its traditional stigma of poverty and dependency.

Means-tested relief was, nonetheless, meant to be the residual element of liberal social policy. The real core was meant to be individual insurance in the market, with voluntary and actuarially sound contracts. In this framework, 'social-policy outcomes' would parallel market outcomes: those who have been frugal, entrepreneurial, and self-reliant will be rewarded.

In historical reality, however, the individual life-insurance model worked poorly, and hardly ever managed to take the kind of hold over peoples' social-security needs that alternative market solutions and/or the state did. As we shall discuss in much greater detail in chapter 4, the private welfare market could grow only if and when the state came to its aid. The more realistic liberal response, therefore, came to incorporate a blend of welfare capitalism in the market, and social insurance in the public sector. The principle that a minimum of collectivism had to blend with individualism emerged in the era of the liberal 'reform movement' around the turn of the century.

The liberal reform movement is usually associated with Lloyd George in Britain, but had its counterparts across the Western world. Its origins are multifaceted. In Britain, the studies of Rowntree and Booth disclosed rampant poverty, disease, and misery among the urban working classes. The Boer War revealed that the condition of the British fighting men was abysmally poor (Beer, 1966; Evans, 1978; Ashford, 1986, p. 62). A more general catalyst was the enfranchisement of the working classes, and the realization that a new type of capitalism was unfolding, a type of economy built around large combines, organization, bureaucracy, human capital, and a more intricate and complex division of labor – in short, an economic order in which progress, efficiency, and profits no longer could be premised solely on squeezing the last drop of sweat from the laborer. It is therefore not surprising that some of the major initiatives came from 'corporate liberals' (Weinstein, 1972), the new scientific managerial school, or liberal reformers such as Albion Small and William James in the United States, people who combined a firm commitment to the market with a belief that its salvage required greater social responsibilities.

The reform liberals were willing to sponsor a larger measure of collectivism with their acknowledgment of the problem of externalities, the need for public goods, and their policy of help to self-help. Reform liberalism was not prepared to open escape-routes from the market, only to take steps to reduce its social pathologies and to realign individualism to the new reality that society was organized in collectivities. The liberals' favored social policy reflects this new logic. Help to self-help was to be nurtured via mass education and sponsored equal opportunity. The idea of occupational fringe-benefits, or welfare capitalism, reflected the acceptance that wage bargains were struck collectively, and the hope that necessary welfare programs could be incorporated in this arena. And social insurance gradually became an acceptable policy to the extent that it remained essentially voluntarist and actuarial, and did not interfere with work incentives and competitiveness. As Ogus (1979) points out, liberals were often surprised to discover that social insurance embodied a host of liberal ideals: the principles of an individual contract, benefits pegged to past effort, self-reliance, and market-conformity. The state could, indeed, be regarded as another type of insurance-carrier. The social rights of citizenship in reform liberalism are patterned on the market.

While these were the favored ideals, in practice liberal reformism often allowed significant deviations. Lloyd George introduced non-contributory and thus not actuarial old-age pensions in 1908. What motivated this unprincipled initiative may, as Keir Hardy and the Independent Labour Party suggested, have been the even more compelling desire to nurture splits between the lower and upper echelons of the working class. Yet benefit levels were kept at a minimum so as to encourage private thrift (Hay, 1975; Pelling, 1961; Gilbert, 1966). A rather similar story unfolded with the US Social Security Act. Meant to adhere strictly to actuarialism, it soon became significantly redistributive, and membership became compulsory. But, as with the British pensions, social security in the US was not meant to crowd out the private-pension market and individualism. Hence, benefits and contributions were pegged to fairly low standards, and the general aim was that the system be as market-conforming as possible (Derthick, 1979; Quadagno, 1988).

To sum up: at its core, liberalism's ideal of stratification is obviously the competitive individualism that the market supposedly cultivates. However, liberalism has had great difficulties applying this conception in state policy. Its enthusiasm for the needs-tested approach, targeting government aid solely at the genuinely poor, is inherently logical but creates the unanticipated result of social stigma and dualism. Its alternative approaches, namely private insurance and bargained occupational welfare on one side, and social insurance on the other side, are equally logical in terms of liberal principles of self-reliance, justice, actuarialism, and freedom of choice, yet these solutions also tend to invoke peculiar class dualisms. Bargained or contracted private welfare will logically replicate market inequalities, but is also guaranteed to prevail mainly among the more privileged strata in the labor force; it will certainly not address the welfare needs of the most precariously-placed workers. In turn, the liberal social-insurance scheme will, if it sticks to principles, also reproduce the profile of stratification of the market, and it will promote private protection for the more fortunate.

If, then, we combine the three liberal approaches, the probable outcome is a curious mix of individual self-responsibility and dualisms: one group at the bottom primarily reliant on stigmatizing relief; one group in the middle predominantly the clients of social insurance; and, finally, one privileged group capable of deriving its main welfare from the market. This is, in fact, more or less the stratification profile that characterizes the US and, to a lesser degree, the British welfare system (Esping-Andersen, Rein, and Rainwater, 1988).

Stratification in Socialist Social Policy

As with conservatism and liberalism, socialist reformism was always pursued with distinct stratification outcomes in mind. For labor movements, it was the construction of solidarity that mattered.

The socialists have always faced the question of how to construct the unity upon which long-term collective mobilization could evolve. Vulgar Marxists often portray the problem as a struggle against bourgeois class society. This is completely misleading: the socialists had to struggle against a multiplicity of historical alternatives, some of which were strongly represented within their own ranks. On one side, they had to fight the exclusionary corporatism of narrow status-solidarity that also permeated early trade-unionism and friendly societies. And they had to attack the paternalism of employers and states, a paternalism that diverted worker loyalties and cultivated schisms. Finally, they had to struggle against the atomizing, individualizing impulse of the market.

As most early socialist writings show, a serious obstacle to collectivism was the dualistic consequence of persistent unemployment. The 'slum proletariat', as Kautsky (1971) termed it in 1891, was universally viewed as a major threat. Demoralized, uprooted, unorganized, and resourceless, it was vulnerable to reactionary demagoguery, difficult to organize, and likely to undercut wages and sabotage strikes. It was a major theme already at the 1867 Lausanne Congress of the Ist International; at that time, the delegates put their faith in the cooperative movements' ability to improve the moral fibre and economic condition of the lumpenproletariat.

A second important obstacle lay in the social divisions institutionalized through earlier conservative and liberal reforms. The old poor law systems were obviously the foremost enemy, since they drove a wedge into the proletariat and because recipients were typically disenfranchised. The abolition of the means-test and less-eligibility rules was therefore a top political priority. Similarly, they opposed employer-sponsored paternalistic welfare for its corporativistic and particularistic consequences, and they attacked state insurance for workers as being social pacifism, divisive and apt to institutionalize inequalities.

The socialists certainly saw the dangers inherent in ruling-class reformism, but were often hard-pressed to formulate genuine alternatives. An embryo of their thinking lay in the early critiques of bourgeois social amelioration. Marx and Engels were preoccupied with the possibility that social-pacifist reforms would retard socialism – a fear that is understandable in light of Napoleon III's, von Taaffe's, and Bismarck's open admissions that this was exactly what they pursued. Yet not even Marx held entirely to this view. In his analysis of the British Factory Acts (1954–6, ch. 10), Marx concludes that bourgeois reforms are both meaningful and will enhance the position of the workers. The concluding pages of the *Communist Manifesto* call for reforms that are hardly at variance with later liberalism.

The socialists had to devise a social policy which both addressed the real need for social relief, and would help the socialist movement come to power. The question revolved around contending principles of solidarity. Corporatism and fraternal associations were one prevalent model, especially among groups of skilled and craft workers. But these were problematic if the aim was to build broad class unity and uplift the 'slum-proletarians'.

A second approach was to place the social question in the hands of the trade unions and win concessions through collective bargaining. But this assumed stable and strong bargaining-power and employer recognition; it also ran the risk of replicating labor-market inequalities or mainly favoring the labor aristocracies. Again, it was a strategy unlikely to produce broad solidarity. Nonetheless, it evolved as the major approach in two kinds of societies. In Australia it came to predominate because the unions there were in an unusually favorable bargaining position. In the United States, its importance has had more to do with the lack of a plausible political ally and an untrustworthy state.

The early socialist movements frequently turned to a third alternative, the micro-socialist 'ghetto strategy', according to which the movement itself became the provider of workers' welfare. This was an attractive avenue, particularly where the socialists found themselves barred from state power. It demonstrated that the leadership could respond constructively to the acute needs of workers. Its attraction was certainly also that a micro-socialist haven could promote organization, membership growth, and socialist education, and present the movement as an attractive spokesman for working-class needs. Micro-socialism was a way to present a practical example of the good society to come, one that would reveal all the more clearly the heartlessness and brutality of the surrounding bourgeois society.

Micro-socialism was pursued with vigor and some success in the early days of socialism. The movements often constructed organizational empires with recreational facilities, chess clubs, theater troupes, music, Boy Scout organizations, sports clubs, and often even productive enterprises such as building societies and cooperatives.

The problem with the ghetto model lay in its own purpose, namely to build class solidarity and power by mobilizing through membership. Since it was financed by the workers themselves, it was vulnerable to prolonged economic crises and costly industrial disputes. But also, micro-socialism was pregnant with the dualism of members versus non-members. The divide was, as always, between the privileged workers and the groups of more precarious status. If, then, the socialists desired broad class unity and parliamentary majorities, they were compelled to adopt a genuinely universalistic idea of solidarity, a universalism that helped unify what in reality was a substantially differentiated and segmented working class.

The principle of a broad popular universalism emerged in tandem with the extension and consolidation of democratic rights. Here, the Scandinavians were pioneers, as manifested in Per Albin Hansson's rhetoric of the 'Peoples' Home' welfare state in the late 1920s. Indeed, it was already explicit in the Danish socialists' pension-proposals in the 1880s, and in Branting's social policy in Sweden in the first decades of the century (Elmer, 1960; Rasmussen, 1933). After World War I, Otto Bauer pursued the idea of a worker–peasant alliance in Austria through broad coverage in social-welfare policy (Bauer, 1919). In such highly corporatist systems as the German, Austrian, and Italian, the socialists or communists have always fought for universalism with calls for *Volksversicherung* and *unificazione*.

The coincidence of universalism and democracy is hardly accidental. Parliamentarism presented the socialists with new reformist vistas, but it also imposed upon them the necessity of mobilizing solid electoral majorities which, almost certainly, the ghetto strategy would fail to produce. The majority problem was accentuated where the working class was likely to remain an electoral minority.

It was this specter that Bernstein raised in 1898 in his classic *Evolutionary Socialism* (Bernstein, 1961), and which electoral socialists began to recognize in subsequent years. They could either respond by settling for a minority opposition status, or they could forge broader political alliances. The latter case required a politics of cross-class universalism.

It was the alliance option which inspired Bauer's thinking and, even more clearly, the Scandinavians' 'People's Home' notion of welfare policy. In the inter-war years, the rural classes were the linchpin of a broad popular alliance, and the socialists tried with varying success to mobilize the agrarian classes. Where the socialist ghetto model was weak – as in Scandinavia – their capacity to make inroads in the rural social structure was vastly better. Where socialism was concentrated in urban working-class enclaves, such as 'Red Berlin' and 'Red Vienna', ideology and rhetoric was more likely to retain its traditional revolutionary, workerist flavor, and a rural outreach would be less likely to receive a favorable response.

The shift to a people's universalism was not merely instrumental vote-maximization. It spoke logically to the prevailing social structure and to the socialists' own comprehension of solidarity. The social structure was dominated by masses of rural and urban 'little people'. Solidarity does not have to be workerist, since many other groups are victims of forces beyond their control, and face poverty and basic social risks. Universalism, therefore, became a guiding principle because it equalized the status, benefits, and responsibilities of citizenship, and because it helped build political coalitions.

Still, universalism occasionally came into conflict with rival labor-movement objectives. In many cases, the labor movements found in the self-financed and controlled welfare funds a great source of both financial and organizational power. To relinquish this for the sake of universal solidarity was not always viewed with favor. In Germany, the trade unions jealously guarded their control over sickness funds. Even the Danish and Swedish labor movements, vanguards of universalism, would not accept loss of control over their unemployment insurance funds.

Australia and New Zealand constitute two cases in which the labor movements, despite being powerful, never fully embraced the universalist ideal. In these countries, labor retained the traditionally widespread preference for targeted income-tested benefits because they appear more redistributive. But the main reason seems to be the outstanding bargaining situation enjoyed by the trade unions for decades. Thus, as Castles (1986) argues, labor's demands for social protection could be equally, if not better, served via wage negotiations.

The socialists' adherence to universalism was put to a major test in the wake of social-structural modernization. In an advanced economy, the 'little people' disappear, only to be replaced by a new white-collar salariat and more prosperous workers who will hardly be content with a basic flat-rate benefit. Hence, unless social security could be upgraded, a massive exodus towards private-market schemes would likely ensue, leading to new inequalities. Thus, to preserve the solidarity of a universalistic welfare state, the socialists were compelled to align social benefits to middle-class standards.

The Swedish social democrats were the first to pave the way for a universalism of 'middle-class' standards. The formula was to combine universal entitlements with high earnings-graduated benefits, thus matching welfare-state benefits and services to middle-class expectations. For the average worker, as social citizen, the result was an experience of upward mobility. For the welfare state, the result was the consolidation of a vast popular majority wedded to its defence. 'Middle-class' universalism has protected the welfare state against backlash sentiments.

Comparative Dimensions of Welfare-State Stratification

If all welfare states participate in the process of social stratification, they do so differently. The historical legacies of conservative, liberal, and socialist principles in their early construction became institutionalized and perpetuated, often over an entire century. The result is a clustering of regimes that is strikingly parallel to the one we discovered in the analyses of de-commodification.

To identify welfare-state clusters, we need to identify the salient dimensions of stratification. The corporatist model is best identified by the degree to which social insurance is differentiated and segmented into distinct occupational- and status-based programs. In this case, we would also expect large variations between the bottom and top in terms of benefits. To identify etatism, the simplest approach is to identify the relative privileges accorded civil servants. In contrast, we would identify liberal principles in terms of welfare states' residualism, especially the relative salience of means-testing; in terms of the relative financial responsibility accorded to the individual insured; and in terms of the relative weight of voluntary, private-sector welfare. And, to capture the socialist ideals, the relevant measure is clearly degree of universalism. The socialist regime ought to exhibit the lowest level of benefit differentials.

The degree to which clearly defined regime-clusters exist depends, then, on the extent to which regime-specific features are exclusively present only in one type. To give an example, we would not expect a conservative-type system (with strong corporatism and/or civil-service privileges) to also harbor liberalist traits (such as a large private market) or socialist traits (such as individualism). Since, however, the real world

TABLE 3.1 Degree of corporatism, etatism, means testing, market influence, universalism, and benefit equality in 18 welfare states, 1980

	Corporatism[a]	Etatism[b]	Means-tested poor relief (as % of total public social expenditure)	Private pensions (as % of total pensions)	Private health spending (as % of total)	Average[d] universalism	Average[e] benefit equality
Australia	1	0.7	3.3	30	36	33	1.00
Austria	7	3.8	2.8	3	36	72	0.52
Belgium	5	3.0	4.5	8	13	67	0.79
Canada	2	0.2	15.6	38	26	93	0.48
Denmark	2	1.1	1.0	17	15	87	0.99
Finland	4	2.5	1.9	3	21	88	0.72
France	10	3.1	11.2	8	28	70	0.55
Germany	6	2.2	4.9	11	20	72	0.56
Ireland	1	2.2	5.9	10	6	60	0.77
Italy	12	2.2	9.3	2	12	59	0.52
Japan	7	0.9	7.0	23	28	63	0.32
Netherlands	3	1.8	6.9	13	22	87	0.57
New Zealand	1	0.8	2.3	4	18	33	1.00
Norway	4	0.9	2.1	8	1	95	0.69
Sweden	2	1.0	1.1	6	7	90	0.82
Switzerland	2	1.0	8.8	20	35	96	0.48
United Kingdom	2	2.0	—[f]	12	10	76	0.64
United States	2	1.5	18.2	21	57	54	0.22
Mean	4.1	1.7	5.9	13	22	72	0.65
S. D.	3.2	1.0	5.1	10	14	19	0.22

ᵃ Measured as number of occupationally distinct public pension schemes. Only major schemes have been included.

ᵇ Measured as expenditure on pensions to government employees as % GDP.

ᶜ Estimates of poor-relief expenditure exclude benefits from normal income-tested schemes (such as housing allowances in Scandinavia, unemployment assistance in Germany, or old-age, unemployment, and sickness assistance in Australia and New Zealand). It should be kept in mind that the borderline between these two types of targeting is difficult to draw. Our estimates here are based on an individual assessment of how the system operates in each nation.

ᵈ Average for sickness, unemployment, and pensions. (Income-tested assistance programs, like the Australian and New Zealand unemployment and sickness benefits, have been scored 0 since none provides full citizen rights to benefits.)

ᵉ Average differential between basic and maximum social benefits for sickness, unemployment, and pensions (based on net, after-tax, benefits). Benefit differentials are based on the ratio of guaranteed basic social benefit to the legal maximum benefit possible in the system.

ᶠ Data are not available.

Sources: G. Esping-Andersen (1987b; table 3); United States Government Printing Office, *Social Security Programs Throughout the World* (1981); ILO, *The Cost of Social Security*, basic tables (Geneva: ILO, 1981); OECD, *Measuring Health Care, 1960–1983* (Paris: OECD, 1985, p. 12); SSIB data files

TABLE 3.2 Bi-variate correlation matrix of stratification attributes for 18 welfare states

	Corporatism	Etatism	Poor relief	Private pensions	Private health	Universalism
Corporatism	1.00					
Etatism	0.55					
Poor relief	0.16	−0.11				
Private pensions	−0.40	−0.64	0.49			
Private health	−0.02	0.01	0.60	0.45		
Universalism	−0.02	−0.03	−0.05	0.00	−0.28	
Benefit differentials	0.40	0.14	0.73	0.21	0.51	0.21

of welfare states is most likely to exhibit hybrid forms, our task is to see to what degree there is sufficient co-variation for distinct regime-clusters to emerge.

In table 3.1 we present data on regime-specific program attributes. Representing *conservative* principles of stratification, the table shows, first, the degree of status segregation, or corporatism, measured as number of (major) occupationally distinct pension schemes in operation; second, it presents degree of 'etatism', measured as the expenditure on government-employee pensions as a percentage of Gross Domestic Product.

Table 3.1 also displays three variables designed to identify key attributes of *liberalism*: first, the relative weight of means-tested welfare benefits, measured as a percentage of total public social expenditure (excluding benefits to government employees); second, it provides data on the importance of the private sector in pensions, measured as private-sector share of total pension spending, and in health care, measured as private-sector share of total health spending.

Finally, table 3.1 includes two attributes most clearly associated with *socialist* regimes, namely degree of program universalism (measured as averaged percentage of population, 16–64, eligible for sickness, unemployment, and pension benefits), and degree of equality in the benefit structure. In the latter case, our measure is an average for the above-mentioned three programs in terms of the ratio of the basic level of benefits to the legal maximum benefit possible. We would clearly expect the socialist-inspired regimes to accentuate benefit equality, while in conservative regimes inequalities should be greatest.

Beginning with the conservative attributes, we discover a basically bi-modal distribution of countries with regard to both corporatism and etatism; the coincidence between the two characteristics is, moreover, quite marked. One group of nations scores very high on both: Austria, Belgium, France, Germany, and Italy, with the possible inclusion of Finland. It is worth noting that this is the very same group which we earlier identified as falling in the conservative tradition on de-commodification.

Turning to our liberal characteristics, the pattern is considerably fuzzier. The poor-relief variable clusters nations into three groups, one scoring very high (Canada, France, and the United States), one with medium levels, and one in which poor relief is truly marginal (the Nordic countries). The private-pension variable, in contrast, distinguishes sharply between one group with a preponderance of private pensions, and another in which they hardly exist at all. The private-sector health variable, like poor relief, clusters into three groups. Here

TABLE 3.3 The clustering of welfare states according to conservative, liberal and socialist regime attributes (cumulated index scores in parentheses)

	Conservatism		Degree of Liberalism		Socialism	
Strong	Austria	(8)	Australia	(10)	Denmark	(8)
	Belgium	(8)	Canada	(12)	Finland	(6)
	France	(8)	Japan	(10)	Netherlands	(6)
	Germany	(8)	Switzerland	(12)	Norway	(8)
	Italy	(8)	United States	(12)	Sweden	(8)
Medium	Finland	(6)	Denmark	(6)	Australia	(4)
	Ireland	(4)	France	(8)	Belgium	(4)
	Japan	(4)	Germany	(6)	Canada	(4)
	Netherlands	(4)	Italy	(6)	Germany	(4)
	Norway	(4)	Netherlands	(8)	New Zealand	(4)
			United Kingdom	(6)	Switzerland	(4)
					United Kingdom	(4)
Low	Australia	(0)	Austria	(4)	Austria	(2)
	Canada	(2)	Belgium	(4)	France	(2)
	Denmark	(2)	Finland	(4)	Ireland	(2)
	New Zealand	(2)	Ireland	(4)	Italy	(0)
	Sweden	(0)	New Zealand	(2)	Japan	(2)
	Switzerland	(0)	Norway	(2)	United States	(0)
	United Kingdom	(0)	Sweden	(0)		
	United States	(0)				

we may note the substantial degree of 'privatization' in countries like Austria and Germany, something which testifies to the ambiguity of private welfare organization. In these two countries, 'private' health care reflects the tradition of the Church's influence (Caritas, for example) rather than unbridled private entrepreneurship. But, all in all, there is one group that systematically scores high on our liberalism attributes: the United States and Canada, and also, slightly less distinctively, Australia and Switzerland.

Considering, finally, our socialist regime measures, we see that universalism is the reigning principle in the Scandinavian social democratic welfare states, and is to a degree approximated in a few liberal regimes such as Canada and Switzerland. At the other extreme lie a number of liberal cases where social rights are unusually underdeveloped (the United States, Australia, and New Zealand). The continental European countries which otherwise tend to score high on conservatism fall in the middle here, a result that is hardly surprising since their emphasis on compulsory membership along occupational lines will result in a situation in which a large share of the labor force has insurance coverage. The benefit-differential measure should in principle facilitate a sharp distinction between the 'socialist' and 'conservative' cases. In the former, an accent on equality should produce low differentials; in the latter, the principle of maintaining status and hierarchy should result in sharp inequalities. To correctly interpret this variable, we should for a moment leave aside Australia and New Zealand. Since their systems are based on the flat-rate social assistance tradition, benefits will, virtually by definition, be equal. Otherwise, the tendency is largely as one would have expected: the Scandinavian social democracies are among the most egalitarian. Yet the table is less able to distinguish the corporative systems (which do show high differentials) and their liberal counterparts (which also exhibit very extreme differentials).

A first attempt to identify to what extent regime-clusters exist is by the zero-order correlation matrix presented in table 3.2. Obviously, for regimes to exist there must be a strong relationship among the particular characteristics that supposedly identify the regime; and, in converse, these must be negatively correlated, or uncorrelated, with attributes of alternative regimes. The correlations in table 3.2 point towards the kind of regime-clustering that we had anticipated. The conservative attributes (corporatism and etatism) correlate positively (0.55), and they are negatively related or unrelated to both the liberal-regime attributes (poor relief, privatization) and to the socialist universalism variable. There is a positive correlation with benefit differentials, indicating that conservative regimes tend to replicate inequalities in the welfare state.

The liberal regime-cluster is equally evident. Poor relief is strongly related to both private pensions and health (r = 0.49 and 0.60, respectively), and the last two are also positively correlated. High benefit differentials are powerfully linked to the liberal-regime variables. We may therefore conclude that high inequalities in welfare benefits emerge both from hierarchal systems and from market adherence. The distinctiveness of the liberal regime is evident in that its traits are all negatively correlated or uncorrelated with both conservative and socialist attributes.

The socialist regime, finally, is more difficult to pin down because its two component variables, universalism and egalitarian benefits, are not strongly correlated. Some countries (like Canada and Switzerland) which are otherwise very liberalistic tend also to approach universalism, and other liberalistic nations (like Australia), whose systems are essentially of the flat-rate minimum-benefit kind, have low benefit differentials. Nonetheless, the universalism characteristic does stand on its own, distinguishing itself (by being uncorrelated) from both conservative- and liberal-regime variables. It is a surprise, nonetheless, that we do not find a stronger association between egalitarian and universalism.

As in chapter 2, these data can be developed into summary indices so as to more clearly and economically identify significant nation-clusters. As before, we will do this (roughly) on the basis of the mean and standard deviation in the distribution along each of our variables. In table 3.3 we present cumulated summary scores for 'conservatism', 'liberalism', and 'socialism'. As explained in Appendix 1, the higher the score, the greater the degree of conservatism, liberalism, and socialism, respectively. We have divided the table into high, medium, and low clusters.

From table 3.3 we cannot but conclude that clusters do exist. The nations which score high on our summary index of conservatism (Italy, Germany, Austria, France, and Belgium) all score low, or at best, medium on our indices of liberalism and socialism. In turn, the countries characterized by strong liberalism (Australia, Canada, Japan, Switzerland, and the United States) score low or medium on conservatism and socialism. Finally, the socialism cluster includes the nations of Scandinavia, and the Netherlands, all countries which score low (or medium) on the two other regime-clusters.

In other words, if we are willing to accept that welfare states play an important role in the patterning of social stratification, and that we have captured attributes of stratification which matter significantly in peoples' real and perceived experience of inequalities, status, and class differences, we find that it is misleading to compare welfare states as merely 'more' or 'less' egalitarian. We discover, instead, entirely different logics of social stratification embedded in welfare-state construction. In this sense, we may speak of regimes as we did with reference to de-commodification.

We can, additionally, begin to see that the clustering of de-commodification and stratification is very similar. Recalling the evidence presented in chapter 2, there is a clear coincidence of high de-commodification and strong universalism in the Scandinavian, social democratically influenced welfare states. There is an equally clear coincidence of low de-commodification and strong individualistic self-reliance in the Anglo-Saxon nations. Finally, the continental European countries group closely together in terms of being corporatist and etatist, and also being fairly modestly de-commodifying.

In chapter 4, we will conclude our specification of welfare-state regime-clusters by analyzing how the boundary between state and market emerged in pensions, the single most important welfare-state program. It is already clear that the public–private mix plays a key role in shaping both de-commodification and stratification. What we wish to explore more fully is the overall structuration of social policy or, more specifically, pensions, in the political economy.

Appendix   Scoring procedure for stratification indices

As in chapter 2, we have developed indices based on the distribution of nations around the mean and standard variation on the individual variables. Conservative-regime attributes are captured via corporatism and etatism variables; liberal-regime attributes through social assistance and the relative importance of private health and pensions; socialist-regime attributes are mainly captured via the degree of universalism. The final variable, benefit differentiation, is expected to score low for socialist regimes.

To construct the index of corporatism, nations with less than, or equal to, two separate occupationally distinct pension programs have been given the score of 0; nations between two and five (inclusive) have been given a score of 2; and nations with more than five occupationally distinct programs are scored equal to 4.

The etatism variable reflects the degree to which the civil service is granted special welfare privileges, and is measured in terms of pension expenditures for civil servants as a percentage of GDP. Where the share is less than (or equal to) 1 percent, we have given an index score of 0; where the share is between 1 and 2.1 percent, we have given a score of 2; and where the share surpasses 2.2 percent, we have given a score of 4.

The index for the relative importance of social assistance is based on data on expenditures on means-tested benefits as a percentage of total social-transfer expenditures. The task of defining exactly the boundary between the classical type of means-tested benefits and the more modern income-dependent transfers is very difficult. We have decided to treat the Australian and New Zealand welfare states as essentially income-tested, and these countries will accordingly score fairly low. Similarly, we exclude housing allowances in Scandinavia. The variable, in other words, has been constructed to try to include program expenditure for what is genuinely means-tested social assistance in the traditional poor-relief logic. It therefore includes programs such as AFDC in the United States, *Sozialhilfe* in the Germanic countries, *socialhjaelp* in the Nordic countries, and so forth. Great Britain poses a special problem because of the way in which both means- and income-tested benefits there have been consolidated under the general heading of 'supplementary benefits'. For comparative purposes, we have chosen (conservatively) to estimate the British share as being equal to 1 percent. The index construction on this variable follows the logic adopted previously: if the expenditure ratio on social assistance, relative to total transfer payments, is less than 3 percent, we give a score of 0; from 3 to 8 percent, we give a score of 2; more than 8 percent is given a score of 4.

The index for the relative share of private-pension expenditures to total pension expenditures is developed as follows: if the share is less than 10 percent, a country is scored equal to 0; if the share is between 10 and 15 percent, the score is 2; and if the share is more than 16 percent, we give the country a score of 4.

For the relative share of private health expenditures, we give a score of 0 to countries where it is less than 10 percent; from 10 to 20 percent, we give a score of 2; and if greater than 21 percent, the country receives a score of 4.

The universalism variable measures the percentage of the relevant population (labor force between ages 16 and 65) covered under the respective programs. A low degree of universalism is defined as less than (or equal to) 60 percent of the population being covered, and scored equal to 0; where coverage lies between 61 and 85 percent, we give a score of 2; and where coverage exceeds 86 percent, we give a score of 4. Note that income-test-based programs, such as the Australian and New Zealand unemployment and sickness benefit schemes, have been scored equal to 0. This is because these types of programs do not grant automatic universal rights.

Finally, our variable on benefit differentials is based on what a normal standard worker will receive as a standard benefit and what is the maximum benefit stipulated in the rules of the system. If the standard benefits are less than 55 percent of maximum benefits, we give the system a score of 0 (reflecting very high differentials); if they lie between 55 and 80 percent, the system is given a score of 2; and if they are above 80 percent, the system is given a score of 4.

4

State and Market in the Formation of Pension Regimes

Introduction

Neither state nor market was predestined as a locus of welfare provision. Yet almost every textbook on social policy will try to convince you otherwise. Sociologists generally equate welfare distribution with government social policy. Liberal dogma and contemporary economic theory want us to believe that the state is an artificial creation and that the market, if left untampered with, is the only institution truly capable of furnishing our various welfare needs. This may be true for automobiles, but it certainly is not true for social security.

In all advanced countries we find some blend of private and public welfare provision, and it is in this relationship that we will uncover some of the most important structural properties of welfare states. In this chapter, the relationship will be explored for pensions, by far the most important in the overall package of social transfers. We will discover that states created markets and that markets created states. For pensions, at least, it required the application of state power to build and nurture a viable private market. In turn, the state's role in furnishing pensions has been decisively shaped by the nature and limits of markets. State and market, or, if you will, political power and the cash nexus, have interacted continuously to manufacture the peculiar blend of social provision that goes into defining welfare-state regimes.

If an analysis of pensions appears somewhat narrow and pedestrian, keep in mind two circumstances: first, pensions account for more than 10 percent of GDP in many contemporary nations; second, pensions constitute a central link between work and leisure, between earned income and redistribution, between individualism and solidarity, between the cash nexus and social rights. Pensions, therefore, help elucidate a set of perennially conflictual principles of capitalism.

Welfare-State Regimes in the Nexus of State and Market

As we discussed in chapters 1 and 2, the concept of welfare-state regimes denotes the institutional arrangements, rules and understandings that guide and shape concurrent social-policy decisions, expenditure developments, problem definitions, and even the response-and-demand structure of citizens and welfare consumers. The existence of policy regimes reflects the circumstance that short-term policies, reforms, debates, and decision-making take place within frameworks of historical institutionalization that differ qualitatively between countries. The boundaries of rights and claims that are attached to social citizenship constitute an example of such institutional parameters, which are relatively historically stable. Thus, the range of human needs that are given the status of a social right is a central definitional issue with regard to the identification of welfare-state regimes. An 'institutional' welfare state in Titmuss's scheme is, in contrast to the 'marginalist', one that recognizes no preordained boundaries for social rights (Titmuss, 1974; Korpi, 1980).

A particularly important element in the identification of welfare-state regimes will, accordingly, be related to the blend of publicly provided social rights, and private initiative. In other words, regimes can be compared with respect to which essential human needs are relegated to private versus public responsibility.

The division of social protection between public and private provides the structural context of de-commodification, social rights, and the stratificational nexus of welfare-state regimes. Private welfare must, ironically, be analyzed in order to identify the welfare state; and as we shall discover, the opposite is equally true. But, besides its relevance for classificatory endeavors, the role of private provision is an analytical precondition for any serious testing of causal theories of welfare-state growth, precisely because state provision is so powerfully intermingled with private provision (Rein and Rainwater, 1986).

The Public–Private Mix of Social Provision in Advanced Capitalist Democracies

Any study of the public–private mix faces formidable obstacles. One is the paucity of reliable data, especially going back in time; another is the difficulty of defining exactly what should be considered private or public.

The definitional question must be resolved in the light of our theoretical concerns. Our first principle for distinguishing systems has to do with the presence of laws, since this is the only meaningful way of differentiating social rights from the varieties of contractual arrangements. This implies that we must include all pensions under the rubric of 'public' a) if they are directly legislated and administered by the state, or b) if there exists a clear and explicit government mandate that the private sector provide a given type of pension. As a consequence, we will consider the Finnish, British, and Dutch second-tier industrial pensions as public; but, given the absence of an explicit government dictum in Switzerland (until 1982), the labor-market pensions there are to be classified as private. The same argument applies to the Dutch 'company pensions'. France is the only ambiguous case: mandating exists but is not formally legalized. Since the gist of French practice is equivalent to the situation prevailing in the truly legislated cases, we have chosen to treat French occupational pensions as 'public'. The year in which government mandating occurred defines the shift from private to public.

A second category that must be isolated is government civil-service pensions. These mirror the government's role as employer and are thus occupational in nature; despite being financed by, and paid out of, government budgets, they have very little to do with legislated social rights but much to do with a particular status demarcation. They reflect the legacy of etatism and corporate privilege.

There remain two classes of 'purely' private pensions: occupational pension plans, and individual annuities. It is important to keep the two types separate due to the differential logic that they espouse. In a strict sense, it is difficult to consider occupational plans as simply market-conforming. They often reflect employer paternalism (in the form of the traditional gratuity pension); they are sometimes the result of collective insurance (in the form of group plans) and are, in this sense, private-sector equivalents to corporatist social insurance; and they are often the outcome of labor-market collective bargaining, and therefore constitute a form of deferred wages. Today, the first type is relatively marginal (except in Japan), and we can therefore view private occupational pensions primarily as a form of group insurance or of trade-unionism. Finally, the category of individual insurance, such as life-insurance plans, reflects the tradition of individual self-reliance within the framework of competitive contracting.

As noted, the empirical problem is formidable because of the generally meager and uneven statistical coverage of private plans. Normally, there is reliable information on life-insurance plans, mandated occupational plans, and funded, or trusteed, labor-market pensions. The major shortcoming is data on unfunded 'gratuity-type' pensions. For some countries, Japan especially, we cannot avoid underestimating the scope of private provision. Historical data are, moreover, almost impossible to assemble. This limits our inquiry to the present. Little information is available for two nations, Austria and Italy, but it is universally agreed that their private plans are truly marginal; we will therefore score them equal to the lowest within the sample (an approximation for Italy is facilitated by known private-pension expenditures for 1970).

In the following empirical overview we present two different indices: first, total expenditure by program category; second, the sources of income among aged households. With respect to the former, expenditure data were preferred to coverage or finance data, since they reflect the actual state of affairs: finance data, given long-term funding, reflect a possible future scenario. And the problem with coverage data is that broad coverage does not necessarily imply that private pensions play any significant role; in Sweden, for example, there is virtually universal coverage by occupational private plans, but the benefits paid out are exceedingly marginal.

With respect to the sources of income among aged households, we have survey data for some nations that allow us to estimate the relative importance of public and private pensions, as well as of work income and individual savings, in the total income package of aged households. This affords us the possibility of examining the continued importance of work as well, and it allows us to compare expenditure-based data with income-source data as a means to ascertain data reliability. Issues of definitions and data sources for pension expenditures are treated in detail in the appendix to this chapter.

State and Market Provision of Pensions

For a few countries, it is possible to trace expenditure developments of occupational plans since the 1950s. Table 4.1 presents estimates of

TABLE 4.1   Estimates of the scope of private occupational pensions, as % of GDP, since 1950

	1950	1960	1970	1980
Australia	0.1	—	—	1.3
Canada	0.13	0.5	0.7	0.6
Denmark	—	—	0.34	0.65
Finland	—	0.2	—	0.1
France	—	0.7	—	0.3
Germany	0.2	0.1	—	0.5
Italy	—	—	0.09	—
Netherlands	0.3	—	0.4	0.8
Sweden	0.4	—	—	0.5
Switzerland	0.25	—	1.1	1.4
United Kingdom	—	1.2	—	1.0
United States	0.14	0.34	0.74	1.4

Source: G. Esping-Andersen, 1988, *State and Market in the Formation of Social Security Regimes*. European University Institute Working Papers, Florence, Italy

occupational pension expenditure as a percentage of GDP between 1950 and 1980 for 12 nations. The table illustrates two important phenomena that we shall return to subsequently. First, it shows that private (funded) occupational pensions played a relatively marginal role until very recently. In 1950, private pensions (as well as public) absorbed a small proportion of national resources. Second, the table reflects the differential trends among nations. In some countries, especially Australia, Switzerland, and the United States, private plans have grown very large. A substantial growth also occurred in Denmark, Canada, and Holland. The opposite is true for Finland, Sweden, and Great Britain, where, of course, government legislation or mandating marginalized the private sector. The bi-modal distribution of private pensions across nations remains when we examine more closely the breakdown of pension expenditures around 1980 in table 4.2.

This table shows the relative importance of social security, government-employee, private occupational, and individual pensions as a percentage of GDP for 18 nations. For all four categories, the cross-national variance is substantial. Social security pensions vary from a low of just above 2 percent in Japan to a high of almost 10 percent in Sweden. Government-employee pensions range from less than 1 percent in Australia and Canada to a high of almost 4 percent in Austria. Private occupational plans are insignificant in Austria and Italy, but very large in Switzerland and the United States. Individual annuities (which may include some group plans, too) play a dominant role in Canada,

TABLE 4.2   Expenditure on public- and private-sector pension schemes and individual life-insurance annuities, as % of GDP, 1980

	Social Security	Government-employee	Private occupational	Individual insurance
Australia	3.8	0.7	1.3	0.6
Austria	8.65	3.8	—[a]	0.3
Belgium	5.6	3.0	0.4	0.3
Canada	2.9	0.2	0.6	1.3
Denmark	6.1	1.1	0.65	0.8
Finland	6.2	2.45	0.1	0.2
France	8.3	3.1	0.3	0.6
Germany	8.3	2.2	0.5	0.8
Ireland	3.4	2.2	0.1[b]	0.5
Italy	6.15	2.2	—[a]	0.1
Japan	2.15	0.9	0.45	0.45
Netherlands	6.9	1.8	0.8[c]	0.45
New Zealand[d]	8.1	0.75	0.35	0.0
Norway	7.1	0.9	0.1	0.55
Sweden	9.7	1.0	0.5	0.15
Switzerland	7.3	0.95	1.4	0.6
United Kingdom[e]	6.4	2.0	1.0	0.1
United States	5.0	1.5	1.4	0.3

[a] Basically non-existent system.
[b] There are no data on expenditure for the 'industrial funds'. This has been estimated on the basis of contribution ratios.
[c] 1981 data.
[d] The data pertain to 1977.
[e] 1979 data. Labor-market pensions have been allocated to the private sector when contracted out, except in the case of public-employee benefits.
Source: G. Esping-Andersen, 1988: *State and Market in the Formation of Social Security Regimes.* European University Institute Working Papers, Florence, Italy

Denmark, and Germany, but are peripheral in Finland, Italy, and Great Britain.

A clearer picture of the relative pension-mix can be established if we present the ratio of each of the four categories to total (private and public) pension expenditure, as seen in table 4.3. Note that we have here set Austria's and Italy's occupational pension expenditure equal to 0.1 percent of GDP.

Table 4.3 shows that nations cluster heavily. Low levels of social security in the overall mix are accompanied by large shares of private-sector provision. But this is almost tautological. Countries are surprisingly bi-modal with regard to their emphasis on public-employee pensions. In one group, their size is enormous: Austria, Belgium,

TABLE 4.3 The public–private pension mix, 1980 (as % of total pension expenditure)

	Social security pensions	Public-employee pensions	Occupational pensions	Individual annuities
Australia	59.4	10.9	20.3	9.4
Austria	67.8	29.8	0.8	2.3
Belgium	60.2	32.3	4.3	3.3
Canada	58.0	4.0	12.0	26.0
Denmark	70.5	12.7	7.5	9.2
Finland	69.3	27.4	1.1	2.2
France	67.5	25.2	2.4	4.9
Germany	70.4	18.6	4.2	6.8
Ireland	54.8	35.5	1.6	8.1
Italy	71.6	26.0	1.2	1.2
Japan	54.4	22.8	11.4	11.4
Netherlands	69.4	18.1	8.0	4.5
New Zealand	87.9	8.2	3.8	0.1
Norway	82.0	10.4	1.2	6.4
Sweden	85.5	8.8	4.4	1.3
Switzerland	71.1	9.3	13.7	5.9
United Kingdom	67.3	21.1	10.5	1.1
United States	60.9	18.3	17.1	3.7

Source: G. Esping-Andersen, 1988: *State and Market in the Formation of Social Security Regimes*. European University Institute Working Papers, Florence, Italy

Finland, France, Ireland, Italy, and Japan. This is, of course, the group of nations we have earlier identified as strongly etatist and corporatist. In contrast, among both our liberalistic and social democratic welfare-state clusters, civil-service pension expenditure is low (Australia, Canada, Denmark, New Zealand, Norway, Sweden, and Switzerland). What primarily distinguishes the latter is the relative position of social security versus private-sector provision. Australia, Canada, and the US are examples of modest social security and strong private commitments, whereas Norway and Sweden (and possibly also Denmark) exemplify the opposite. A preliminary classification of 'pension regimes' is thus possible:

1 Corporative state-dominated insurance systems, in which status is a key element in the pension-program structure. In this regime, the private market is generally marginal, and social security tends to be highly occupationally segregated with particularly

TABLE 4.4   The sources of income among households, head 65+ years

	Work incomes	Property assets interest	Private pension	Social security transfers[b]
	% of total household income			
Canada (1980)	27.0	22.6	11.3	37.0
Denmark (1977)	27.7	11.1	10.4	46.9
Finland (1980)	15.3	7.1	0.3	77.3
Germany (1978)	11.9	11.6	3.9	68.5
Ireland (1980)	49.1	3.9	12.3	34.7
New Zealand (1980)	13.9	18.9	4.4	59.4
Norway (1982)	20.4	7.2	0.8[c]	71.5
Sweden (1980)	11.1	8.8		78.1[d]
United Kingdom (1980)	23.8	9.1	5.5	54.6
United States (1980)	26.8	15.4	5.5	37.3

The category of 'other unspecified' income sources has been omitted from the table; thus figures do not necessarily add up to 100 percent. For Canada, Germany, Sweden, the UK, and the US, the data refer to households with head aged 65–74. Note that for Norway and Denmark, where retirement age is 67, the data refer to heads 67+. The Danish data are a weighted average of single male, single female, and married households, recalculated from source (below).

[a] Work incomes include income from self-employment.

[b] Social security pensions and other public-sector income-transfers to the aged, including civil-service pensions.

[c] The Norwegian private pension figure includes civil-service pensions within the household income statistics. We know from national accounts that the ratio of civil service pensions to private occupational pensions is 9:1, and have adjusted accordingly – allocating 90 percent to 'social security transfers'.

[d] This includes also private occupational pensions, which cannot be estimated separately.

Sources: For Canada, Sweden, the UK, and the US, the data derive from the LIS files. For Denmark, from H. Olsen and G. Hansen, De Aeldres Levevilkaar 1977 (Copenhagen: SFI, 1981, pp. 263ff.). For Finland, from direct correspondence with Finland Central Statistical Office. For Ireland from J. Blackwell, Incomes of the Elderly in Ireland (Dublin: NCA, 1984, table 12), and from direct communication with Dr M. Macquire, OECD, Paris. For New Zealand, from New Zealand Household Survey 1980–1981 (Wellington: Department of Statistics, 1983, table 10). For Norway, from Inntektsstatistik 1982 (Oslo: Statistisk Sentralbyra, 1985, p. 58). For Germany, recalculations from Einkommens- und Verbrauch Stichprobe. 1978 (Wiesbaden: Statistisches Bundesamt, 1983, p. 308).

pronounced civil-servants' privileges: Austria, Belgium, France, Germany, Italy, and Japan, with the possible inclusion of Finland.

2 Residualist systems, in which the market tends to prevail at the expense of either social security or civil-service privilege, or both: Australia, Canada, Switzerland, and the United States.

3 Universalistic state-dominated systems, in which population-

wide social rights eradicate both status privilege and markets: New Zealand, Norway, Sweden, with the possible inclusion of Denmark and Holland.

This classification leaves us with only one really mixed case, Great Britain. In Britain, the basic flat-rate state pension was never adequately supplemented with a public-sector second-tier earnings related scheme; at the same time, the principle of contracting out has led to some growth in private pensions. But in neither case has the evolution been strong enough to decide the system's overall pattern.

A similar kind of clustering ought to emerge from the data on income sources among aged households. Hence, work, investment, and private-pension incomes should play a relatively larger role in the overall income-mix of households within the residualist regimes.

With a few exceptions, this is confirmed in table 4.4. Unfortunately, the data do not allow us to distinguish civil-service pensions from general social security. Work incomes are important in the countries where we would expect it: Canada and the US, but also in Denmark, Ireland, and Britain. For Denmark and Britain, the reason is probably the straightforward one that the social security system offers only modest flat-rate pensions, and that a second tier either does not exist, or is too recent to provide sufficient pension income. For Ireland, the reason would primarily have to do with the continued importance of rural self-employment. However, given that the table refers to households, the work income might, in large measure, refer to spouses' earnings.

The distinction between investment income and private pensions in table 4.4 corresponds to the relation between individual self-reliance and collective bargaining. In this sense, individualism appears especially pronounced in Canada, New Zealand, and the United States, and least so in Norway, Sweden, and Finland. For a few of these countries we have household-income survey data for the early 1960s as well. This permits us to trace major structural changes for Denmark, Canada, Britain, and the US. The primary trends are a fall in the significance of work, especially in Denmark and Canada; the rise of social security; and also a rise in the role of investment income, especially in Denmark and Canada (OECD, 1977; Goodman, 1986).

The statistical correspondence between our two types of indicators is fairly strong. Based on the ten-nation sub-sample for which household-income data are available, the zero-order correlation between the private pensions' share in household income and occupational pension expenditure as a percentage of total is + 0.602. Similarly, the correlation between the two indicators of the social-security share is + 0.683. Both work-incomes' share, and private-pensions' share of household incomes is strongly negatively correlated with the social security variable (− 0.694, and − 0.636, respectively).

The evidence suggests a good empirical correspondence among our various indicators of the public–private mix in pensions. This also implies that the relevance of a 'regime approach' to the cross-national comparison of welfare states may be fruitful. The clustering along our basic dimensions is both sufficiently clear on single indicators, and is upheld when we cumulate different indicators.

We now turn from a quantitative overview of the contemporary pension-mix to the question of how differential public–private structures evolved historically.

The Historical Origins of Pension Structures

We should not impose upon the nineteenth century the conceptual meaning of pensions and retirement that we have today. Retirement was a marginal phenomenon until World War II (Graebner, 1980; Myles, 1984a). Neither public policy nor private choice assumed that a person would normally withdraw from active working life at a certain specified age, and henceforth enjoy old age in leisure. There were of course persons drawing a pension, but it was hardly ever meant to replace earnings or savings. It was not until very recently that a majority of the aged were secured a level of retirement income that guarantees against dependency, poverty, or the compulsion to work.

Social security pensions emerged at the close of the nineteenth century, and spread more rapidly in the inter-war decades. But until after World War II, they hardly even constituted an institutionalized means of retirement (Perrin, 1969). This does not imply, however, that the world of pensions was once a predominantly private domain to be successively crowded out by the state. Indeed, from their origins to the present, pensions have continuously progressed through an intricate mix of private and public; the state has been instrumental in developing both spheres.

Income security for the aged in the nineteenth century was a question of protection against impaired working capacity or loss of breadwinner. Besides working (the norm), the principal sources of old-age income-protection lay in family care, thrift, or charity within the private sector, and poor relief within the public sector. As actual pension plans emerged, the state was on center stage. In its role as employer, the state often pioneered the idea of occupational pensions. The British government introduced civil-service pensions as early as 1834. This, ironically, was the same year in which the new Poor Laws established the principle of less eligibility. New York City began to provide pensions for its employees in 1857. Taxation policy came to play a critical role in boosting private-sector pension plans; government regulation of early friendly societies as well as of rules pertaining to tax-exempt pension payments has directly shaped the structure of private-pension developments. And, finally, the state's indirect stimulus has naturally been formidable; the absence of legislated pensions, insufficient coverage, meager benefits, or restrictive eligibility-conditions would almost automatically inspire private alternatives.

Any discussion of the history of pensions must take into account the radically different structural conditions that prevailed in early industrial capitalism. Due to class structure and demographic conditions, objective needs have continuously changed.

A large bulk of the nineteenth-century population was rural; self-employment remained significant. Thus, in 1870, agriculture's share of total employment usually surpassed 50 percent (65 percent in Austria, 52 percent in Denmark, 50 percent in Germany and the United States, but only 23 percent in Britain). The relatively marginal commodification of labor that this implies means that dependence on wages or insurance incomes in old age would be somewhat peripheral.

Employment structure notwithstanding, prevailing demographic conditions would have subdued massive demands for old-age pensions. Around 1820, life expectancy at birth was normally well below 40 years; by 1900, it was still below 50 years (in comparison to contemporary societies with a life expectancy of more than 70 years). To adjust for high rates of infant mortality, we may note that life expectancy at age 20 around the turn of the century hardly surpassed 60 years: 60 years in Austria, 61 years in France, 62 years in the US, and 66 years in Sweden (United Nations Statistics Office, 1949). In other words, it was hardly usual for someone to survive beyond the age of 65. This, of course, directly shaped the age profile. The population ratio of those 65 years and older was, around 1870, between 3 and 5 percent (as compared to 11–15 percent in the mid-1970s) (Maddison, 1982).

The need for old-age pensions in nineteenth-century industrial societies was perhaps modest, but certainly not absent. With the consolidation of the commodity-status of labor emerged the risk that incapacity to work would jeopardize survival. Widows, the disabled, and the old were easily the victims of extreme poverty. Von Balluseck (1983, p. 219) reports that the vast majority of those receiving alms in

Berlin in 1867 were widows, or persons over 60. But abject or prospective need for protection was hardly matched by any sustained capacity to ensure that it be met.

In the nineteenth century, old-age income-protection was managed in a variety of ways. First, most people continued to work, a norm that was pervasive well into the twentieth century. Ball (1978, p. 80) reports that almost 70 percent of American males over age 65 worked in the 1890s; Guillemard (1980) reports similar figures for France. In fact, the early social security schemes or employer plans were not meant to replace work income, but rather to compensate for diminished working capacity (Myles, 1984). Employers would often provide sheltered jobs for their aged and less productive personnel – a practice that, incidentally, still enjoys widespread usage.

The family was the second major means of securing a livelihood in old age. The importance of family was twofold: first, the means of production were traditionally passed on to the younger generation; and with this went the expectation that the aged would live off the 'dividend'; and second, the family was the provider of a general welfare function. A 1929 New York survey showed that more than half of aged persons depended on support from family and friends (Weaver, 1982, p. 42).

The third avenue was charity, in many nations predominantly organized by the Church. The New York survey cited above showed that 3.5 percent of the aged were solely dependent on charity, but this misrepresents its real significance. As late as 1927 in the United States, total private charity payments were six times greater than total public welfare expenditure (Weaver, 1982, p. 20).

Publicly provided poor relief constituted a fourth avenue. This, as discussed above, remained practically the only government income-maintenance program, at least until the turn of the century. As the German example showed, the relief rolls were often swelled with old workers who had neither work nor property. Even as late as 1954, there were 1 million aged Britons dependent on social assistance (Brown and Small, 1985, p. 136). However, where political adherence to hard-core liberalism held sway, poor relief was not a particularly dependable source. In the United States, there were many states which refused to grant cash assistance to the needy (Weaver, 1982); in Britain, the reign of the poorhouse ensured that all but the most desperate would turn elsewhere.

The fifth and sixth avenues, namely either state or private pension schemes, are today dominant, but were in the nineteenth century extremely marginal. Bismarck's pioneering pension-insurance first came in 1889, and most nations failed to introduce public pensions for workers until well into the twentieth century. This does not mean that the state was wholly inactive; indeed, states pioneered the principle of occupational pensions (for their own civil service), and frequently mandated them in selected high-risk or high-priority occupations, such as for seamen or miners. But, clearly, these kinds of plans failed to cover those citizens with the greatest potential need, namely the growing masses of propertyless wage-workers. Veterans' pensions were occasionally of some importance, especially in the United States. Skocpol and Ikenberry (1983) argue that the surprising lack of popular pressure for pension legislation in the US was due to the rather promiscuous disbursement of Civil War pensions.

Private-sector insurance was not capable of substituting for the huge gaps left by family, charity, and state. Our nineteenth-century ancestors normally faced two private-sector pension options. First, and most important, were friendly societies and their kindred. These were generally thrift organizations for distinct social groups, whether defined by occupation or by trade union; they often evolved out of the ancient guilds. In some nations their scope was considerable. Gilbert (1966) has estimated that about 50 percent of working-class males in Britain in 1880 were members of friendly societies; in the United States around 1890, there were 3.7 million members – equivalent to about 5 percent of the labor force (Weaver, 1982, p. 46). Ashford (1986, p. 151) notes that the French mutual societies counted 2 million members in 1902. Friendly societies were, on the other hand, only marginally involved in old-age pension disbursements. Their activities centered on sickness protection, unemployment, burial costs, and survivors. Moreover, their membership largely consisted of the better-off, skilled sections of the working class: those capable of furnishing the required weekly contributions. As a result, their capability of securing pension incomes among the aged was somewhat less than impressive. This is clear in the United States during the 1920s; while membership had grown to more than 5 million, the total number of pension recipients in 1928 was only 11,000 (Weaver, 1982).

The alternative source of private-sector pension protection was employer plans. There were a small number of industries that established private pension plans at an early date, notably the railroads and mining, and among seamen. These early forerunners of the industrial pension were, moreover, often sponsored by governments. In addition, a handful of private firms began in the nineteenth century to establish company pensions. These were almost universally corporate vanguard firms, such as American Express, ATT, Carnegie Steel, and Kodak in the United States, Krupp, Siemens, and Hoechst in Germany, and

Cadbury, Lever, and Rowntree in Britain. Such plans, however, were primarily addressed to salaried staff and were, above all, paternalistic and gratuituous. Benefits were discretionary, usually contingent on lifelong and loyal service, and were financially precarious. Thus, rather than being premised on contractual entitlement principles, they were paid out of current company revenues. As such, a person's pension prospects were intimately connected to the vagaries of company fortunes.

The Historical Evolution of the Public–Private Mix

The nineteenth-century pension market was clearly residual and undeveloped. The first emergence of state pension insurance could therefore hardly have any major 'crowding-out' effect. The nineteenth-century private market had, in fact, not discovered much of a niche for pensions.

Paradoxically, public and private pensions emerged and grew in tandem. What were gradually crowded out were the legacies of pre-capitalist social protection such as the family and charity, together with poor relief and friendly societies.

The causal structure of pension evolution rests on a combination of sociological variables (demography and employment) and political transformation. The demographic structure began to change dramatically around the turn of the century, particularly with respect to family structure and life expectancy. In the three decades after the turn of the century, male life expectancy at age one jumped by almost ten years in most nations; the ratio of citizens of 65 and older thus grew (United Nations Statistics Office, 1949). It was also in this era that the shift from self-employment to wage labor, and from agriculture to industry, was particularly powerful. In countries like Germany and the United States, the share of agricultural employment declined from 50 percent in 1870 to about 33 percent in 1910. Hence, neither the family nor the farm would afford much old-age protection for the average worker of the new social order. And, meanwhile, need continued to grow.

It was also an era in which the meaning of work and employment was recast, from artisan-type shops and small manufactures to modern mass production, and from a stress on labor intensity to a growing concern with maximizing productivity. The Progressive Era in the United States, and its equivalent in Europe, inaugurated ideas of scientific management and optimal efficient use of labor power; thus the desire of management to shed itself of ageing workers also arrived (Myles, 1984a; Graebner, 1980).

While need for pensions obviously grew, so did citizens' collective capacity to demand them. Over the course of the nineteenth and even eighteenth centuries, there had been countless proposals and plans for both public and private pension plans. Daniel Defoe had proposed a 'pension office' as early as 1697; Thomas Paine suggested that pensions be one of the basic rights of man, and proceeded in fact to present actual legislation to the Lower House; both revolutionary and Napoleonic France debated old-age protection (Alber, 1982, pp. 32–3; Ashford, 1986). These plans all came to naught because there was no political will, and probably only timid popular pressure. The period around the turn of the century, however, changed the conditions under which political will could find expression. In the labor market trade unions and, gradually, industry- and nation-wide labor associations emerged. Their legal recognition was generally established during the closing years of the nineteenth century, and their growth was almost everywhere explosive. Universal suffrage spread around World War I, allowing representation and some leverage to the rising labor parties. In other words, the 'social question' became political.

In this historical nexus emerged the modern blend of private and public old-age protection. In the private sector, the movement was towards two basic systems; one was individual (life) insurance; the other, collective types of occupational and industrial pensions. In the public sector civil-service pensions usually emerged first, and social security pensions only much later.

Early social legislation followed two avenues: one a basic, usually flat-rate, minimum with its roots in the social-assistance tradition (Denmark and Australia, for example); the other, actuarial insurance schemes based on individual contributions and a demonstrable employment record. In a nutshell, the thrift element shifted from the friendly society to the modern insurance company; the employer gratuity pension was gradually transformed into a contractual fringe benefit in collective bargaining; government poor relief became social security.

The early initiatives within both public and private pensions were frequently motivated by desires to weaken the labor movements. Private-sector employers instituted pensions as a means of dividing the employees and glorifying management (Myles, 1984a; Graebner, 1980; King, 1978; Jackson, 1977). Employers utilized pensions as a means of upholding status- and authority-distinctions among its workforce, either by favoring their white-collar, salaried personnel, or by developing visibly differentiated plans. Partly because the motive was to win workers' loyalties, and partly because the initiatives cultivated divisions, the trade unions were typically antagonistic. Nonetheless, restrictive occupational unions often favored exclusionary fringe-benefit plans.

Similarly, early state legislation of pensions was typically undertaken as a means to arrest the growth of labor movements, and to redirect workers' loyalties towards the existing order (Rimlinger, 1971). This was the clear rationale behind the early German, Danish, and Austrian reforms; this was also what guided the 1891 Papal Encyclical, *Rerum Novarum*. It was hardly ever labor which initiated early pension developments.

Given their relative powerlessness in either the state or the market, labor movements naturally concentrated on developing their own systems for social protection. It was during the turn of the century that these came to enjoy a fast pace of growth. As noted, the American trade-union societies grew from 3.7 million to 5.3 million members between 1890 and 1900; they continued to grow until the Great Depression, when they suffered severe financial difficulties and gradually lost out to private insurance companies, employer plans, and public pensions (Weaver, 1982, pp. 46ff.). It should be kept in mind that probably only a quarter of the large numbers included under trade-union plans were covered for pensions (Weaver, 1982, p. 48), and very few actually became recipients. The situation was fairly similar in Britain, where trade-union fund membership grew to 5.5 million by 1938 (Brown and Small, 1985), a figure that is equal to 24 percent of the British labor force of that period.

From the point of view of labor movements, the friendly-society strategy was discovered to be less than optimal. As we have already seen, it risked segmenting the working class by excluding its weakest elements. Besides, it was prone to financial difficulties due to recurrent unemployment, costly strike action, and business cycles. Weaver (1982) argues that the decay of trade-union funds in the United States was primarily caused by their inability to weather the Depression.

The institutionalization of private and public pensions coincided during the early decades of the twentieth century. Public policy was decisive in nourishing market expansion. First, governments began in earnest to build up occupational plans for their employees at both central and local levels. In Britain, for example, all local governments had instituted teachers' pensions by 1898; by 1937, this was extended to all local-authority employees (Brown and Small, 1985). In the United States, there was a rapid growth of both federal-employee pensions and state/local government coverage. By 1928, total coverage of public employees reached about 1 million, or about 25 percent of all (King, 1978, p. 200; Weaver, 1982, p. 48). In the same year, veterans' pensions were still the greatest source of pension income, benefiting almost

500,000 individuals, or close to 85 percent of all pension recipients in the US (Weaver, 1982, p. 48). This was also the era in which many public utilities such as transportation, gas, and electricity were nationalized; as a consequence the membership of government-employee plans grew. In the United States, the federal government even came to the rescue of the railroads, leading to the nationalization of their industrial pension plans in 1935.

The direct impact of government occupational plans on private-sector growth was twofold. They were important as agenda-setters, stimulating demands for equal protection among other employee groups; also they helped bolster insurance companies as key institutions in the further growth of private-sector pension protection in terms of individual, group, and industrial schemes. In brief, government-employee plans helped construct the private market.

Government was also influential through its fiscal and regulatory policies. Especially in the inter-war period, governments introduced the idea of tax expenditures to help induce private entrepreneurship in the field of social protection. The typical technique was to allow tax deductions for insurance contributions (as did the 1921 Finance Act in Britain; the 1922 and 1924 Revenue Act in Denmark, and the 1926 Revenue Act in the US). In turn, when governments granted tax privileges, they were motivated also to regulate private-sector plans so as to ensure that they were financially solid, accountable, and honored contractural rights. In this manner, governments came to further bolster the importance of insurance companies; concomitantly, they helped reshape the nature of employer pensions, discouraging the traditional discretionary-gratuity principle and encouraging the rise of regular, negotiated, and contractual fringe-benefit plans.

Legislated social-insurance schemes, either by design or by default, left ample room for private pensions. Where legislation was slow to emerge, as in the United States, the incentive was obvious. Where it did happen, the private sector was often antagonistic at first, fearing a crowding-out effect. When Germany, for example, legislated pensions for salaried employees in 1911, the insurance industry was vehemently opposed (Jantz, 1961, p. 149).

The effect of pension legislation on private-pension growth is in no way clear cut, however. The social security reforms that were intro-duced before World War II offered very meager benefits and incom-plete coverage, and, where the insurance model was adopted, the contribution requirements entailed that basically only future genera-tions would have a chance of benefiting. Thus in Britain, the 1908 law provided only means-tested benefits to aged citizens beyond the age of

70; the subsequent contributory pension of 1925 assumed 40 years' of contribution and was, at any rate, designed so as to provide only a minimum, to be supplemented with alternative incomes. The German workers' pension insurance was launched as a disability pension for those unable to work, targeted for workers over 70, and premised on 35 years of contributions. As Myles (1984a) shows, those Germans who did receive a pension were probably unable to live on it. Sweden presents a similar picture. Old-age pension insurance was legislated in 1913, but provided hardly any benefits at all for decades. In all three cases, then, social security's role in securing pension incomes remained marginal at best. Yet the private pension market did not help fill much of the glaring gap.

Generally speaking, government pension-legislation before World War II was in the spirit of strict actuarialism and minimalist protection, so as not to thwart markets and discourage labor supply; it was assumed that necessary pension supplements should be purchased in the private market. In the United States, the spirit of minimalism was unusually extreme. But the same basic principle applied also to European practice. 'Welfare capitalism' was a slogan that depicted well the definition of government responsibility for the era as a whole.

The evolving pension-mix of the first decades of the twentieth century mirrors a welfare-capitalist model. It embodies a matrix of developments that bridge the largely pre-capitalist terrain of the nineteenth century, and the welfare-statism of the period after World War II. Objective need for pensions had clearly asserted itself; wage-earners' power to demand action was increasingly an inescapable reality; industry's new productivism diminished the value of aged workers; states had taken decisive steps to encourage and even create a market for pensions; social security had been set in motion, but was not permitted to dominate.

Private pension schemes grew at a respectable pace during the first decades of the twentieth century. But more important than their growth was their transformation. They changed from discretionary gratuities to contractual arrangements, from unfunded plans to insured, trusteed schemes; and from catering to narrow strata of upper-echelon staff, they were slowly extended to manual workers. Within this process also occurred a transformation of the age-old tradition of thrift. The friendly societies (or the family piggy-bank) gave way to the modern insurance company's life-insurance plan. More slowly, the savings embodied in the family farm gave way to urban home-ownership.

It was hoped that welfare capitalism would allow the modern capitalist enterprise to become a substitute for the unpleasantly communistic flavor of social insurance. It spoke to the new world of the Progressive Era, of the emerging modern corporation, scientific management, and a heightened sensitivity to good labor relations.

In the United States, both companies and whole industries began to establish funded and trusteed pension plans, increasingly in collaboration with insurance companies. By 1930, the insurance industry held a total of 83 million policies (including individual, group, and company plans), and was paying out benefits amounting to $2 billion (more than charity, public-employee plans, and the scattered state-pension plans paid out together) (Weaver, 1982, p. 42). This staggering amount mainly included risks other than pensions, but it was in the pension field that the life-insurance industry's fastest growth occurred. In 1915, group plans (almost exclusively contracted by individual manufacturing firms) accounted for 1 percent of its business; the figure was 15 percent by 1935 (Weaver, 1982, p. 47).

Industrial pensions that were aimed at manual workers grew at a fast pace in the 1920s. By 1928, they had outgrown trade-union plans, covering four times as many workers. Their total assets grew ten-fold from 1920–1929; the number of plans grew from 15 in 1900 to 440 in 1929 (Weaver, 1982, pp. 47ff.). Yet the high growth rates departed from a base of close to zero, and welfare capitalism remained, by the Depression, little more than an article of faith. Total coverage on the eve of the Depression was 4 million policies (including the railroads), or 7.5 percent of the labor force. Counting all types of pension insurance, coverage totalled 14 percent (Weaver, 1982, p. 48). And coverage ratios disguise the fact that the probability of actually receiving a pension was extremely low. The lack of portability rights, long-service requirements and other contingencies meant that, in practice, only a minority of perhaps 10 percent of those covered actually came to enjoy the benefits (Latimer, 1932). When they did, the benefits were typically too meager to live on. In 1927 prices, the pension averaged $45 per month (in 1980 dollars equal to $200 per month.

American welfare capitalism was a failure, and it was not even especially market-conforming. Its thrust was, by and large, corporativist, with differential privileges accorded a variety of status groups and echelons in private industry; long-service requirements and lack of portability translated easily into corporate serfdom. The corporatist flavor was not merely a result of managerial strategy, but also the outcome of early collective bargaining: trade-unionism was, before World War II, largely dominated by exclusive skills and crafts unions.

The American story was more or less paralleled elsewhere, even in nations which legislated old-age pensions. In Germany, it is true, the

1889 and 1911 laws probably stymied private-sector pension growth. But not altogether; both the traditional unfunded provident funds (*Unterstutzungskassen*) and company plans have remained a stable part of the pension-mix. In 1933, life-insurance payments amounted to 0.6 percent of GDP. This compares with 1.9 percent in the United States for 1929. In 1933, German private pension-plan expenditure equalled 0.2 percent of GDP, compared to a US figure of 0.3 for 1940 (Skolnick, 1976; Munnell, 1982; Statistisches Bundesamt 1972, p. 217). In Germany, private-sector plans grew steadily in terms of coverage, but remained marginal in terms of benefit size.

In Great Britain, private occupational plans also grew rapidly, in spite of social security legislation. Membership in occupational plans rose from about 1 million in 1908 to 2.6 million in 1936 (about half being in public-employee plans). The labor force coverage compares with that of the United States, namely 10 to 12 percent. A peculiar feature of the British model was its reliance on contributions from both employers and employees. Also, for manual workers both contributions and benefits were of the flat-rate kind. The weekly pension in 1936 was normally around 20 shillings (about 25–30 percent of a worker's normal wage). The social security pension was about 10 shillings per week (Brown and Small, 1985). The pension-mix that was offered in Britain was, thus, a slightly superior welfare capitalism to that of the United States.

The private pension plans that emerged in the 1920s were surprisingly resistant to the impact of the Depression; the victims were primarily trade-union societies. Indeed, in the two nations most seriously afflicted, Germany and the United States, private-sector plans sustained their momentum of growth. For one thing, they were increasingly reinsured and funded; also, they were still heavily biased in favor of white-collar employees whose risk of unemployment was significantly lower. In addition, they were supported by government tax policy and, occasionally, by direct government rescue operations

Restructuration in the Post-War Era

The hope that a minimalist state and a buoyant market would complement one another in a harmony of capitalism and welfare was falsified even before the Depression shattered it entirely. This was something of which the aged in the United States were keenly aware. By 1940 (when Social Security had just begun), the estimated total pension protection (including all types of private and public pension payments) was 33.5 percent of the population 65 and older. Private plans benefited only 1.8

percent of the aged; social security 1.2 percent. Twenty-three percent of the aged received old-age assistance (OAA), and another 4 percent, veterans' benefits (estimated from Bureau of the Census, 1976; section H). A little under half of the male population 65 and older continued to work in this period, but the gap in protection was by any definition enormous. The majority was obviously not able to benefit from the market, and we would have to conclude that probably a third had to seek help from family, charity, or perhaps from local poverty-assistance.

In most other countries, too, there was neither enough market nor enough state coverage. Table 4.5 shows the pension take-up rate among the population 65 and over for the combination of social security and government-employee pensions in 1939. In only a few countries did a majority of the aged receive a pension. Some, like France, had not yet introduced social security. The table also shows that the average pension amount was too small as a sole source of old-age income. For this period, there are virtually no data on private pension coverage. In the Swiss case, which approximates the American in terms of extremely low social security coverage, it is known that in 1940 there were only

TABLE 4.5   % of population 65+ receiving social security pension, and net (after-tax) pension as % of average worker wages, in selected countries, 1939

	Receiving pension in population 65+	After-tax pension replacement rate (% of net wage)
Australia	54	19
Austria	35	—
Belgium	46	14
Canada	24	17
Denmark	61	22
France	0	—
Germany	66	19
Italy	16	15
Netherlands	52	13
Norway	53	8
Sweden	79	10
Switzerland	5	—
United Kingdom	67	13
United States	5	21
Average	40	15.5

Pensions include social security and government-employee pensions, but exclude public assistance. After-tax replacement rates refer to average old-age pension payment as a percentage of average production worker wage.
Source: SSIB data files

about 29,000 annuities paid out by life-assurance companies (Statistisches Bundesamt, 1982, p. 335). In Denmark, which appears in table 4.4 to be somewhat above average, the coverage in private pensions immediately after the war was under 100,000 people (OECD, 1977). In Britain, there were only 200,000 occupational-pension recipients of which half were in the public sector (Brown and Small, 1985, p. 13).

World War II was a watershed for pension development. It had demanded and created a level of national solidarity that catapulted labor movements into the center of political decision-making; strict wartime wage–price controls under conditions of over-full employment pushed employers to offer attractive fringe benefits and unions to demand them. The war either disrupted old social-insurance systems (as in Germany) or it established the framework for a post-war welfare-state promise; it had also demanded extraordinarily high public expenditure and tax levels that, even when subsequently scaled back, helped establish a new plateau of popular fiscal tolerance for the post-war decades.

The 1940s were a growth era for private pensions for the reasons stated above, and also because social security remained insufficient. In the United States, the movement was especially dramatic. There, only a minority could count on social security checks in the foreseeable future, and even with the 1939 (and subsequent) 'blanketing-in' provisions, the benefits were at any rate too low (on the average $25 per month in 1939). The labor reforms of the New Deal had finally permitted the rise of mass unionism, and the war gave rise to full employment. Under conditions of wage–price controls, the stage was set for a growth of fringe benefits (which were exempt from the controls) (Ball, 1978; Myles, 1984a; Graebner, 1980).

The rise of private pensions was in many cases spectacular. In Great Britain, membership in private-sector plans grew from 1.6 million in 1936 to 3.1 million in 1953 (and 5.5 million in 1960). In contrast to its stance in the pre-war era, the TUC began seriously to encourage its union-affiliates to bargain for pensions. In the United States, the war years brought an additional 2.5 million workers under private-scheme coverage (King, 1978, p. 200), and the pace continued through the 1950s and after. Private-pension benefit expenditures grew by 68 percent from 1945 to 1950, and by 364 percent from 1950 to 1960 (Munnell, 1982, table 8.4). Indeed, through most of the entire post-war era, but particularly in the late 1960s and early 1970s, private-pension expenditures grew almost as fast as social security. The new phenomenon of bargained industrial pensions spread in almost all advanced capitalist countries (the few exceptions being Austria, Germany, and Italy); in

France, this took the form of a labyrinth of complementary plans, subsequently to be incorporated under the ARRCO and AGIRC systems; in the Netherlands there emerged industrial and company plans, the former being eventually subject to government mandate; Finland and Sweden likewise nationalized the second-tier pensions.

The war also altered the institutional form of pensions in at least two decisive directions. First, as noted by Munnell (1982), private pensions became a key object of union bargaining strategies, a means of deferring present wage-gains for future promises. Second, with the institutional entry of unions (in the United States, following the 1948 National Labor Relations Board ruling), the traditional gratuity pension withered away in favor of collectively bargained, contractual pension plans (Rein, 1982). In a sense, the unions helped accelerate the demise of remnants of the pre-capitalist system, and put in their place collectivistic market contracting.

The post-war surge in occupational pensions was not solely a by-product of the war and trade-union power; it was nursed along by a variety of government initiatives. The state's role in post-war capitalism has, if anything, been even more potent than ever before. First and foremost, its decisions regarding social security have had profound effects. There emerged two basic types of state pensions. The first was the universal flat-rate pension, which usually amounted to little more than upgrading the old minimum pension. Benefits were equal but low, and the assumption was that they would be complemented by private pensions. This was explicit in the British 1944 White Paper and in the Danish 1956 reform, and was certainly assumed in the Australian, Norwegian, and Swedish systems as well.

The second type, based on the social-insurance pension, determined benefits on the basis of contributions, clung to the idea of actuarialism, and premised eligibility on employment performance. In this arrangement, many citizens (such as women and mobile workers) were left out, and system maturation was often too long for most workers to be able to anticipate a satisfactory pension; as a result, this, too, helped stimulate the private market. This was clearly the situation in the Netherlands and the United States. Therefore, in either case, public policy had left ample scope for complementary private pensions.

The taxation policy of governments has been a second crucial precondition for private-pension growth. Many, if not most, countries enacted post-war tax legislation that vastly improved the tax-exempt status of private pension contributions, and sometimes also granted special deductions to recipients. Via tax expenditures, governments thus helped finance the private pension market in a major way. Today, private-pension-related tax expenditures, as a percentage of GDP, are around 1 percent in countries such as Australia, Denmark, and the United States, and about 0.7 percent in Great Britain (OECD, 1984a; Vestero-Jensen, 1984). Accordingly, private pensions may be a form of deferred wages, but they are certainly also a deferred tax. The high marginal tax rates that were inflicted upon post-war citizens certainly added to the attraction of occupational pensions as fringe benefits.

One of the most important, yet typically neglected, taxation effects has to do with home-ownership. In the United States, home-ownership among the elderly is, without doubt, a vital source of 'income'. Today, almost 75 percent of aged couples own their own home, of which 80 percent are mortgage-free. This implies that 60 percent of aged households enjoy a *de facto* income supplement of perhaps 15 to 20 percent (Ball, 1978, p.92; and author's calculations).

With tax concessions came increased government regulation of the pension market. As Brown and Small (1985) put it, British social policy came to be made by tax officials, following the 1947 Finance Act's requirement that pension schemes be separately funded and approved. Governments both opened and closed markets in decisive ways. In many cases, the state actually took the initiative to create new markets for pension savings, as was the case with the Danish 'Index Contracts', and the American Keogh and IRS individual retirement accounts. When, in 1972, the German and American governments introduced legislation to regulate occupational pensions by requiring guarantees to employees, it was believed that this would seriously impair the prospects for further growth. Yet in neither case was this belief warranted.

When governments began to mandate private pensions, they also helped create markets, as happened in Britain, the Netherlands, and Switzerland (after 1982); in the case of France, one could speak of quasi-mandating. The result, of course, is a major increase in complementary occupational pension provision. In other countries, the decision was to legislate complementary pensions (Norway, Sweden, Finland, and Denmark). But it is exceedingly difficult to determine whether the latter implies crowding-out, while the former expands markets. The mandated system obviously imposes a collectivist type of compulsion upon private enterprise that is not much different from legislation. Where nationalization implies funding and administration in governmental institutions, as happened in Norway and Sweden, the market is unequivocally marginalized; where nationalization allows private-sector management, as in Finland, the result is ambiguous.

In light of our historical synopsis, the considerable cross-national variance in the public–private mix would appear to be a function of two types of state intervention: first, governments' tradition of granting a privileged status to their civil service and employees; second, governments' decision to legislate (or directly mandate) the second-tier pension that, virtually everywhere, was growing in the private market.

Conclusion

In our examination of pension structuration, the state has been the principal link between inputs and outcomes. We have seen that market-biased regimes, as in the United States, were made possible by active and direct government policy; status privilege, of course, is a legacy of corporatism and authoritarian etatism; and the universalist social-citizenship model is clearly only possible where the state crowds out both markets and corporatism. The state thus stands in the center of how we define regime-types.

Our examination has also shown that welfare states must be identified not solely in terms of what they do, how much they spend, or what they have legislated, but also in terms of how they interact with the market and alternative private arrangements. From the perspective of the pensioner this will usually be obvious enough. A retiree will have a good grasp of how his retirement incomes are packaged. The mix is often less clear from the point of view of governments. A large, and perhaps even decisive, sphere of state involvement is hidden behind the walls of the revenue service; only a few countries have any precise idea of how much private pensions are subsidized via tax expenditures.

In any case, the logic of any welfare system can only become clear when we examine the interplay of public and private provision. It is the interplay that defines the overall distributional structure, the relation between social rights and private contracts, inequalities of class, gender, or status, and, in the final analysis, defines welfare-state regimes.

When we consider both private and public provision, we will also arrive at drastically different assessments of nations' 'welfare effort'. This is important for theory-testing. Whether one adheres to an economic-growth theory, a demographic theory, or to a working-class-mobilization theory, one's argument should not be tested solely against levels of public-sector welfare effort. In some nations, the level of pension output in the public sector may be quite modest, but concomitantly heavy in the private sector. If we have a theory that argues, say, that economic development or demographic structure determines pension expenditures, it would seem a mistake not to examine both private- and public-sector pension outlays.

More generally, if our concerns are to explain welfare-state differences it is obvious that the public–private interplay must be included in our specification, and that it constitutes one of the objects to be explained. It is to these queries that we turn in chapter 5. We shall find that conventional hypotheses about welfare states must be seriously reconsidered once we begin to specify more carefully the institutional properties of welfare states, and once we examine public and private provision together.

Appendix   Explanations and data sources for chapter 4

Under 'pensions' are included old-age and disability pensions (excluding work-injury pensions). Where lump-sum retirement payments are a typical feature (usually only in private occupational pensions or in individual plans) they have been included. Note, however, that the Japanese data exclude the kind of lump-sum payments made directly by employers.

Data for social security pensions and public-employee pensions are derived from ILO, *The Cost of Social Security, 1980* (Geneva: ILO, 1983). For New Zealand, from ILO, *The Cost of Social Security, 1977* (Geneva: ILO, 1979). For the United States, from *Statistical Abstract of the United States, 1981* (Washington, DC: Government Printing Office, 1982).

Data for private occupational plans and for individual life-insurance annuities are derived from governmental sources within the countries included. A detailed overview of all these sources can be obtained from Esping-Andersen, 'State and Market in the formation of Social Security Schemes', European University Institute Working Papers, No. 87/281 (Florence, 1987).

5

Distribution Regimes in the Power Structure

Why is social protection more marketized in some nations than in others? Why is universalism so prominent in the Nordic countries, and corporatism in continental Europe? Why do some states define their social-policy responsibilities very narrowly, while others see the right to employment as a minimal obligation, and officially bind themselves to commitments that would dazzle the imagination of any nineteenth-century liberal (or socialist, for that matter)? And why, finally, do nations crystallize into distinct regime-clusters?

The task of this chapter is to identify what forces propel welfare-state development. In the protracted controversy around this issue, functionalist modernization theories have generally been pitted against power theories. The issue is theoretically important because it highlights paradigmatic schisms in the social sciences. Power-centered theories rest on a particular view of the nexus between politics and society. Foremost, they assume that government is no neutral arbiter, nor is it inherently responsive to emerging social needs; its actions are dictated by the exercise of power. Hence, the balance of power in a society is decisive for what a welfare state will look like. The contrasting view holds that welfare states emerge under virtually any conditions of power. The starting point, following Marshallian economics (Marshall, 1920), is that redistribution can only occur with a certain level of economic development. But the real source of social policy growth is found in industrialism, urbanization, and population change. These establish new urgent social needs that cannot easily be met by the traditional family, community, or market-place.

The debate is difficult to settle, to a degree because we confront two sharply divergent research styles. The historical approach, such as that of Rimlinger (1971), Ashford (1986), Gilbert (1966), Weir, Orloff, and Skocpol (1988), and Flora's collection of European nation studies (1986), is rich on detail but generally short on national comparisons. The quantitative, usually cross-sectional, correlational research has come to represent the main alternative. Cutright (1967) and Wilensky (1975) represent a first generation of this approach, in which social expenditures constituted the main variable, and cross-sectional analyses of many countries the main methodology. Over the past decade a second generation has evolved, applying either more sophisticated techniques (such as pooled time-series analyses) (Hicks, 1988; Griffin, O'Connell, and McCammon, 1989; Pampel and Williamson, 1988), more elaborated specifications of salient welfare-state differences (Korpi, 1980; Myles, 1984a; Esping-Andersen, 1985b), or both (Korpi, 1987; 1988).

If all this research fails to add up to any unequivocal conclusion, it is not because of lack of effort, but largely because of methodological incompatibilities. It is analytically difficult to confront detailed historiography with a table of regression coefficients. The former paints a dense portrait of how myriads of events impinged upon social-policy formation; the latter seeks economy of explanation, and reduces reality to a minimum of variables. From the former, it is difficult to generalize beyond any particular case; in the latter, we have no history.

The dominant correlational approach is additionally marred by a frequent mismatch between theoretical intent and research practice. First, most use data solely on expenditure as a surrogate for 'welfare stateness'. Earlier, we have argued why expenditures present a circumspect and possibly misleading picture of welfare-state differences. If what we care about is the strength of social rights, equality, universalism, and the institutional division between market and politics, social-spending levels may camouflage more than they reveal.

Second, the standard correlational approach holds a questionable assumption of linearity: that countries' welfare states can be compared in terms of 'more' or 'less' (spending, redistribution, or whatever). We cannot exclude the fact that certain dimensions of welfare states are linearly comparable, but many of those that we have found to be salient are clearly not. Hence, in terms of stratification, the public–private mix, and the strength of social rights, we find clusters and regime-types. The problem with most studies of the correlational variety is that they test their hypotheses without pausing to specify the nature of the beast to be explained; the welfare state remains almost always under-theorized.

The under-theorization of the welfare state is understandable in light of the fact that most scholars are less interested in the welfare state than in the validity of their explanatory theories of power, modernization, or industrialization. Welfare states are often little more than another vehicle for testing theories. The problem of under-theorization, nonetheless, applies also to the explanatory variables. Take the role of power. The power-explanation of welfare states normally assumes that working-class mobilization is the driving force behind social reform. Hence, countries with strongly mobilized and unified working classes should produce more advanced welfare states. Yet, with rare exceptions (such as Korpi, 1983, Wilensky, 1981, or Castles, 1981), there is hardly any attention given to whether it is unionization or parties (and what kind of parties) that matters, or what is a reasonable length of time before labor-movement power can be expected to translate itself into substantive results. The structuration of power is usually ignored.

Even cursory reflection makes the last point obvious. Take the period leading up to the crisis of the 1930s. The difference in measurable working-class power (unionization, left-party votes) between, say, Britain, Germany, Austria, Sweden, and Denmark was not that great. But differences in the structure of power within which labor was compelled to struggle were decisive for the entire progress of Western civilization. Or, take the post-war era. Almost all studies score Austria, Sweden, and Norway almost identically on working-class power. But social democracy's capacity to utilize 'similar' power resources in these three countries was subject to different constraints. Scandinavian social democracy was blessed with a chronically divided right; Austrian social democracy was not (Esping-Andersen and Korpi, 1984; Castles, 1978). Perhaps this results in decisive welfare-state differences?

How, then, do we formulate theoretically satisfactory propositions about the causes of welfare-state variations? The task must begin with a re-examination of the way we ask the questions. When we hypothesize about the impact of working-class mobilization, we must first identify welfare-state characteristics that have some identifiable relationship to working-class interests and demands. In this light, social-expenditure levels are epiphenomenal, since labor probably never demanded more spending as such. It is also necessary to specify more precisely how any given level of working-class power is likely to produce relevant social-policy outcomes. This must certainly include considerations of the parliamentary system, of divisions within labor movements, and of the relationship between the various political forces in society. If we wish to do good sociology, we are required to view power as a relationship, not as a thing.

The Social Democratization of Capitalism

The working-class mobilization theory must therefore begin with a specification of what, concretely, workers want and can be mobilized to struggle for. It must, subsequently, provide evidence that there is a relationship between working-class power and welfare-state outcomes that corresponds to such identifiable wants.

On this kind of voyage, we immediately face a paradox: the first steps towards a welfare state were almost always taken by the old ruling classes who, be they conservative autocrats or bourgeois liberals, should be regarded as the true architects of the modern welfare state's foundations.

Most historians will tell us that the conservative reformers were motivated by concerns that were quite far removed from workers' demands. Bismarck saw the *Sozialstaat* as a prescription against socialism, and as a means to win the new proletariat's loyalties for the Wilhelmine autocracy (Rimlinger, 1971). The working classes were usually the objects rather than subjects of early social policy. In some cases, ruling-class reformism even preceded the birth of a labor movement. This was the case in Sweden.

When we theorize about the role of working-class mobilization, therefore, we must remember that our welfare states were founded in opposition to both labor and socialism. This is evident in the design of early welfare policies. The corporatist model in Germany and Austria, for example, was intended to fragment and divide what appeared as an emerging collectivist threat. Tellingly, these countries were among the world's leading welfare spenders both prior to, and after, Nazism, but under conditions which were sharply at odds with trade-union and social democratic party policies.

A confirmation of the working-class mobilization theory of welfare states cannot therefore begin with the beginning. Neither can it presume that workers, or their collective expression, have a historically impermeable model for an ideal social policy. Does this leave us with a paralysis of specification? No, because it is possible to identify properly the characteristics relevant for a working-class mobilization thesis from an understanding of pressing needs that emerge from workers both as individuals and as a political collectivity.

From the perspective of the individual, it is clear that the insecure status of wage-earners will lead them to demand income security, social relief, and greater immunity from forces beyond their control. Being captive to market forces, workers are irrational if they do not seek a modicum of 'de-commodification'.

Social rights, however, can be granted in numerous ways, and it is here that we must also consider the exigencies of collective action. Workers have organized in a multiplicity of ways and have evolved a variety of social-policy models. The traditional guild- or crafts-community most likely produces narrow fraternal societies and occupational welfare schemes. Christian and especially Catholic workers' movements naturally strive for a familial model in which corporatism and the Church figure more prominently than broad class solidarity. The reigning theory of working-class mobilization, however, is essentially premised on the laborist, socialist, or social democratic model of collective action, a model that was far from being dominant until well into the twentieth century.

There are certain, albeit quite few, principles of social policy common to virtually all kinds of labor movements. One is clearly de-commodification from the whip of the market place. Without this, collective action itself becomes hardly possible. Workers need a basic command of resources in order to be prevented from acting as strike breakers or from underbidding fellow workers, and in order to be effective and reliable participants in a solidaristic community. The early labor organizers did not need Karl Kautsky or Rosa Luxemburg to tell them that the lumpenproletariat constituted a formidable danger to collectivism.

A second principle is that social policy helps define the relevant boundaries of collective identity because, for workers, it constitutes such a vital element in their livelihood. Thus, the ways in which social protection schemes are organized comes to delineate social identities, status communities, and solidarities. It was for precisely these reasons that the emerging working-class mass parties opposed narrow occupational schemes, corporatism, and status-differentiated privileges, and instead struggled for comprehensive, egalitarian, and universalist social security.

It is therefore mistaken to assume that workers or working-class movements will naturally, or inevitably, arrive at one patent model for a welfare state. We plunge into a world of fallacies if we define our relevant actor as being either the 'working class' (as does Therborn, 1978) or 'working-class mobilization' (as does almost everybody).

A workable theory of 'working-class mobilization' must, instead, define its actor in terms of a peculiar kind of political class formation. In this way our analytic task is more manageable because of the clear convergence towards wage-earner mass movements that characterizes the post-war era. Whether under the banner of a social democracy, communism, or laborism, almost all parliamentarian labor movements converge with respect to their principles for social policy and designs for welfare-state reforms.

In essence, the convergence is around what might best be called the social democratic model. In practice, any leftist party committed to winning power via parliamentary majorities is hard put to avoid embarking upon what we earlier have identified as the social democratic regime-model. The ideal of a nationally defined solidarity and universalism is, perhaps, the clearest example. Left parties' power, indeed, depends on their capacity to eradicate status differentiation and dualisms that arise when large groups tie themselves to market provision, and to minimize group stigmatization. The universalist, full-employment welfare state such as the Scandinavian ones has in practice become the referent for labor parties internationally.

We know already that a variety of historical forces has played a decisive part in the formation of welfare states; this is almost certainly why they differ, yet cluster as they do. The extraordinary power of the Church, the aristocracy, and an authoritarian state in early continental European capitalism is certainly a key to the explanation of this regime-type; in converse, the weakness of absolutism and the dominance of a laissez-faire-inspired bourgeoisie in the Anglo-Saxon nations goes a long way in accounting for the 'liberal' regime. In both cases, social policy was never neutral, but part of a more general campaign to weaken, or absorb, the socialist impulse and to secure a lasting institutionalization of politically preferable principles of social organization.

With this in mind, it is defensible to examine the working-class mobilization thesis in terms of a process of social democratization of the welfare state. By this we mean the capacity to substitute for the characteristics dominant in either a liberal or conservative regime, a comprehensive, universalistic, 'de-commodifying', full-employment welfare state.

Formulated in this way, a certain degree of linear analysis is warranted, but only up to a point. It is clear that international variations in welfare-state development cannot be ascribed solely to different levels of power mobilization, but must be understood in terms of power structuration. Within the context of modern parliamentarism, this involves two conditions in particular: the patterns of political coalition-formations, and the structuration of labor movements – especially the relationship between unions and parties. We must, in particular, be attentive to the ways in which denominational-based political mobilization has filtered working-class demands into policies, and the ways in which Catholic and Christian parties have affected the position of socialist and labor parties. In countries like the Netherlands, Italy, Germany, and Belgium, the Christian Democratic parties of the post-war era gained prominence in part because of their electoral success among workers; being capable of long-term governance, they have also been decisive in the interpretation of labor's social-policy needs.

Measuring the Influence of Power

Since power finds a host of expressions and resides in all levels of society, we must choose among a variety of approaches. We may, for example, identify patriarchy in both the family and business enterprise, and in the state. Or, we may follow the lead of the 'neo-corporatism' literature, and see the peak level of organized interest-intermediation as the key mode of power articulation. However, neither appears optimal when our chief concern is welfare-statism. In social-policy making, interest organizations and bureaucracies may have great influence; yet it is parliamentary and cabinet power that constitute the most obvious, direct, and visible focus for analysis, and it is on this level of power articulation that we shall focus.

Our study is limited to the 18 major industrialized capitalist democracies. We need to assure ourselves that we are studying political systems, economies, and social structures that are comparable. Ours is therefore not a sample, but a universe of comparable nations. Hence, no conclusions can be generalized beyond this rather unique group of political economies.

The models we test will present measures that have some bearing on differences in structuration. First, our working-class mobilization variable consists of a weighted average of legislative and cabinet seat shares for left/labor parties, for either the period 1918–33, 1918–49, or 1949–80. The name of the variable is 'Weighted Cabinet Shares' (WCS). As many studies suggest, trade unions may also influence policy, but they are largely omitted here: first, because trade-union strength is empirically substitutable by party strength (the correlation is 0.816); second, because our real analytical focus is on parliamentarism.

Many studies present dubious ways of measuring power. It is, for example, common to measure party strength in terms of vote shares. But this is questionable, since electoral rules often do not assign seats proportionally to votes. It is also too often the case that studies measure party power over brief time-periods, something which risks a 'Blum' effect: a leftist party comes to power only to be ousted a few years later, having had little or no lasting influence.

We also introduce variables that capture the role of Catholic and Christian Democratic mobilization. For analyses that pertain to years prior to 1950, our measure is simply the percentage of Catholics in a nation. It is not until later that the phenomenon of Christian Democratic mass parties fully emerged. But the specification also rests on the presupposition that where Catholicism is strong, the dominant ideals of social justice are likely to be colored by the world-view of the Church – in effect, the variable seeks to capture a general presence of the Catholic teachings on social policy. For our analyses of the contemporary era, we use the proportion of legislative seats held by Catholic parties over the period 1946–80. Indeed, the choice of either one or the other makes little difference: the zero-order correlation between the first and second measure is 0.848.

It is clear that we need to identify the historical impact of neo-absolutism and authoritarian etatism. To condense the complexity of such historical experiences into something reasonably measureable, we have identified two basic features: 1) the strength and durability of absolutist rule; 2) delays in the granting of full political democracy. Our measure of the former derives from Rokkan's classification (1970, ch. 3), and results in three groups: 1) strong and durable; 2) weak absolutism; and 3) no absolutism. The scores given by this classification have, in turn, been weighted by the year in which full universal (male and female) suffrage was institutionalized.

In every model, we control for the two most influential and convincing non-power-based theoretical causes of welfare-state development. The first is economic development, which can be argued to have an effect either because a) the rate of economic growth allows resource redistribution or, b) the level of economic progress summarizes overall industrial maturation and social modernization. In the former case, our measure is the average annual rate of real GDP growth, 1960–80 (the period in which modern welfare states really grew and matured); in the latter case, our measure is GDP per capita. Second, we include the percentage of the aged (65 and over) in the population as a demographic variable most obviously related to social policy (pensions usually account for a major share of social transfers).

Economic development and demographic pressures were usually identified as the principal explanations in the 'first-generation' studies of welfare-state causes (Cutright, 1965; Wilensky, 1975; 1987). In addition, Wilensky (1975; 1987) advocates a bureaucratic-incrementalist theory which presupposes that once a bureaucracy has been put in place, it will have both an interest in, and the powers of promoting, its own aggrandizement. Indeed, decisive events in the history of social policy have been traced directly to the actions of welfare-state bureaucracies (Derthick, 1979; Skocpol, 1987; Weir, Orloff, and Skocpol, 1988). In a quantitative, comparative study like this one, bureaucracy's influence is exceedingly difficult to identify in a measurable way – the argument presented in most accounts is too closely tied to the critical intervention of key historical personalities. Moreover, if the explanandum concerns entire welfare states, it is hard to construct a meaningful bureaucracy variable, given that particular social programs emerge over a wide range of years. In the analyses to follow, we will identify the effect of bureaucracy solely on pensions. In this way, bureaucracy is more immediately recognizable as potentially influential.

Measuring Welfare-State Regimes

It should be obvious by now that the present study attaches only limited validity to aggregate-expenditure measures in welfare-state research. We have argued in favor of structural and institutional features, and it is on these that our analyses will center. The following tests of welfare-state causes progress through four distinct phases. We first present a limited series of analyses of aggregate welfare-state measures: social security expenditures as a percentage of GDP (for 1933, 1950, and 1977), and total (private- and public-sector) pension expenditure. In these two cases, the causal importance of demographic and economic variables is most likely to emerge.

In the second analytic phase, our attention centers on pensions and, in particular, on the structuration of pension provision. The decision to focus especially on pensions rests partly on the fact that they constitute by far the most important element of welfare-state activities, and partly on the wish to shift from a highly abstract and aggregate level of welfare-state specification to a level at which more detailed institutional characteristics can be identified. For pensions, our analyses will distinguish what we argue are critical differences between regimes. We will thus examine degree of program corporatism (number of status-defined separate pension plans); the etatist bias (expenditure on civil-service pensions as a percentage of GDP); the relative importance of private-sector pensions (individual and occupational pension expenditures as a percentage of total pension spending); and what might be called the social security bias (proportion of total pension spending that is neither private nor civil service).

In the third phase, we examine general structural and institutional features of welfare states, again with the aim of isolating key characteristics of conservative, liberal, and socialist welfare-state regimes. Here we will focus on the following variables: the relative significance of targeting and means testing, i.e. welfare-state residualism (measured as means-tested social-assistance spending as a percentage of total social transfers), the inegalitarianism of benefit structures, decommodification (all as measured in chapters 2 and 3), and the welfare-state's role in guaranteeing full employment (adjusted average unemployment, 1960–80, and growth of public-sector employment, 1970–80).

Finally, in the fourth stage, we turn to an explanation of the welfare-state regimes identified in chapter 3; that is to say, the three principal models of welfare states as systems of social stratification.

Methodological Design

Most theories of welfare states propound dynamic, historical arguments. But they are almost always tested with purely cross-sectional data. Herein lies a major obstacle to adequate empirical corroboration. Using cross-sectional designs to address dynamic hypotheses can only be undertaken with severely compromising assumptions. Chiefly, we are substituting cross-national differences at any given point in time for differences over time. To illustrate the point, it is almost always the case in comparative studies that Sweden scores highest on any given welfare-state attribute (expenditure, egalitarianism, generosity, etc.). When we do cross-sectional research, we are implicitly assuming that other nations would approach Swedish levels had they commensurably more of the causal attributes with which Sweden is so happily blessed (social democracy, trade-union strength, neo-corporatism, economic development, or old people).

Given that one country, like Sweden, will always be a welfare leader in any study of the impact of power, cross-sectional designs are especially prone to the fallacy of Swedocentrism or 'social democratism' identified by Shalev (1983). A cross-sectional study will focus its attention on the variance explained by any given causal variable (say, power). Yet it is often the case that theories are formulated such that it is the degree of association (the B, or slope of the regression) that constitutes the statistic of interest: we want to know, for example, how much an augmentation of left-party power results in a growth of social equality.

For reasons of data scarcity, proper time-series studies are few and far between. And, if we choose to study the few variables for which long series do exist, we often run into the problem of heavy autocorrelation – the best explanation of this year's spending is last year's. Nonetheless, on the basis of the few time-series-based studies currently available, we do know that many assumptions from the cross-sectional studies must be revised. Griffin, O'Connell and McCammon (1989) show, for example, that the correlation between social democratic control and unemployment is −0.544 on a cross-sectional basis, but only an insignificant −0.150 on a time-series basis.

In this study we are condemned to rely mainly on cross-sectional analyses. For virtually all our variables, proper time-series are either impossible to construct, or the data are so heavily trended that statistical identification is rendered impossible. In other words, conclusions of a dynamic nature will have to be considerably hedged.

The Welfare State as an Aggregate

THE SOCIAL WAGE

As we have noted, social security expenditure as a percentage of GDP has been the most commonly used indicator of degree of 'welfare statism'. It reflects in a crude way the total social wage, i.e. the share of a nation's resources that is distributed according to social rather than strict market criteria. Following the gist of our argument, there is no reason to believe that expenditure commitments, as such, should be related to left-party power. A large social wage could emerge as well from authoritarian regimes or from Catholicism. Indeed, to the extent that left-power mobilization were to influence social expenditures, it would have to be relatively late in the development of welfare states. Left cabinet-participation, let alone power, was marginal and sporadic prior to the post-war era.

The size of contemporary welfare states cannot be predicted from how large they were before World War II. Indeed, the zero-order correlation between social expenditures (as a percentage of GDP) for 1933 and 1977 is a negative −0.120. For 1950 and 1977, however, the relationship is considerably stronger (0.617). If the size of welfare states in past years were a powerful predictor of today's, clearly there would be little left to explain other than what once caused their variation. However, something has occurred between the 1930s and today that has altered fundamentally the distribution of nations along the dimension of social expenditures.

The fact that the social wage has grown in all nations is not very surprising; our concern is to explain what has intervened to produce contemporary differences between nations. Today, welfare states diverge more in terms of size than they did before. Thus, the standard deviation from the mean has increased from 2.7 (with mean = 4.6 percent of GDP) in 1933, to 2.6 (with mean = 7.2 percent) in 1950, to 6.0 (with mean = 18.3 percent of GDP) in 1977.

If we disaggregate the historical panorama, we see better why today's national rankings have little correspondence to the situation earlier. In 1933, the social-wage leaders were Germany, Britain, and Austria; the laggards were Finland, Holland, and Italy – today among the leaders. And the United States ranked in the middle, despite having then introduced virtually no single social security legislation. The ranking of the 1930s mirrors an almost entirely different social program-mix than exists today. Dominant were means-tested poor relief, civil-service benefits, and, especially in the United States, patronage-flavored veterans' pensions. But, before we turn to the structural differences of welfare states, let us examine the validity of some main explanations of the social wage.

In table 5.1, we present bi-variate regression results on the impact of economic, demographic, and political variables on the social wage (social security expenditure – SSE – as a percentage of GDP) for the years 1933, 1950, and 1977.

Perhaps the most important result that emerges from table 5.1 is that none of our explanatory variables is significant until we arrive at the post-war era. For 1933 and 1950, most variables normally considered influential on welfare-state development are inconsequential. The lack of a left-power effect (WCS) is, of course, to be expected, but the lack of an effect of Catholicism and absolutism in 1933 (and again in 1950) contradicts our expectations. As we have discussed earlier, it is largely to these two historical forces that one must credit the early establishment of welfare-state schemes.

There are two variables that emerge as important in accounting for the changed distribution of welfare spending. One is percentage aged in the population (% aged) which is significant in both 1950 and 1977; the other is left-power mobilization (WCS), which becomes important in 1977.

In other words, political forces influence spending commitments only in the post-war era. This is also what we should expect. It is only after World War II that all our nations had established full democracy, and that working-class and socialist parties had a genuine chance of possessing or, at least, sharing governmental power. It is evident that

TABLE 5.1   Cross-sectional (OLS) analysis of the social wage in 1933, 1950, and 1977

	r	B	R sq.[a]	F
Dependent variable				
SSE/GDP (1933)				
GDP/capita (1933)	0.078	N.S.	—	—
% aged (1930)	0.178	N.S.	—	—
WCS (1918–33)	0.287	N.S.	—	—
Catholic party	0.122	N.S.	—	—
Absolutism	0.070	N.S.	—	—
Dependent variable				
SSE/GDP (1950)				
GDP/capita (1950)	−0.106	N.S.	—	—
% aged (1950)	0.613	0.892 (3.10)[b]	0.336	9.61
WCS (1918–49)	0.254	N.S.	—	—
Catholic party	0.262	N.S.	—	—
Absolutism	0.289	N.S.	—	—
Dependent variable				
SSE/GDP (1977)				
GDP/capita (1977)	0.088	N.S.	—	—
% aged (1977)	0.727	1.823 (4.23)	0.498	17.89
WCS (1950–76)	0.558	0.236	0.268	7.23
Catholic party (1946–76)	0.251	N.S.	—	—
Absolutism	0.270	N.S.	—	—

[a] R sq. adjusted.
[b] t-statistics in parentheses.
Source: SSIB data files

'economic growth' explanations do not fare well; in no year does GDP explain social-expenditure performance. But the strength of the % aged variable suggests that a demographic-functionalist theory has a degree of validity.

For 1950 and 1977, the % aged variable is the strongest, explaining respectively 34 and 50 percent of the variance in social spending. For 1977, the Weighted Cabinet Shares variable explains about 27 percent of the variance. For the post-war era, then, we are confronted with the classical juxtaposition of a power-based and a functionalist-demographic theory. To estimate their relative stength, the two variables are entered simultaneously in a simple multivariate OLS model:

$$SSE/GDP\,(1977) = -2.860\,C + 0.058\,WCS + 1.596\,\%\ aged\ (R\ sq. = 0.477)$$
$$(t = 0.42)\quad (t = 0.58)\quad\ \ (t = 2.72)$$

When we control for aged population, left power loses its explanatory strength: the demographic structure, as Wilensky (1975) and Pampel and Williamson (1985) also show, is the most powerful explanation of cross-national variations in social spending.

This is a result that is quite consistent with the argument put forth in this book: there is no convincing theoretical argument for why social-expenditure levels, as such, should mirror the aspirations of workers and the achievements of labor parties. The absence of any 'Catholic' or 'absolutist' effect is more surprising, especially for the early years. After World War II, of course, both social democratic and Christian Democratic forces expanded welfare spending in tandem – the socialists perhaps more strongly – and this alone might account for the absence of an independent 'Catholicism' effect after 1950. But in 1933, and again in 1950, the Catholicism and the absolutism effects should have emerged more clearly. While this contradicts our expectations, it does not destroy our argument. The crucial issue is not aggregate expenditures, but welfare-state structuration. It is when we turn to analyses of structural differences that our argument concerning political forces is put to a real test.

Pensions

There are many reasons why we should choose to disaggregate the social wage into its component parts. There are some items in the total welfare-state package that are more crucial than others for working-class welfare, and demographic factors (such as ageing) do not pertain equally to all social programs. A test for the relative impact of power and demographic–economic variables is better done by focusing strictly on pensions.

Myles (1984a) and Pampel and Williamson (1985) represent, so far, the most sophisticated approaches along this line. The ways in which the two studies measure pensions differ considerably. Myles focuses primarily on the qualities of pension schemes, and finds that left-power variables offer a decisive explanation of cross-national differences; Pampel and Williamson concentrate on pension expenditures, and find that demographic structure is the most powerful explanation (the aged constitute a powerful voting bloc). This kind of approach is, nonetheless, implicitly biased. Taking only welfare-state expenditures on pensions, as Pampel and Williamson do, means that one is studying only a part of the entire pension-world – the public sector. Implicitly, this means that one is studying the structuration of pensions.

It seems obvious that a proper test of the impact of population ageing must include all types of pension expenditure, public and private. In this way, we are not concerned with structuration, but with macro-economic resource allocation. And, in this way, we maximize the chance that economic and demographic forces over-determine the political variables. In brief, we are more likely to arrive at a convergence argument when we study pension expenditure in terms of both private- and public-sector outlays. In contrast, we would be more likely to discover a significant influence of political variables when we study the structural differences in pension arrangements.

Table 5.2 summarizes our findings with respect to total pension expenditure. The dependent variable includes spending on four types of programs: individual private plans, collective occupational pensions, civil-service pensions, and social security pensions. For this variable, we have data only for 1980.

As we anticipated, population ageing is the driving force behind combined total pension spending – a result that would appear quite logical, if not almost tautological. However, the difficulty arises when we attempt to interpret the significance of the proportion of the aged. It can be analyzed in terms of a functionalist theory, according to which needs are satisfied when they arise or, alternatively, in terms of political pressures that the elderly voters exert on the political system.

The functionalist interpretation would be more plausible if a) political variables were completely irrelevant, and b) economic variables were causally important. As to the former, table 5.2 does indicate that none of our political-power variables influences pension-spending in any significant way. As to the latter, we discover surprisingly that economic level (GDP per capita) is completely insignificant, while the rate of

TABLE 5.2   Cross-sectional (OLS) analysis of total private and public pension expenditure (as % of GDP), 1980

Independent variable	r	B	R sq.[a]	F
GDP/capita (1980)	0.052	N.S.	—	—
GDP growth, 1960–80	−0.557	−0.23 (−2.69)[b]	0.267	7.21
% aged (1980)	0.791	5.170 (5.17)	0.602	26.69
WCS (1946–76)	0.423	0.072 (1.87)	0.128	3.49
Catholic party	0.329	N.S.	—	—
Absolutism	0.217	N.S.	—	—

[a] R sq. adjusted.
[b] t-statistics in parentheses.
Source: SSIB data files

post-war economic growth is significantly, but negatively, related to pension-spending. This indicates that the size of total 1980 pension-spending is more likely to be large when economic growth has been sluggish. How can we best interpret this seemingly paradoxical result?

We should first bear in mind that pension-spending is calculated in terms of GDP. Hence, if GDP grows slowly and the percentage of aged grows rapidly at the same time, pensions will almost surely grow faster than GDP. To put it differently, demographic pressures persist regardless of economic conditions. This hypothesis is treated in the following OLS model:

$$\text{Total pensions} = \underset{(t = 0.61)}{1.580\,C} + \underset{(t = 4.14)}{0.679\,(\%\text{ aged})} - \underset{(t = -1.58)}{0.010\,(\text{GDP growth})}$$

This model explains 64 percent of the variance ($F = 15.84$), and since GDP growth loses its significance, it confirms the singular causal importance of the demographic variable.

But, as we argued earlier, the crucial impact of political variables is not likely to emerge in models of aggregate welfare outputs, but rather when we examine structural biases. It is to this examination that we now turn. First, we begin with a series of analyses of the three types of pension arrangements that reflect our welfare-state regimes. The 'liberal' regime is measured by the share of private-sector pensions relative to total. For the 'conservative' regime, we will analyze both degree of etatism, measured as civil-service pension expenditures as a percentage of GDP, and degree of program corporatism, measured (as in chapter 3) as the number of status-distinct, public pension plans. Finally, the 'social democratic' regime is identified in terms of legislated social security pension expenditure as a percentage of total.

Pension Regimes

The 'liberal' market bias

For reasons of solidarity, unity, and de-commodification, it is to be expected that left political parties will attempt to supplant private-sector pensions with legislated social rights. We would, accordingly, anticipate a strong and negative effect of WCS on private-sector pensions in the total pension-mix. For similar reasons of de-commodification, and also because of their preference for status and hierarchy, we would expect similar effects for Catholic parties and for nations with strong absolutist and authoritarian state traditions.

Private pensions contain two distinct types: individual pension contracts (usually of the life-insurance variety), and (typically) collectively negotiated occupational plans. The two may easily reflect diverse logics. While the former most closely adheres to strict market individualism, the latter may, in its own right, grow large where labor is strongly organized – in particular under conditions where trade-unionism is substantial while labor-party power is weak. In other words, occupational pensions may, for organized workers, constitute an alternative strategy to the parliamentary road. We will thus test separately for trade-union strength. In table 5.3, the dependent variable is combined private-sector (individual and occupational) pension expenditure as a percentage of total pension spending in the economy (% market pensions) for 1980.

The results from table 5.3 are consistent with our general theoretical argument. Although none of the political variables achieves real statistical significance, the signs, as expected, are all negative. The role of trade-unionism has been analyzed separately only for occupational pensions as a share of total. The regression coefficient is negative and insignificant, with B = −0.179; t = 1.48. While it is worth recalling that trade-unionism and WCS are highly intercorrelated (and thus substitutable), this result nonetheless indicates that private occupational plans do not constitute a major labor-movement alternative.

Table 5.3 shows that the market bias in pensions is mainly associated with two variables: it is positively related to GDP per capita (although not to GDP growth), and strongly negatively related to population

TABLE 5.3   Cross-sectional (OLS) analysis of the market bias in pensions, 1980

Independent variable	r	B	R sq.[a]	F
GDP/capita	0.508	3.330 (2.36)[b]	0.212	5.58
GDP growth	0.262	N.S.	—	—
% aged	−0.530	−2.209 (−2.50)	0.236	6.26
WCS (1946–80)	−0.412	−0.290 (−1.81)	0.118	3.27
Catholic party	−0.405	−0.229 (−1.77)	0.112	3.14
Absolutism	−0.348	N.S.	—	—

Dependent variable is private pensions (individual and occupational) as % of total combined public and private pension expenditure in 1980.
[a] R sq. adjusted.
[b] t-statistics in parentheses.
Source: SSIB data files

age-structure. While the economic-level variable is difficult to interpret, the % aged variable's strong negative effect points to an interesting addendum to our earlier findings. It now appears that the demographic 'push' theory does not apply equally to all kinds of pensions – that the aged, in a sense, are not neutral in the way their influence is exerted upon pension spending. The coefficients suggest that the aged harbor a negative preference for private-market pensions.

These reflections call for two additional model tests. First, we need to establish whether the (negative) aged-effect holds also when controlling for GDP per capita. Second, if it is correct that the aged have negative preferences for private pensions, this would conceivably influence the role of left parties. Below, we first test the explanatory effect of the aged, controlling for GDP:

$$\% \text{ market pensions} = 12.150 \, C + 3.615 \, (\text{GDP/capita}) - 2.381 \, (\% \text{ aged})$$
$$(t = 0.96) \qquad (t = 3.30) \qquad\qquad (t = 3.42)$$

With an (adjusted) R sq. of 0.528 (F = 10.49), it is clear that the additive regression, including both the % aged and the GDP variable, performs far better than either of the former bi-viriate models. Also, both variables remain statistically significant. Our second model, however, indicates that there is no simple 'transmission' of the aged's pension preferences into left-party effects:

$$\% \text{ market pensions} = 38.860 \, C - 0.076 \, (\text{WCS}) - 1.910 \, (\% \text{ aged})$$
$$(t = 2.76) \quad (t = -0.37) \qquad (t = -1.58)$$

The variance explained in this model is actually less (20 percent) than in the bi-variate model with just % aged. In other words, it mis-specifies the relationship between age structure and private-pension biases.

The lack of a stronger negative impact of left-party power on private pensions raises a theoretical concern. The lack of an effect may have to do with the essentially bi-modal way in which nations are distributed on the private-pension variable: in one cluster, the private-pension ratio is very high (the US, Canada, Switzerland, and Australia), while in another, the ratio is very low. Here, then, is a clear case where the linear approach is of limited utility.

THE ETATIST BIAS IN PENSION PROVISION

The etatist bias was earlier defined as a propensity to grant civil servants special privileges. Etatism is, in our argument, associated with the conservative model of welfare states, and we would accordingly expect Catholicism and absolutism to be strongly and positively related to high levels of etatism. Conversely, following our social democratization theory, left-party power mobilization (WCS) should influence etatism in a negative direction. It is hard to see how either age structure or economic development could influence a state's special treatment of civil servants. In table 5.4, the dependent variable is defined as expenditures on government-employee pensions as a percentage of GDP (in 1980). The demographic and economic variables are, as expected, of little or no importance for etatism. For left-party power (WCS), the relationship is, as hypothesized, negative but also entirely insignificant. Since both trade unions and left parties usually attack special-status privileges, we can interpret this to mean that labor parties in government have been generally unable (or unwilling) to diminish civil servants' advantages.

In turn, table 5.4 shows quite powerful effects of both Catholic-party strength and strong absolutist legacies. This is precisely what one would have expected. The next question is what happens when Catholicism and absolutism are entered simultaneously in the model? One theoretical possibility is that one variable overpowers the other; a second is that they both independently add up to a total explanation. In the model below, we test for the additive effects of both absolutism and Catholicism:

$$\text{Etatism} = 0.599 \, C + 0.014 \, (\text{Catholic party}) + 0.127 \, (\text{Absolutism})$$
$$\quad (t = 1.76) \qquad (t = 2.84) \qquad\qquad (t = 1.82)$$

The combined additive model explains 54 percent of the variance ($F = 8.65$), and is thus superior to either of the two bi-variate models in table 5.4. Yet, when entered together, it is evident that the Catholic-

TABLE 5.4   Cross-sectional (OLS) analysis of etatist privilege, 1980

Independent variable	r	B	R sq.[a]	F
% Aged	0.458	0.187 (2.06)[b]	0.160	4.24
GDP/capita	−0.385	N.S.	—	—
WCS (1946–80)	−0.060	N.S.	—	—
Catholic party	0.667	0.037 (3.58)	0.397	12.21
Absolutism	0.534	0.198 (2.53)	0.241	6.39

[a] R sq. adjusted.
[b] t-statistics in parentheses.
Source: SSIB data files

party variable overpowers absolutism – the latter has essentially lost its significance.

This generally confirms our expected correspondence between conservative welfare-state regime characteristics and their political expression. This kind of correspondence will be re-confirmed in the following section of program corporatism in pensions.

CORPORATISM IN SOCIAL SECURITY PENSIONS

As we have argued repeatedly, the emphasis on status differentials and corporatism has been very strong in both Catholicism and in the policies of authoritarian states. We should not forget, however, that occupational corporatism also pervaded many early labor movements.

The theory of social democratization would lead us to expect that labor parties will work actively to dismantle status differentiation. In converse, Catholic-party strength and a legacy of absolutism should both affect corporatism positively. Aside from the likely opposition from rightist and Catholic parties, a labor party's efforts to de-corporatize will also be opposed by institutionalized interests entrenched in the preservation of status segregation and privilege. Thus, we should expect a negative, but not very powerful, effect of WCS on corporatism.

There is no genuine theoretical reason why either age structure or economic development should influence program corporatism. In table 5.5, we present analyses of pension-program corporatism, defined and measured as in chapter 3: number of separate, occupationally defined, public-sector pension progams. The results from table 5.5 are exactly as we predicted. Left parties (WCS) have a negative, albeit insignificant, effect on corporatism; whereas the effect of Catholicism and, par excellence, absolutism is colossal. Indeed, the explanatory power of

TABLE 5.5   Cross-sectional (OLS) analysis of corporatist social stratification in pensions, 1980

Independent variable	r	B	R sq.[a]	F
WCS (1946–80)	−0.178	N.S.	—	—
Catholic party	0.463	0.085 (2.09)[b]	0.166	4.38
Absolutism	0.923	1.124	0.843	92.54

[a] R sq. adjusted.
[b] t-statistics in parentheses.
Source: SSIB data files

absolutism alone (84 percent of the variance) is startling. As before, we need to examine the relative causal relationship between absolutism and Catholicism in an additive multivariate model:

Corporatism = 1.072 C + 0.014 (Catholic party) + 1.054 (Absolutism)
            (t = −1.85)   (t = 1.66)   (t = 8.87)

The model confirms that absolutism constitutes the truly decisive variable. The variance explained in this model increases only marginally compared to the bi-variate model with absolutism (86 percent; $F = 52.68$), and the Catholic-party variable becomes insignificant.

THE SOCIAL SECURITY BIAS IN PENSIONS

A social security bias in the pension mix should be most closely associated with a 'social democratization' of the welfare state. Measured as social security pensions as a percentage of total (private, public, and civil-service), a high score will obviously also mean a crowding-out of private plans, although not necessarily of etatism or corporatism.

It is with respect to social security pensions that the 'bureaucracy' theory is most appropriate. The argument, as put forward by Wilensky (1975), rests on the assumption that, once established, bureaucracies will amass independent powers and crystallize egoistic organizational interests in their own perpetuation and growth. Hence, in line with Parkinson's law, we would anticipate that the older the system (measured as year in which it was founded), the larger it becomes. In table 5.6, we test for political, economic, demographic, and bureaucratic

TABLE 5.6   Cross-sectional (OLS) analysis of social security bias in the pension mix, 1980

Independent variable	r	B	R sq.[a]	F
% aged	0.443	1.812 (1.98)[b]	0.146	3.90
GDP/capita	0.050	N.S.	—	—
Bureaucracy	−0.078	N.S.	—	—
WCS (1946–80)	0.706	0.488 (3.99)	0.468	15.94
Catholic party	−0.164	N.S.	—	—
Absolutism	−0.150	—	—	N.S.

[a] R sq. adjusted.
[b] t-statistics in parentheses.
Source: SSIB data files

variables on the international variation in social security bias.

From table 5.6, it is clear that neither bureaucracy nor economic development influence a social security bias. It should be kept in mind that Wilensky's argument for the bureaucracy effect was tested on the basis of social security spending as a percentage of GDP, not on our structural-bias variable. Still, if we instead test the thesis against social security pensions as a percentage of GDP for 1980 among the 18 nations included in our study, the effect of bureaucracy remains nil.

Population ageing has a small, but insignificant, effect on the social security bias. This comes as something of a surprise when we recall the negative effect it had on the private-pension bias. At that point, we offered the hypothesis that the aged were a political pressure group in favor of legislation rather than market dependency. Alone, the WCS variable explains 47 percent of the variance. This is consistent with our notion that labor parties will work energetically to solidify citizenship-rights and diminish the reliance on private provision.

The importance of left power is additionally confirmed when we control for % aged. In the multivariate OLS model below, the % aged variable loses significance altogether, thus confirming the robustness of the WCS explanation. The total variance explained is 43 percent ($F = 7.50$), which is inferior to the simple bi-variate model of WCS and social security bias.

$$\text{Social security bias} = 63.750\,C + 0.508\,(\text{WCS}) - 0.185\,(\%\ \text{aged})$$
$$(t = 5.54) \quad (t = 3.02) \quad (t = -0.185)$$

Our predictions are upheld with regard to the influence of political variables: indeed, the only identifiable force behind the social security bias is labor parties in power.

The Structuration of Welfare States

Having examined the causal mechanisms behind welfare states in terms of size, and pensions in terms of structural biases, we now turn to explanations of structural differences in welfare states more generally. We shall in this section concentrate on three features, all of which have been core issues in the history of labor movements' social policy. We first examine the relative importance of means-tested poor relief – a feature which is especially characteristic of the residual, liberal welfare-state regime, and which has always been violently opposed by labor. Thus, left power should help marginalize poor relief. Subsequently, we shall analyze de-commodification and full-employment performance, since both represent cornerstones in the 'social democratic' welfare state.

THE IMPORTANCE OF MEANS-TESTS

The old poor-relief tradition was opposed by labor movements, both because they fought for solid citizens' rights, and because means-tests tend to stigmatize and socially divide the population. Among our 18 nations, the poor-relief tradition has been almost entirely eliminated in the social democratically dominated Nordic countries; it is still fairly prominent in countries like the United States and Canada, and is moderately present in the continental European nations. The relative importance of means-tested assistance benefits in total social security expenditure constitutes a very appropriate measure of welfare-state structuration, because it highlights the principles embodied in traditional liberal social policy.

In table 5.7, we present analyses of the poor-relief bias on the basis of 1977 data. There are clearly only two variables of any statistical importance: GDP per capita, which, surprisingly, is positively and significantly related to poor relief; and WCS, which, as we predicted, has a strong and negative effect. Catholic-party strength and absolutism, as well as the % aged, are all insignificant (although the signs point in the expected direction).

In light of GDP/capita's strong explanatory power, we should enter it as a control variable with WCS. In the model presented below, both WCS and GDP/capita remain as powerful as ever; jointly the two

TABLE 5.7   Cross-sectional (OLS) analysis of means-tested poor relief in the welfare state, 1977

Independent variable	r	B	R sq.[a]	F
GDP/capita	0.580	1.860 (2.85)[b]	0.295	8.12
% aged	−0.380	N.S.	—	—
WCS (1946–80)	−0.652	−0.224 (−3.44)	0.389	11.83
Catholic party	0.118	N.S.	—	—
Absolutism	−0.063	N.S.	—	—

[a] R sq. adjusted.
[b] t-statistics in parentheses.
Source: SSIB data files

variables now explain a full 72 percent of the variance ($F = 22.38$).

$$\text{Poor relief} = -6.922 \, C - 0.221 \, (\text{WCS}) + 1.830 \, (\text{GDP/capita})$$
$$(t = -1.86) \quad (t = -4.97) \qquad (t = 4.40)$$

The strong additive, linear effect of GDP/capita on the poor-relief bias is best interpreted as spurious: the very same countries which score highest on GDP/capita (US and Canada) also score highest on poor relief. This conclusion is, in fact, borne out by an inspection of the residuals. What is important is that the model confirms our argument about the centrality of left-party power for 'social democratization'. WCS is clearly decisive for restricting the means-tested bias in welfare states.

DE-COMMODIFICATION IN THE WELFARE STATE

Our measure of de-commodification derives from the composite index developed in chapter 2. The variable seeks to measure the degree to which social programs have the capacity to free workers from the constraints of the cash nexus.

Clearly, we should expect left political power to have a very strong and positive effect on de-commodification; if not, much of our entire theoretical framework collapses. The effect of WCS should also remain strong when controlling for economic development. This is important because the goal of decommodification ought to be pursued even under adverse macro-economic conditions.

Our understanding of conservative politics leads us to expect that their influence on de-commodification would be slightly more positive than negative. Clearly, the strongest opposition ought to come from liberalism, for which, alas, we have no unambiguous measure. As a second best, in table 5.8 we include poor relief as a proxy for liberalism.

Table 5.8 shows that only two explanations are significant in a bi-variate relationship: WCS is, as we expected, strongly and significantly related to de-commodification – it explains 43 percent of the variance; the % aged in the population has an almost equally strong impact. The GDP variable is completely insignificant and changes absolutely nothing when entered together with the WCS variable.

The poor-relief proxy for liberal political power is, as we thought, negatively correlated with de-commodification, but does not reach significance. The most appropriate test, then, is whether the strong performance of the % aged variable is due to the fact that it has independent explanatory power, or whether its effect is mediated through WCS.

TABLE 5.8   Cross-sectional (OLS) analysis of de-commodification in the welfare state, 1980

Independent variable	r	B	R sq.[a]	F
GDP/capita	−0.026	N.S.	—	—
% aged	0.672	2.173 (3.63)[b]	0.417	13.18
WCS	0.681	0.371 (3.72)	0.430	13.81
Catholic party	0.161	N.S.	—	—
Absolutism	0.284	N.S.	—	—
Poor relief	−0.412	−0.654 (−1.81)	0.118	3.27

[a] R sq. adjusted.
[b] t-statistics in parentheses.
Source: SSIB data files

The model below suggests the former to be the case, since both variables retain (in equal degree) their respective status *vis-à-vis* de-commodification; however, both lose considerably in terms of statistical significance. The total variance explained in this model is 49 percent ($F = 9.18$), i.e. hardly more than in either of the bi-variate models with WCS and % aged, respectively.

$$\text{De-commodification} = 7.898\,C + 0.229\,(\text{WCS}) + 1.275\,(\%\text{ aged})$$
$$(t = 0.92) \quad (t = 1.81) \qquad (t = 1.71)$$

Clearly, then, the % aged effect is not solely transmitted via WCS (the zero-order correlation between the two is 0.663, which might help explain the poor performance of both variables in the model), but neither is de-commodification best explained by the additive effect of the two variables.

Regardless, our findings lend substantial support to the underlying theory that de-commodification is an important, if not central, goal behind the process of working-class power mobilization. The lack of any influence of economic variables suggests that the 'industrialism' thesis has little validity. On the other hand, since demographic forces clearly count, we cannot here dismiss entirely the functional view of welfare-state evolution

FULL-EMPLOYMENT PERFORMANCE

Full employment is not only a good that benefits individual wage-earners. Kalecki's (1943) belief that sustained full employment would significantly push the balance of power in favor of the working classes was probably shared by all labor movements. Their strength derives substantially from tight labor-markets.

In many countries, a public commitment to full employment was proclaimed and even written into the constitution in the aftermath of World War II. However, the commitment was unevenly granted and even more unevenly applied. It has varied from a constitutional guarantee, as in Norway, to a general Keynesian counter-cyclical strategy, as in Germany between 1967 and 1974, and to a practically passive governmental role, as in Denmark until 1958, Germany before 1967, and the United States throughout most of the post-war era.

Douglas Hibbs (1977) has shown that left political power favors full employment over price stability. The shortcoming of his otherwise unusually sophisticated study is that the data cover a limited number of countries, and then only for the growth decades. The task of maintaining full employment after 1973 will most likely require substantially more power mobilization. Active employment policies must be financed and require financial solidarity among the employed.

Many countries responded to post-1973 unemployment with programs designed to reduce labor supply, including early retirement, exportation of foreign workers, and encouraging women to return to the family. Obviously, this is a much softer version of the binding full-employment commitment compared to a case where participation levels remain maximal.

The following analyses seek to control for national differences in

TABLE 5.9   Cross-sectional (OLS) analysis of full-employment performance, 1959–1983

Independent variable	r	B	R sq.[a]	F
GDP growth	0.160	N.S.	—	—
WCS	0.557	5.880 (2.68)[b]	0.267	7.18
Catholic party	−0.448	−3.806 (−2.00)	0.150	4.01
Absolutism	0.014	N.S.	—	—
Poor relief	−0.492	−15.137 (−2.26)	0.195	5.11

The full-employment index = average level of unemployment 1959–78 plus average level of unemployment 1978–83, multiplied by the ratio of inactives in the population aged 15–64. Note that the index has been inverted so that a positive sign indicates a good performance.
[a] R sq. adjusted.
[b] t-statistics in parentheses.
Source: SSIB data files

labor supply. The measure is the long-term average rate of unemploy-ment (according to the standardized OECD definition), weighted by the level of labor-force participation. Nations with low participation rates are thus 'punished', while countries that have produced an expansion are 'rewarded'. The index thus captures not merely unemployment, but also performance in terms of job-creation.

Clearly, in the analysis of full-employment performance, the relevant economic variable is average rate of real GDP growth. Since our argument holds that a residual welfare state is much less likely to be committed to full employment, we introduce the poor-relief variable in the models: see table 5.9.

That left power is an important precondition for full employment emerges clearly from table 5.9. WCS explains almost 27 percent of the variance. A similar, but less significant relationship emerges if we correlate unemployment (1978–83) with WCS: the zero-order correla-tion is −0.384. The table also reveals that economic-growth rates have no influence whatsover on full-employment performance. This gives added evidence to the argument that full employment performance is largely a question of political will.

The 'political' hypothesis gains additional support from the significant negative effect that poor relief and Catholic-party strength have on full-employment performance. In the former case, the role of poor relief (either as a proxy for liberalism or for welfare-state residualism) was expected to be negative, since a hallmark of laissez-faire ideology is to avoid interference in the (labor) market. In the latter case, the negative effect can be said to reflect Catholicism's particular brand of social policy: a willingness to subsidize family well-being, but not to guarantee employment.

To identify the explanatory power of WCS in relation to rival political forces, we have run two separate models: one in which we control for poor relief; a second in which we control for Catholic-party strength.

$$\text{Full employment} = -293.015 \, C + 4.337 \, (\text{WCS}) - 6.909 \, (\text{poor relief})$$
$$(t = -3.35) \quad (t = 1.48) \quad (t = -0.81)$$

This model explains only 25 percent of the variance (F = 3.84), and although it reduces the significance of WCS (and eliminates the in-fluence of poor relief), it can be dismissed. The model performs more poorly than the bi-variate regression with just WCS. In the second model (below), the combined effect of Catholicism and WCS results in a more robust explanation. The variance explained increases to 40 percent (F ≐ 6.64), and Catholic parties' negative effect clearly over-powers WCS's positive effect on full employment.

Full employment $= -253.100\ C + 3.681\ (\text{WCS}) - 1.860$ (Catholic party)
$\qquad\qquad\quad (t = -4.14) \qquad (t = 1.64) \qquad\qquad (t = -2.13)$

We can interpret this to mean that, on balance, left-power mobilization is less effective in maintaining full employment when in competition with a strong Catholic/Christian Democratic party.

COMMITMENTS TO FULL EMPLOYMENT

The maintenance of full employment, as our low percentage of explained variance suggests, obviously depends on a host of factors both within and outside of left parties' control. A country's international vulnerability may be so great that a major shock (such as in the 1970s) produces levels of mass unemployment that even the best of efforts will fail to redress. Still, left parties can engage their best efforts, and it is to these that we now turn.

In a market economy, labor governments have recourse to an array of policies with which to counter business cycles and unemployment. Among the most important are active manpower policies (retraining, labor mobility, and sheltered employment), and public-sector employment growth.

To assess left-power mobilization's effect on active manpower-program development is not easy. Using expenditures on such programs (excluding spending on unemployment benefits, of course), we must limit our analysis to 15 nations. We have regressed active manpower-program expenditures as a percentage of GDP (for 1975) on WCS, and the results indicate a strong and significant effect: the zero-order correlation is 0.695, and WCS explains 44 percent of the variance.

Turning to public employment as an alternative strategy, we have

TABLE 5.10   Cross-sectional (OLS) analysis of public-employment growth (annual averages, 1970–1980)

Independent variable	r	B	R sq.[a]	F
GDP/capita	−0.152	N.S.	—	—
GDP growth	−0.259	N.S.	—	—
WCS	0.748	0.109 (4.51)[b]	0.532	20.33
Catholic party	−0.018	N.S.	—	—
Absolutism	−0.009	N.S.	—	—

[a] R sq. adjusted.
[b] t-statistics in parentheses.
Source: SSIB data files

calculated the average rate of public-employment growth, 1970–80, for the 18 nations. The analyses presented in table 5.10 indicate that nations' capacity to increase public employment is not a function of either richness (GDP/capita), nor real GDP growth, but almost solely of left-power mobilization (WCS).

In summary, we seem to face a scenario in which left power has been instrumental in developing policies to boost job growth and avert unemployment, but it has been much less capable of actually assuring full employment in the long haul. The question that presents itself, then, is whether variations in full-employment performance can be explained by the labor-market policies of left parties. To examine this question, we present below an additive regression model with WCS and rate of public-employment growth, 1970–80.

$$\text{Full employment} = -330.011 \, C + 8.360 \, \text{WCS})$$
$$(t = -6.76) \qquad (t = 2.53)$$
$$+ 22.618 \, (\text{public-employment growth})$$
$$(t = 1.00)$$

The model explains 27 percent of the variance (F = 4.09), but it shows that the policy of increasing public employment has no independent effect on employment performance.

Explaining Welfare-State Regimes

We have now arrived at the point we can test the impact of political variables on the stratification dimensions of welfare-state regime differences identified in chapter 3.

THE CONSERVATIVE WELFARE-STATE REGIME

In chapter 3, the conservative regime was identified as one in which corporatist organization and etatism were especially pronounced. We argued that Catholic-party strength and a history of strong absolutist and authoritarian statehood were principal forces, while left power should have a negative effect. In a study of the stratification dimensions of welfare states, there seems to be no reason why economic and demographic variables should play a role, and they have been omitted from our analyses. The dependent variable in table 5.11 is the index of conservative stratification attributes developed in chapter 3.

Since the conservative-regime characteristics that we are examining

TABLE 5.11   Cross-sectional (OLS) analysis of conservative welfare-state regime stratification, 1980

Independent variable	r	B	R sq.[a]	F
WCS	−0.149	N.S.	—	—
Catholic party	0.608	0.111	0.331	9.40
		$(3.07)^b$		
Absolutism	0.705	0.859	0.456	15.81
		(3.98)		

[a] R sq. adjusted.
[b] t-statistics in parentheses.
Source: SSIB data files

were largely institutionalized at an early date (usually in efforts to weaken labor), they would also have become ingrained structural elements in society, with powerful interests concerned with their preservation. It is therefore not surprising that the WCS effect, although negative as anticipated, is small, and insignificant. We can interpret this to mean that left parties have been unable to alter in any fundamental way the corporatism and etatism they inherit when (and if) they come to power. This, at least, is consistent with previous analyses (Esping-Andersen and Korpi, 1984).

Conservative stratification attributes are, however, powerfully related to both Catholic-party strength and absolutism. This is exactly what our overall theory would have predicted. Nonetheless, there is no reason to believe that the two are interchangeable political forces. Strong Catholic parties, it is true, tend to be concentrated in nations with a protracted and strong authoritarian and /or absolutist heritage; but not wholly so. Absolutism was extraordinarily weak in Ireland and the Netherlands.

A closer inspection of the relative influence of the two variables is warranted because their social-policy principles diverged to a degree. While 'absolutist-authoritarian' social policy accentuated the centrality of the state, Catholicism's subsidiarity principle has always insisted that private organizations (mainly the Church) be prominent in social services. In an effort to isolate the relative importance of the two, we present two models, one in which Catholic-party strength and absolutism are entered simultaneously, and one in which we test for an interaction-effect between the two.

$$\text{Conservative regime} = -0.069\,C + 0.071\,(\text{Catholic party})$$
$$(t = -0.07) \qquad (t = 2.26)$$

$$+\,0.670\,(\text{absolutism})$$
$$(t = 3.19)$$

This additive model explains 57 percent of the variance (F = 12.47), and is thus superior to either of the bi-variate models in table 5.11. Both Catholicism and absolutism remain significant, and both contribute independently of one another. The addition of an interaction term (absolutism × Catholic-party strength) weakens the significance of the variables, adds nothing to the model's explanatory power, and shows, at any rate, that there is no case to be made for an interactive influence of the two. The considerable decline in significance can partly be ascribed to model 'overloading'. By testing a regression model with three independent variables on a sample of only 18, the error-term becomes very large.

$$\text{Conservative regime} = 0.426\,C + 0.035\,(\text{Catholic party})$$
$$((t = 0.40) \qquad (t = 0.77)$$

$$+ 0.475(\text{Absolutism})$$
$$(t = 1.74)$$

$$+ 0.005\,(\text{Catholic party} \times \text{absolutism})$$
$$(t = 1.11)$$

In summary, we conclude that our single best estimation of conservative 'regimeness' is the combined additive influence of Catholicism and absolutism.

THE LIBERAL REGIME

In terms of stratification, we identified liberalism with the prominence of means-tested targeting and with private-market reliance. As noted, we cannot develop a direct measure of the laissez-faire liberal political forces; and the use, as in earlier analyses, of the poor-relief variable as a surrogate is obviously ruled out, since it enters as part of the definition of the dependent variable.

As a consequence, our test of the liberal welfare-state regime can do little more than test for the straight 'social democratization' hypothesis; that is, the degree to which left-power mobilization results in a lessening of liberal welfare-state attributes.

Table 5.12 indicates that only two variables play an important role in explaining degree of liberal stratification: WCS and GDP/capita (1980). While WCS has a predictably strong and negative effect on liberalism, the positive effect of GDP/capita is probably to be regarded as spurious: as already noted, the liberal regime is more likely to be found among the richest nations (the United States, Canada, and Australia, for example). The negative effect of left mobilization (WCS) is much more powerful

TABLE 5.12   Cross-sectional (OLS) analysis of the liberal welfare-state regime stratification, 1980

Independent variable	r	B	R sq.[a]	F
GDP/capita	0.524	1.326 (2.46)[b]	0.230	6.07
WCS	−0.738	−0.200 (−4.38)	0.517	19.16
Catholic party	0.100	N.S.	—	—
Absolutism	0.000	N.S.	—	—

[a] R sq. adjusted.
[b] t-statistics in parentheses.
Source: SSIB data files

than was the case in our analysis of conservative stratification. Against liberalism, WCS explains a full 52 percent of the variance, indicating that left-power mobilization is potentially much more effective in eradicating liberal than conservative stratification elements. This, again, was to be expected. The 'absolutist' nations generally introduced social policy much earlier than the liberal ones. As a result, it is likely that conservative principles became more powerfully institutionalized and immunized against change. The 'liberalist' nations, in contrast, were later and more feeble social reforms, and often left a great void of social legislation when labor parties emerged as powerful forces. In such cases, therefore, the left would have had substantially more scope for aligning welfare-state evolution to their particular principles.

In the model presented below, the negative influence of WCS also remains decisive when we control for GDP. The model explains a full 78 percent of the variance ($F = 31.41$), and is thus superior to either of the bi-variate tests in table 5.12.

$$\text{Liberal regime} = -2.304\,C - 0.198\,(\text{WCS}) + 1.295\,(\text{GDP/capita})$$
$$(t = 0.90) \quad (t = -6.44) \quad (t = 4.52)$$

Accordingly, we can offer two conclusions: that the single most forceful explanation of liberal 'regimeness' is the negative impact of WCS, and that a combination of WCS and GDP/capita is the best model, but difficult to interpret in light of the theoretical ambiguity of GDP/capita.

THE SOCIALIST REGIME

To the socialist regime, universalism and equality are leading principles of welfare-state solidarity. Our hypothesis is clearly that the degree of 'socialism' depends on the strength of left-party mobilization (WCS),

TABLE 5.13   Cross-sectional (OLS) analysis of the socialist welfare-state regime stratification, 1980

Independent variable	r	B	R sq.[a]	F
GDP/capita	0.036	N.S.	—	—
WCS	0.698	0.115	0.455	15.22
		(3.90)[b]		
Catholic party	−0.384	N.S.	—	—
Absolutism	−0.359	N.S.	—	--

[a] R sq. adjusted.
[b] t-statistics in parentheses.
Source: SSIB data files

and that absolutism and Catholicism are its natural 'enemies'.

This is also what table 5.13 suggests. WCS is the single most important variable, and explains more than 45 percent of the variance. Absolutism and Catholic-party power are insignificant, but show the expected negative signs. The simple conclusion, therefore, is that left-party power is a precondition for the development of the socialist regime.

Conclusion

Proceeding through several stages of analysis, we have tried to identify the impact of political variables on welfare-state characteristics. The results give substantial comfort to our underlying theoretical argument. They may, so far, be summarized as follows.

First, when we examine non-structural features of social policy, the influence of politics and power remains marginal, while economic and, especially, demographic variables play a leading role. This is consistent with the argument that social (and/or private) provision will emerge in tandem with economic development and population ageing. This also suggests that social spending *per se* was hardly ever at the center of major political conflict.

Second, it is when we begin to identify the structural differences in welfare states that political power relations gain explanatory momentum. This we found to be the case with regard to pension systems and also to more general welfare-state features, such as degree of de-commodification, commitment to full employment, and residualism. It is on such issues that the interplay of working-class power mobilization, Catholicism, and state tradition comes into play. The analyses leave little doubt that left-party power is decisive for de-commodification, full-employment efforts, and general social democratization. It is also clear that Catholic parties and a historical legacy of authoritarian statehood influence corporatist and etatist biases.

Third, we have been able to identify a fairly clear correspondence between welfare-state regimes and political forces. Conservative stratification principles are decisively explained by the presence of Catholic-party strength and the history of absolutism; socialist stratification depends, in turn, on strong social democracy. And, finally, strong labor movements appear to be a good guarantee against liberalist welfare-state stratification.

Data scarcity and methodological constraints have, nonetheless, limited the degree to which our analyses could follow the prescriptions of our theory. Our ability to consider the impact of power in relational terms has been confined to analyses of the joint impact of left and Catholic power, and of 'absolutism' as a reflection of nations' history of state-building.

What such linear models cannot accomplish is what, in the end, must be answered; namely, is political power a decisive or only a spurious historical variable? When we identify the singular influence of working-class mobilization (WCS) on, say, de-commodification or universalism, to what extent are socialist parties mediating forces? Are there alternative historical influences which pre-determine a particular welfare-state outcome? Answers to these kinds of questions must await new break-throughs in the statistical analysis of welfare-state development.

PART 2

The Welfare State in the Employment Structure

In the first part of this book, our concern was with the specification of crucial welfare-state differences and the testing of leading hypotheses about their crystallization into three distinct regime-types. In a sense, we addressed long-standing issues in the social sciences. The present challenge for comparative research is to study welfare states in their role as independent, causal variables: how do different types of welfare states systematically influence social and economic behavior in advanced capitalism? It is to such questions that we turn in Part 2.

Those who are familiar with the sociological literature on the family, social stratification, or social organization, or those who have studied the literature on labor markets, will easily recognize the analytical absence of the welfare state. Yet, be it in contemporary Scandinavia, western Europe, or even North America, the welfare state is becoming deeply embedded in the everyday experience of virtually every citizen. Our personal life is structured by the welfare state, and so is the entire political economy. Given the magnitude and centrality of the welfare state, it is indeed unlikely that we shall understand much of contemporary society unless it becomes part of our models.

Of the many social institutions that are likely to be directly shaped and ordered by the welfare state, working life, employment, and the labor market are perhaps the most important. On one side, the core idea of social policy was always to safeguard persons against the exigencies and risks that confront them in their life-cycle, especially when their working capacities fail. The philosophy of the traditional, minimalist welfare state was to establish a safety net, a haven of last resort, for those demonstrably unfit or unable to work.

On the other side, the modern, advanced welfare state has deliberately abandoned the minimalist philosophy, and espouses entirely new principles with regard to its proper role in the life-cycle, now often committing itself to optimize people's capacities to work, to find work, and even to count on a good job with good pay and working environment. The goal is to allow individuals to harmonize working life with familyhood, to square the dilemmas of having children and working, and to combine productive activity with meaningful and rewarding leisure. In some countries, at least, this philosophy has buttressed recent decades of social-policy development; indeed, it often underpins the legitimacy and common understanding of many contemporary welfare states.

This is not to say that these principles enjoy undisputed consensus. Some conservative parties, many employers, and most economists invoke the classical fear that welfare rights distort the work incentive, and that active government involvement in the shaping of employment outcomes will only disequilibrate the economy.

Our concern in Part 2 of this book is not with the work-incentive effects of welfare programs. The aim, instead, is to explore how such a central institution as the welfare state has come to influence events outside its traditional domain.

In the following three chapters, we apply our findings on welfare-state regimes to the study of major ongoing transformations in the sphere of employment. Few will question the fact that contemporary capitalist economies are undergoing a series of fundamental structural changes, of which many, if not most, turn upside down our conventional notions of working life: women's natural place is no longer at home, but in the labor market; the welfare state pays thousands or even millions of able-bodied people not to work; most people no longer find themselves in a factory, but rather in an office or in a fast-food outlet. Today, a typical worker may face the prospect of spending the largest slice of the life-cycle outside work, in education and leisure. The great promise of full employment that permeated the optimistic post-war era has become a big black cloud over the majority of advanced nations. But full employment, as a political guarantee, has also been revolutionized. To Lord Beveridge and his fellow post-war reformers, the concept was assumed to apply only to the masculine half of the nation. Contemporary politicians must commit themselves to a full employment that recognizes no gender boundaries.

We will investigate the ways in which different types of welfare states influence employment change by focusing on three select issues. First, in chapter 6 our aim is to explore systematic connections between welfare-state regime-types and general characteristics of labor-market behavior. Our principal hypothesis is that the peculiarities of welfare states are reflected in the ways in which labor markets are organized. We will suggest that each of our three welfare-state regimes goes hand in hand with a peculiar 'labor-market regime'.

Second, in chapter 7 we shall examine how nations' capacity to maintain full employment over the post-war period has been decisively influenced by the welfare state. And, finally, in chapter 8 we turn to the much broader and more ambitious task of tracing welfare states' influence on contemporary employment shifts and social stratification in the emerging 'post-industrial' society.

In the second part of the book, we will change gears, methodologically speaking. Instead of our previous 18-nation comparisons, our strategy is now based on a comparison of three nations, sampled from each of the regimes identified in Part I: the United States serves as a representative of the liberal regime, Sweden of the social democratic regime, and Germany as a convenient (if not perfect) illustration of the conservative regime.

6

Welfare-State and Labor-Market Regimes

The objective of this chapter is to undertake a first conceptualization of welfare-state/labor-market interactions. Our task is organized around three principal cornerstones of the labor market: 1) the conditions under which people exit from the labor market and enter into the status of welfare-state client (here, the focus is especially on retirement); 2) the conditions under which people claim paid absence from a job; and 3) the conditions under which people are allocated to jobs, that is, enter into employment.

If it can be argued that the labor market is systematically and directly shaped by the (welfare) state, it follows that we would expect cross-national differences in labor-market behavior to be attributable to the nature of welfare-state regimes. This view contradicts prevailing models of labor markets found in standard neo-classical economics, where typically the labor market is treated as a closed and autonomous system: its actors are discrete and independent, responding primarily to price signals. The standard assumption is that labor markets will clear and move towards equilibrium by themselves.

When mainstream economists do consider the influence of the modern welfare state, it is generally under two headings: 1) its overall 'Keynesian' stimulus on demand and 2) its potential for distorting the automatic clearing-mechanism by affecting wages, labor supply, or labor costs. The neo-classical model has very little room for the welfare state.

This problem is perhaps less present in many of the contemporary 'institutionalist' economic models. But, it is nevertheless rare that the state is examined as an endogenous variable. Be it in dual or segmented labor-market theory, insider–outsider models, or efficiency-wage contract theories, the principal focus has been on industrial organization and industrial-relations arrangements. A theory of what role the welfare state plays for mobility behavior, job tenure, and more generally, for labor-market rigidities and stratification, has yet to emerge.

In recent years, a few institutional economists have begun to pay closer attention to the importance of the 'social wage' for worker behavior and the cost of firing (Shore and Bowles, 1984; Bowles and Gintis, 1986). This may be regarded as a first stepping-stone towards more systematic analyses.

Economics has obviously not ignored the relationship between labor-market behavior and social policy entirely. There is, for example, an enormous literature on the negative-incentive effects of social benefits on labor supply and mobility at the micro-level, and also a few attempts to argue their effects at the macro-level (Danziger et al., 1981; Lindbeck, 1981). There is also an emergent literature in which employment behavior, especially women's, is related to government programs such as tax laws, social service provision, and the like (Blundell and Walker, 1988; Gustavsson, 1988). But, generally, the welfare state in this research is taken for granted, or seen as a disturbance in the autonomous clearing-process. Most studies are limited to one country and, typically, also to one area of policy. Their intent is to estimate to what extent social benefits affect a given worker's labor supply.

For similar reasons, our approach also deviates from prevailing sociological models of the labor market. Sociology boasts a long tradition of studying the institutional mechanisms of occupational and job attainment. On one side, its emphasis has been on socially inherited labor-market chances and/or on the mediating effects of upbringing and education. The critique of the economists' view is that social forces preclude the possibility that actors in the labor market a) act independently, and b) start equally in the competition for jobs and rewards. Instead, this literature identifies sociological dividers in the labor market, such as the tendency for fathers' class positions to affect sons' chances of mobility (representative examples of this approach are Blau and Duncan, 1967; Featherman and Hauser, 1978; Jencks et al., 1982; Colbjornsen, 1986).

On the other side, sociology has focused on structural dividers in the labor market; in particular, on organizational features within and between industries and firms (Berg, 1981; Baron, 1984; Baron and Bielby, 1980). This approach is very much a sociological parallel to dual and segmented labor-market theory in economics. In the sociology of professions it has also been found that social institutions influence labor-market outcomes. It is, for example, typical that entry into, as well as conduct within, professional positions is decided by corporate monopolistic practices. But, except for the role of education in mobility studies, in sociology job attainment has rarely, if ever, been related to the welfare state.

In recent years, the social sciences have begun to pay closer attention to the role of government in labor-market performance. This has perhaps been clearest in recent years' research on the determinants of cross-national differences in full-employment performance. For example, Manfred Schmidt (1982; 1983) and Therborn (1986b) show how nations' capacity to maintain full employment varies with the role of active labor-market policies, Keynesian demand-management, trade-union structure, and with their capacity for neo-corporatist interest mediation. Recent studies on the comparative growth in service-sector employment have demonstrated the centrality of welfare states in accounting for international differences in service-sector employment (Rein, 1985); Sharpf (1985) suggests that taxation levels play a role in explaining welfare states' capacities to expand social service employment. Cusack, Notermans, and Rein (1987) have related this to welfare states' budgetary structures.

From a Marxist perspective, there have also emerged a few attempts to reconceptualize class theory. Van Parijs (1987), for example, suggests that the growing army of jobless welfare-state clients be analyzed as a social class in its own right.

The labor market as autonomous from politics is a myth, sustained by ideology and defended by antiquated theory. But as a myth it was given material life in historical practice. Hence, the traditional norm was that social policy should not pervert the mechanisms of the labor market. The architects of early welfare policies were adamant about the principle that social protection was to be limited to those unable to function in the labor market: the old, infirm, sick, and unemployed. The principle of prohibiting welfare policy from shaping labor-market decisions was obvious in nineteenth-century poor relief, with its ideology of 'less eligibility'; in the early social-insurance laws, with their strict actuarialism and long employment or contribution requirements; and also in early social-assistance schemes, where means-tests and low benefits assured that the marginal utility of working remained substantially higher than that of depending on welfare.

When we examine post-war social policy, we discover no immediate break with the philosophy of non-intervention. The Beveridge-model for Britain, or the People's Home model for Scandinavia, were not meant to encourage exit from the market; on the contrary, they were designed to promote maximum labor-market dependence. And, mirroring the intellectual influence of the social-administration tradition, the underlying principle of social reforms was that the welfare state and the labor market were to remain separated. Thus, when governments committed themselves to a 'Keynes plus Beveridge' formula after World War II, they systematically kept the bureaucracies and administration of social protection and labor market sharply separate.

The case for the sharp, albeit fictitious, separation of the labor market from state and societal institutions was premised on classical liberal theory, especially on its assumptions about the equality–efficiency trade-off. Be they the hard-core laissez-faire advocates, or the more tempered and reasoned liberal political economists such as Mill or, later Alfred Marshall, such theorists universally agreed that governments' attempts to augment equality would impair economic performance.

Still, many of our theoretical forebears recognized that institutions were a necessary (and often desirable) way to achieve positive-sum outcomes in this trade-off. Thus, as we have seen, conservative political economy was adamantly against the idea of workers as commodities. Its answer to the call for efficient allocation and productivity was 'Soldaten der Arbeit': loyalty, integration, and hierarchy. Nazi Germany was unwilling to put its faith in a free labor market and preferred instead to assign or conscript people to jobs, and to control their mobility with a mandatory work-book. The reformist socialist tradition held that efficiency and optimal productivity presumed not just educated, healthy, and well-fed workers, but that modernization and rapid technological change were easier to promote when workers were in command of adequate income guarantees.

Thus, in much of our theoretical and political heritage, social policy was regarded as integral to labor-market behavior. It is therefore astonishing that contemporary scholarship ignores it. Over the past decades, three creeping 'revolutions' have fundamentally altered the nexus of work and welfare in such a way that the welfare state has become directly inserted in labor markets.

The Three Creeping Revolutions

The welfare-state edifice that was constructed in the post-war era based itself upon certain, increasingly outdated, assumptions regarding economic growth and full employment. In the era of high industrialism, economic growth could once be counted on to furnish a large number of new jobs. Today, however, we witness the phenomenon of jobless economic growth. This not only implies greater difficulties of managing full employment with given levels of investment, but also poses serious problems for welfare-state finances.

In this context, a silent but significant revolution has occurred in our conception of full employment. When Beveridge (and his contemporaries in other countries) launched a full-employment commitment, their reference was only to able-bodied men. One of post-war capitalism's most remarkable events is the broadening of the base for full employment to encompass also all women and, indeed, anyone who wishes to work. This implies a huge increase in the population for which a full-employment guarantee obtains, and a substantially greater task of political management.

It is in the context of this new dilemma that traditional welfare-state programs increasingly have come to serve new purposes. Education and retirement programs, for example, help reduce the economically active part of the working population. Welfare-state social services can become a vehicle for the absorption of new, especially female, labor-force entrants.

As we discussed, the modern welfare state was designed in such a way that a clear line of demarcation between the labor market and the welfare state should be maintained. Thus, the welfare state should only cater to those absolutely incapable of work; it was not supposed to induce anybody to leave work for welfare. Here, again, has occurred a silent revolution. For one thing, retirement programs have not just been upgraded, but have also been vastly extended. Thus in Western Europe early retirement has in recent years induced perhaps millions of able-bodied persons to leave the labor market and enter the welfare state.

In many cases, early retirement became a response to rising unemployment. But when the welfare state aids a mass exit from working life into retirement, its finances are obviously additionally strained. Early retirement also came to serve as an instrument of firm rationalization and restructuration. In this sense, what we observe is that the social collectivity helps both to organize and to finance improved firm competitiveness. The result is a growing tension between the micro-rationality of the firm and the collective good. The welfare state aids micro-level efficiency but creates at the same time, macro-economic dis-utilities: under-utilization of manpower capacity, and public-budget deficits. If, on the other hand, the welfare state had adhered to the classical dogma of non-interference with the labor-market mechanism, it is possible that countries would have been hard pressed to maintain industrial competitiveness.

We can identify a third important silent revolution. Modern welfare states are no longer systems of social provision only. They have, in many nations, become virtual employment-machines, often being the only significant source of job growth. Today, the Danish and Swedish welfare states employ about 30 percent of the labor force. Again, this is a remarkable departure from the theory of the labor market as a self-regulating organism. Thus, the welfare state absorbs labor supply not only to uphold promises of full employment, but also because the welfare state's own economic logic demands that as many work as possible. For the welfare state it may be more cost effective to employ excess labor than to subsidize it not to work.

Taken together, the emerging new patterns of welfare-state labor-market relations are characterized by considerable strains. Be they for employment or more general economic objectives, the welfare state's traditional responsibilities have been extended and changed. As a result, social policy and the labor market have become interwoven and mutually interdependent institutions. To an extent, the welfare state has become a major agent of labor-market clearing. It eases the exit of women, with family programs; of older people, with early retirement. It upholds labor demand by employing people in health, education, and welfare. It facilitates female labor-supply by providing necessary social services. It helps people reconcile their role as economic producers, social citizens, and family members by granting workers paid vacations and temporary absence from work.

In the following, we will examine more closely the three instances ('windows') where working life and social policy are most evidently interwoven. We select these in terms of the work-contract. First, we focus on the conditions for labor supply: what determines whether people remain in, or exit from, the labor force? Our empirical case here is mainly the retirement behavior of older workers.

The second window examines the conditions that shape behavior within the labor contract. In principle, the work contract stipulates the exchange of labor time for pay. This time is in principle 'owned' by the employer, and the worker has little authority over the allocation of his time. The relevant question is to what extent and under what conditions can workers exercise their own choices under the contract? To what degree is their status, then, de-commodified? The appropriate empirical case here is paid absence from work.

The third relevant window concerns the demand for labor, the conditions under which labor enters into employment. With few exceptions, prevailing theory assumes that labor demand is a function of marginal productivity and price. Much of Keynesian macro-economic theory assumes, of course, that the welfare state's aggregate demand-effect influences labor demand. Economists also recognize wage-subsidy effects. But the welfare state's role as a major employer has been vastly under-researched.

Exit and Labor Supply

There is nothing especially new in the recognition that social policy shapes labor supply. Graebner (1980) argues that the principle of retirement emerged as a means to manage unemployment problems, and as a mechanism to permit employers to shed their less productive workforce.

Economists have studied retirement as a function of leisure–work trade-offs (Aaron and Burtless, 1984; Danziger *et al.*, 1981; Boskin and Hurd, 1978). These kinds of studies are typically couched at the micro-level, and are therefore unable to see how micro-level choices and macro-level outcomes interrelate. What may be an inefficiency in economic theory (people choosing leisure over work with the incentive of pension benefits) may translate into efficiencies for the firm (higher productivity and profits, financed by taxpayers). At the macro-level, early retirement may concomitantly lower labor supply, raise aggregate productivity, and siphon resources towards activities that yield zero productive output (retirement).

Existing scholarship has paid very little attention to the ways in which welfare-state variations may influence the structure of labor supply differently. It is hard to believe that international differences in the exit of older males are due solely to relative pension-benefit levels or ease of access. The demand for early retirement will depend on available alternatives (part-time work, sheltered employment, retraining, unemployment insurance), on the nature of industrial-relations systems (job security), and on the status of the economy; these alternatives also owe much of their existence to welfare-state activities.

Cross-national variations in the scope of early retirement are astonishingly large, and they have increased over the past decades. The proper focus is on male workers in the age group 55–64. The retirement convention in most nations has normally been around age 65, and women's traditional role as housewives makes comparisons of women's retirement difficult. Table 6.1 suggests a systematic relationship be-

TABLE 6.1   Trends in labor-market exit among older males: labor-force participation rates of males, 55–64 (percentages)

	1960/62	1970	1984/85	Change
Norway	92	87	80	−12
Sweden	90	85	76	−14
France	80	75	50	−30
Germany	83	82	58	−25
Netherlands	85	81	54	−31
Canada	86[a]	84	71	−15
United Kingdom	94	91	69	−25
United States	83	81	69	−14

[a] For Canada, we use 1965 instead of 1960 data.
Source: ILO, *Yearbook of Labor Statistics*, current volumes; and *National Statistical Yearbooks*

tween our previously developed regime-types and labor-force exit: the Nordic cluster is characterized by low exit; the continental European by very high exit; the Anglo-Saxon world, except for Britain, by moderate exit. Is this just a function of the quality of pension programs and the availability of early retirement? To an extent it would seem so. Germany, Holland, and France have, since 1970, been frontrunners in the development of flexible and early-retirement programs, while access to early retirement has remained far less attractive in the United States, Great Britain, and Canada. We should note also that Norway still offers only a disability-based early-retirement program.

The pension-program-based explanation is consistent with the findings of other studies that view retirement as induced by attractive welfare benefits (Boskin and Hurd, 1978; Feldstein, 1974; Parsons, 1980; Hurd and Boskin, 1981). Other studies, however, conclude the opposite. This is especially the case with comparative research. Both Havement *et al.* (1984), Diamond and Hausman (1984), and Pampel and Weiss (1983) conclude that cross-national pension-benefit variations cannot explain differences in retirement behavior. Pampel and Weiss argued that retirement is mainly a function of economic modernization, a somewhat vaguely defined and measured phenomenon; Diamond and Hausman, in turn, emphasized the importance of unemployment among older workers. In the case of the United States, they found that 33 percent of laid-off older workers opted for early retirement because they had no employment alternative.

To pinpoint the regime characteristics salient to patterns of retirement, we need to dig a little deeper. Two factors seem especially relevant: the risk of long-term unemployment among old workers, and the probability of receiving a retirement income.

The probability of long-term unemployment among older workers (i.e. long-term unemployment as a percentage of total unemployment within the group of older workers) has been very high in countries such as Germany, France, the Netherlands, and Britain (35–50 percent), and quite low in Scandinavia, and in Canada and the United States (10–12 percent). This, of course, confirms the 'unemployment-management' hypothesis. On the benefit side, Canadian and American pensions are meager; however, Swedish and Norwegian pension legislation compares very favorably with the continental nations, with respect both to largesse and ease of eligibility. Hence, we seem to confront an interaction-effect. Where labor-market chances for the elderly are poor, early retirement may be massive, but only if benefits are attractive: this is the continental scenario. Benefits may be good, but will not induce retirement when labor-market conditions are good: this is the Scandinavian situation. And, finally, benefits may be rather mediocre and still induce retirement because of very poor labor-market conditions, as in Britain.

If differences in labor-market exit depend on the configuration of unemployment risks and retirement benefits, we must consider the welfare state's role in a broader context. First of all, part of the trend in older-worker exit can be explained solely by the fact that when early-retirement provisions were passed (usually in the early 1970s), there existed a latent pool of partially disabled workers waiting for an opportunity to retire. This can explain the common trend, but hardly cross-national differences.

Job rights are a second feature which affects the unemployment–retirement nexus. Where job rights are strong, older workers are difficult to lay off. But differences in job rights can hardly explain variations in retirement since they are more or less equally strong in Scandinavia and on the continent, and rather weak in the United States. Probably more salient are the welfare-state alternatives offered under conditions of threatening unemployment among older workers. It is here that the Scandinavian–continental European contrast best finds an explanation. Whereas in Sweden older workers are offered an array of labor-market alternatives within the active labor-market policy system, in the continental European countries this is not so. In Sweden an older (redundant) worker can choose partial retirement, combined with part-time work, paid re-training, and sheltered employment. In Germany, this is not an option.

But the retirement nexus is also embedded in the nations' strategies with respect to rising unemployment and massive industrial restructuration in the 1970s–80s. Early-retirement provisions were rarely introduced specifically to cope with the economic crisis. It was usually later that they came to serve as instruments of crisis-management. In countries where trade unions are powerful and seniority rules are strict, early-retirement provisions came as a godsend to employers searching for strategies to slim their workforce and rid themselves of their older, and frequently less productive, employees. Here, the quality of early-retirement provisions was a precondition for industrial rationalization.

But, early retirement (and other means of reducing labor supply, such as repatriating foreign workers and encouraging women to remain at home) also came to serve broader aims of maintaining full employment, especially in countries such as Germany, Holland, France, and Belgium, where fiscal and monetary policies were restrictive, and active manpower policies marginal. In these countries, also, the welfare state is biased strongly against the expansion of government social services, and, hence, against welfare-state employment as an alternative strategy for employment promotion. In contrast, in countries like Sweden and Norway, a policy of diminishing labor supply was regarded as inappropriate. In reality, it was not needed, given the commitment to full employment, the active policies against the business cycle, and the massive expansion of social service employment in the 1970s.

Paid Work Absence

Like pensions, sickness and related benefits were originally meant to help only the truly incapacitated. The idea of paid absence from work has undergone a decisive transformation in terms of both quality and scope. In most European countries, sickness benefits today equal normal earnings. In some countries, notably Scandinavia, legislation has deliberately sought to emancipate the individual from work-compulsion by extending high benefits for a broad variety of contingencies, including sickness, maternity, parenthood (for mother and father), education, trade-union and related involvement, and vacation. Controls and restrictions have been eliminated or liberalized; waiting days have been abolished, a medical certificate of illness is required only after one week, no previous work-experience is required to qualify, and benefits can be upheld for very long periods.

It is clear that liberal access to paid absence from work can fundamentally alter employers' exercise of control. And, not surprisingly, related transfer benefits have been a favorite topic for the 'negative work-incentive' literature. In many cases, absenteeism mirrors nothing more than objective incapacitation, and the issue of negative incentives is trivial. But if the programs offered to workers are such that they can exercise a modicum of discretionary choice as to whether to work or to pursue alternative activities that they, personally, give priority to, social policy will have transformed the entire logic of the employment contract.

Most studies addressing the work-disincentive issue predict that overall rates of absenteeism rise as a function of the relaxation of rules and the extension of eligibility (Salowski, 1980; 1983). But any adequate understanding of absenteeism must take into consideration a host of alternative explanations. Where medical certification is required, medical discretion becomes crucial; when workers fear unemployment, or when the employer is tough, people may refrain from exercising their right to paid absence; poor working conditions may promote frequent illness, but they may also incite workers to utilize absenteeism as a 'coping strategy'. Paradoxically, employers may 'encourage' their workers into absenteeism as a labor-hoarding strategy under conditions of slack product-demand, especially if benefits are paid out of taxpayers' money. Finally, absenteeism may reflect peoples' efforts to equilibrate their roles as workers and as family or community members.

It is clear that the phenomenon of absenteeism is extraordinarily complex. This is why almost all empirical studies, especially those of the 'negative-incentive' variety, provoke controversy and remain largely inconclusive.

It is often thought that sickness absenteeism has increased steadily. This is, however, not the case. Aggregate data show that sickness absence rose sharply from the 1960s to the 1970s. This may support a program-based explanation, since it was typically in this period that sickness schemes were liberalized and improved. The lack of change in the United States could be interpreted along these lines, too, since this is the only case where no legislation occurred. Yet in Germany, absenteeism failed to grow, despite program updating in the late 1960s.

Cross-national variations in absenteeism are staggering. A recent OECD study suggests that nations cluster into three groups. In one (Sweden and Britain), we find very high sickness-absenteeism rates, with an average of 20 sickness days per year per worker. In a second group (the United States and Canada), the rates are extremely low, with an average of 5 days lost per worker. Countries like Germany, France, and the Netherlands fall in between, with about 10–13 days lost (OECD, 1985). The study also shows that absenteeism has not risen monotonically over the years. Indeed, it has declined in five out of six countries since the mid-1970s.

Most studies focus solely on sickness absenteeism, but this is far too narrow if we want to understand the welfare state's influence on labor-market behavior. If we broaden our horizon and include all types of paid absenteeism, the rates may actually double. In table 6.2 we provide data on both sickness and total absenteeism (but excluding holidays and vacations) expressed in number of hours absent as a percentage of total hours worked.

Table 6.2 reveals that paid absenteeism in Scandinavia has come to serve functions largely outside the conventional realm of illness; that the welfare state, in a way, has taken upon itself to permit employees to pursue non-work-related activities within the work contract. Next to paid holidays, by far the greatest non-sickness progam is maternity and parental leave – a program which in effect permits women to reconcile working life with fertility. Thus, the aggregate data presented here mask the fact that in Sweden, on any given day, more than 20 percent of employed women are absent with pay. In Sweden, maximum female labor-force participation is a principle of social policy. It has found practical expression in the world's highest participation rates, more than 80 percent. But the associated cost is obviously high rates of absenteeism.

In Sweden, the participation rate of mothers with infant children (0–2 years) was almost as high as the average for all women. It jumped from 43 percent in 1970 to 82.4 percent in 1985. But in this same group of women, close to half (47.5 percent) were absent from work on any given day. This is twice the average rate for women, and four times the national average.

In a separate study (Esping-Andersen and Kolberg, 1989), we have

TABLE 6.2   Paid absence from work: annual hours absent as % of total hours worked, 1980

	Sickness absence	Total absence	Sickness as % of total
Denmark	3.9	8.8	44
Norway	3.2	7.0	46
Sweden	4.3	11.2	38
France	5.1	6.6	77
Germany[a]	6.1	7.7	79
United States	1.3	—	—

[a] The German data are based on number of persons absent as % of total persons employed.

Source: WEEP data files, based on data from National Labor Force sample surveys

studied both the time-series and industry cross-sectional absenteeism behavior of men and women in Scandinavia. Our findings confirm the scenario presented here. Not only are women two to three times as likely as men to be absent from work, but the tendency is strongest in the public sector where, on any given day, more than 30 percent of female employees are absent. This suggests that we cannot approach the problem of absenteeism and work in the conventional manner. In the Nordic countries, the nexus of work and 'leisure' is decided by an intricate web of welfare-state activities, ranging from provisions to maximize female employment (public-sector employment and wide-spread services to facilitate labor supply) to provisions to facilitate absenteeism.

This Scandinavian model can be contrasted with the German. The latter's much lower absenteeism rates must be related to the much lower female-participation levels, and the much higher rates of early retirement among older workers. But nations like Germany or the Netherlands are less puzzling than the United States, where female labor-force growth has been almost as explosive as in Scandinavia. With no benefit legislation, highly uneven coverage through collective bargaining, and often very modest benefits for sickness or maternity and parental leave, American women have very high participation rates in all ages.

When, as in Sweden, on any given day approximately 15 percent of workers are absent yet paid to work, it is difficult to sustain the logic of a labor market guided solely by the pure exchange principle. A very large share of what normally is regarded as labor time is in fact 'welfare time'. The range of alternative choice is such that Swedes are relatively de-commodified: they do not just hand over their time to the employer; the employers' control of the purchased labor-commodity is heavily circumscribed.

The social-policy features that determine such de-commodification possibilities are many. The presence of social legislation is a first precondition, and the very low American absenteeism rates may simply reflect the non-existence of a legislated program. Clearly, waiting days (ranging from zero in Norway and Sweden, to 14 days in Canada), and compulsory medical certification matter. In Sweden, a medical certificate of illness is not required until the seventh day; in Norway, the fourth. In other countries, it is mandatory on the first day. Compensation levels are obviously decisive: the degree of discretionary choice depends on whether a worker can maintain his or her living standards. Furthermore, it ought to make a decisive difference whether benefits are paid by the employer or whether the costs are socialized. In Germany and the United States, benefits are paid by the employer; in

Sweden, by the state. This will certainly influence how absenteeism comes to figure in the matrix of micro- and macro-level utilities. For the Swedish firm, absenteeism is less costly and may, in fact, provide benefits. It can serve as a relatively cost-less labor-hoarding device in slack times. For Sweden as a collective actor, however, it is macro-economically a high, yet necessary, cost to pay for maximizing full employment. In countries like Germany or the United States, the utility-mix will be different. For the employer, the system gives an incentive to minimize absenteeism. This also means that German firms should be less keen on hiring women workers, and it gives them an added incentive to shed their older workers. For Germany, then, there is a macro-economic savings on absenteeism that, however, is made at the expense of low manpower-utilization and heavy pension burdens.

The Welfare State as Employer

State employment is, in itself, nothing new. But its expansion begs a re-examination of its significance. The public sector may pay wages and offer labor contracts like any other employer, but it is not a genuine market, and conventional market principles operate only marginally. Tenured appointments and the lack of a profit motive (surplus value, if you wish), salaried status, and the sheer inoperability of the convention-al productivity-logic mean that orthodox economic models of the labor market hardly apply.

Aside from their time-honored role as direct employers, governments have traditionally influenced employment-entry through a host of instruments. These range from temporary works-programs, wage sub-sidies, and aggregate-demand management, to industrial subsidies and full-scale active manpower policies. The most direct approach to the study of the welfare state's influence on labor demand and employment allocation is, nonetheless, its role as employer. It is also in this role that it most fundamentally alters the ways in which we must understand labor markets.

What, then, is the welfare state's role in shaping the process of employment-entry and the structure of labor demand? What concerns us here is not the public sector as such. If we are interested in welfare-state/labor-market interactions, public industrial enterprises, transport, or communications are irrelevant; so are traditional areas of public administration, and law and order. Our concern is the extent to which collective social-welfare criteria dominate over the market in the allocation of employment.

TABLE 6.3   The welfare state's role in the employment structure: total and public-sector share of health, education, and welfare service employment, 1985 (percentages)

	HEW employment as share of total	Public share of HEW total employment	Public HEW as share of total employment
Denmark	28	90	25
Norway	22	92	20
Sweden	26	93	25
Austria	10	61	6
France	15	75	11
Germany	11	58	7
Italy	12	85	11
Canada	15	44	7
United Kingdom	16	77	12
United States	17	45	8

Source: WEEP data files

To obtain a first idea of cross-national variations, let us examine two indicators: the welfare state's share of total social-service employment (health, education, and welfare services), and welfare-state social-service employment as a share of total employment. The first measures the public–private mix; the second the overall national bias in favor of welfare-state employment: see table 6.3.

Once again, our nations cluster. The Nordic countries, with their extraordinarily large welfare-state employment, form one group, occupying 20–25 percent of all employment. A second group of countries is equally homogeneous. These are nations in which social-welfare employment as such is vastly underdeveloped and where the public sector's welfare-state role is only marginal in overall employment allocation: Austria, Germany, and Italy are the clearest cases. And there is a third cluster, in which welfare-service employment is fairly well developed, but quite dominated by the private sector. This includes Australia, Canada, and the United States.

In chapter 8, we shall examine the welfare state's role in employment change in much more detail, but even at present it seems evident that these three clusters correspond almost totally to the three welfare-state regime-types we have developed.

The Crystallization of Regime-Clusters

When we combine the evidence from our discussion of exit, absentee-ism, and entry, there is considerable support for the argument that welfare-state structures are systematically related to labor-market out-comes. First, some welfare states are strongly biased in favor of maximizing labor supply; their exit rates among older males are modest and their participation rates for women are very high. The prime cases here are Norway and Sweden. In contrast, there are welfare states that strongly nourish exit and reduced labor supply. Here we find Germany, the Netherlands, Italy, and France. Finally, there is a third group, with the United States and Canada as examples, where the welfare state does rather little to encourage either exit or female participation. Both phenomena do happen, but hardly because social policy provides the main incentives. Welfare-state policies may not explain the entire story, but differences in the provision of child-care and related services will affect women's supply of labor, and so will absenteeism programs and tax policy. In Scandinavia, there is no tax-disincentive for two-earner couples; in Germany the disincentive is quite strong (Gustavsson, 1988).

But the welfare state's commitment to social-service delivery also affects employment in another way. Where, as in Scandinavia, the welfare state has been actively and deliberately engaged in social-service expansion, it also provides a phenomenal multiplier-effect for female employment: social services both allow women to work, and create a large labor-market within which they can find employment. On these counts, too, Scandinavia's welfare states represent one extreme; the continental European countries, the other.

The Anglo-Saxon nations are cases where both total and female labor-force participation are high, but where the welfare state's direct effect is demonstrably marginal. When we combine the cross-national behavioral characteristics within each 'window', the result is a powerful degree of nation-clustering. This indicates to us that welfare-state regimes and employment regimes tend to coincide.

There are, consequently, reasons to uphold our initial hypothesis, and regard welfare states as fundamental forces in the organization and stratification of modern economies. To the extent that this will be borne out in the following empirical analyses, we are left with the formidable theoretical task of recasting prevailing theories of the labor market and social stratification. Such a task cannot be undertaken at this point, yet we can begin to identify some necessary parameters for such a project.

First, the lines of demarcation which once created and maintained a firm separation between the welfare state and the labor market no longer operate. The 'silent revolutions' of the welfare state have effectively undermined not only the ideology, but also the reality, of an autonomous market-mechanism. It is not just that social programs increasingly influence peoples' and firms' choices with respect to labor supply, labor demand, and work–leisure trade-offs within the labor contract. The really fundamental point is that social policy has been systematically transformed so as to deliberately reshape the clearing mechanisms in the labor market.

The transformation that has come about in the wake of the silent revolutions is far from trivial. If we briefly return to our 'windows', this becomes clear. Beginning with 'exit' from employment, according to both economic theory and historical practice, the price signal constituted the key mechanism that guided both firm and worker behavior. Today, firms are – at least in many countries – unable to rationalize and shed labor without recourse to the welfare state, whether through early retirement, unemployment, or active manpower policies. For the worker, the decision to quit, retire, or change jobs is similarly guided by the menu of social policy. The decisions of women (who now begin to approach half of the total labor force in some nations) to enter the labor force are even more intimately patterned by the welfare state, in terms of its service delivery (child care), transfer system (ability to utilize the option of absenteeism), tax system, and its labor demand (social-welfare jobs).

Turning to employment 'entry', the story is a mirror-image of exit. In some cases, more than a third of the 'labor market' is no market at all in the normal sense, but instead is a politically organized system of collective goods-production. Welfare-state employment, of course, is also organized around the labor contract, exchanging labor-time for wages. Yet its logic is qualitatively different. The concept of productivity hardly obtains; wages are to a degree determined politically; jobs are typically tenured; and employees normally enjoy substantially more autonomy, freedom, and authority over how they allocate their time, do their jobs, and make their work–welfare choices. Rather than being a (perhaps odd) partner within the whole economy's labor market, the welfare state may, indeed, constitute a separate and distinct job 'market', or even ghetto. Its growth may signal the formation of a new type of dual economy. And, if this be the case, we arrive at a strange paradox: the seminal disintegration of the traditional state–economy boundary, brought about by the modern welfare state, is replaced with novel lines of demarcation. It may be that these will replace the time-honored axis of industrial class conflict around which our societies are organized, our politics are mobilized, and our theories are forged. This, indeed, is what we will discover in chapter 8.

7

Institutional Accommodation to Full Employment

Institutional Problems of Full Employment

Pre-war reformist writers foresaw that full employment with welfare policies would establish a capitalism that was both more humane and more productive. Liberals, such as Beveridge, and social democrats, such as Wigforss and Myrdal, were in basic agreement on this point. They placed their faith in the promotion of Keynesian welfare-state policies.

It was to these issues that Michael Kalecki addressed his now-classic analysis of the 'political aspects of full employment' (Kalecki, 1943). In his view, the principal problem was how capitalism could be accommodated to the new balance of class power. Kalecki identified two distinct responses, one a regime in which the 'political business cycle' constitutes the favored stabilization policy. In this model, the pressures of wages and decaying worker discipline are managed by government-induced slumps. Accordingly, full employment is attained only intermittently, during business-cycle peaks. Kalecki is unfortunately vague with regard to the alternative regime, and makes only the claim that full-employment capitalism must develop new social and political institutions which will reflect the increased power of the working class.

In economies with private enterprise and with public commitments to full employment and social justice, the issue of institutional accommodation condenses into the problem of how labor's redistributional power will not jeopardize the need for balanced economic growth. The central question is how to turn potential zero-sum conflicts into positive-sum trade-offs that are consistent with both sustained price stability and full employment. What kind of institutional framework will permit private enterprise and a powerful working class to coexist?

The question confronted all the advanced industrialized capitalist democracies over the post-war era. In most nations, the leap into peace was taken with strong ideological commitments to sustained full employment – though, to be sure, their articulation ranged from a *de facto* constitutional character (as in Norway) to generally good intentions (as in the United States and West Germany).

Promises notwithstanding, nations faced the practical task very differently. In some countries, like Great Britain, the United States, and Sweden, the distributional dilemmas of full employment emerged immediately after the war, while in others the issue would not surface for many years.

In reality, a genuinely sustained full-employment performance has been both temporally and cross-nationally infrequent. Only very few nations (Norway, Sweden, and Switzerland) have been capable of consistently securing unemployment levels below 2–3 percent over the entire post-war era. For the majority of cases, full employment has been confined to the brief interlude between 1960 and 1974.

Bordogna (1981) makes a useful distinction between the handful of countries in which a binding full-employment commitment actually obtains (such as Norway and Sweden) on the one hand, and nations which, on the other hand, have typically resorted to stop–go policies with associated unemployment as a means to regulate wage pressures. The distinction follows Kalecki's original regime-scenarios, but, in light of post-war developments, it inspires new questions. First, what conditions a nation's choice between these two alternative regimes? Second, which institutional arrangements and, equally salient, which policy instruments, are adopted to contain the wage pressures that a fully employed working class is likely to exert? New institutional structures may, as Kalecki anticipated, be necessary requirements. But they are unlikely to be sufficient unless they are capable of producing policy instruments, on the basis of which zero-sum conflict can be overcome. Third, there are at least two crucial conditions that fundamentally alter the original conception of how to deliver full employment. One is the emergence of global economic integration. It is analytically necessary to distinguish the full-employment issues of the phase of international economic expansion (between the late 1950s and 1973) from those of the post-1973 era. In this perspective, the remarkable post-1973 performance of nations such as Norway and Sweden demands special attention. Have these nations, via institution-building and policy solutions, managed to cut the Gordian knot of the Phillips-curve? The other condition, as discussed in chapter 6, is the radically altered meaning that full employment has been given by the inclusion of women as normal participants in the labor market. Statistically, this might entail a revolutionary augmentation of the full-employment clientele.[1]

In this chapter, our analysis will produce pessimistic conclusions. Despite fundamental differences in institutional accommodation and policy choice (especially since the late 1970s), advanced capitalist democracies appear to converge in one respect; namely, in their incapability of ensuring both full employment and balanced economic growth. This holds for 'political business-cycle' regimes as well as for the notable Swedish and Norwegian examples. The principal reason has to do with the limited means available (within any kind of institutional framework that has, so far, been tried in capitalism) to channel zero-sum conflicts into workable bargains. Within the range of limited means, the welfare state came to play a dominant (and problematic) role.

In the final analysis, the kind of bargain, or accord, required in the pursuit of full-employment policy objectives presumes the preservation of private entrepreneurial discretionary powers. Thus, the tools available to obtain wage restraint or other sacrifices will be largely limited to the public domain. Not surprisingly, social policy became the chief arena within which distributional solutions were sought. However, this has come to place the welfare state in a double bind: it is given responsibility for both full employment performance *and* distributional harmony. The two functions, as we shall discuss, are inherently incompatible.

Institutional Models and Policy Regimes in the Post-War Era

For most nations, the period between the 1930s and the 1950s was a historical watershed for socio-political realignment. Novel institutional arrangements were built to manage distributional conflict. Several distinct models are discernible. One, exemplified by the celebrated Swedish case, was premised on powerful, all-encompassing, and centralized trade unions that, usually in liaison with a governing (or governable) labor party, were willing to engage in central national-level, or industry-wide, negotiations with employers. This institutional matrix was based on labor's recognition of the rights and prerogatives of private industrial ownership, implying that neither unions nor labor governments would interfere with decision-making of private firms.

Conflicts were therefore limited to issues of how to distribute the social product. In brief, it was recognized that labor's power resources would not, and could not, be mobilized to alter the boundary between public and private. In this model, the power of labor compelled strongly phrased commitments to both full employment and social rights: the presence of powerful, cohesive, and class-encompassing interest organizations secured an institutional arrangement of stable 'social accords' with only modest free-rider and prisoner-dilemma problems. Distributional conflicts could, in large measure, be managed through sophisticated and long-term modes of political exchange.

The other basic model of post-war institutional alignment, perhaps best exemplified by the United States, is characterized by incomplete or fragmented class-organizational formation in both markets and politics. Lacking institutional means for comprehensive negotiations of distributional issues, both free-rider and prisoner-dilemma problems are likely to be pervasive, and distributional struggles will tend to be particularistic and temporally short-sighted. Under such conditions, labor is likely to favor maximization-strategies in bargaining, thus augmenting the need for occasional strong anti-inflationary measures. Further, lacking undisputed institutional recognition from employers, labor-movement strength becomes, in itself, an object of conflict. In this kind of system, organizational power will indeed be viewed as a major obstacle to balanced economic growth.

These two polar cases closely resemble the distributional coalitions identified in Olson (1982), and two of the full-employment models in Schmidt (1987), and they each represent one of our welfare-state labor-market regimes. They obscure, of course, a rich variety of post-war institutional expressions. The majority of nations exhibit complex mixes of both, each nation following its own unique path through the post-war decades. The task here, however, is not to elaborate an exhaustive catalogue of institutional models, but to trace how distinct 'contrast-cases' pursued solutions to the full-employment problem.

The following examination will focus predominantly on the following three regimes: the United States, Scandinavia, and Germany; the last is of particular interest, since it moves in the Nordic direction following the rise of labor in the late 1950s and early 1960s, but reverts back to anti-inflationary priorities in the 1970s.

The Crystallization of Institutional Arrangements in the Post-War Era

Many countries emerged from World War II with sweeping promises of social democratization, by which was meant commitments to social citizenship and the abolition of unemployment. In the United States, this was established with the New Deal reforms in social security, agrarian subsidies and active employment promotion. The Democratic Party, under Franklin D. Roosevelt, installed itself as an American equivalent to the Scandinavian 'red–green' alliance of farmers and workers, and one with a largely similar programmatic platform. But lacking in the United States were nationally strong and cohesive 'red' and 'green' class organizations. The coalition was, instead, brokered by the political system, and it remained fragile due to the South's insistent rejection of welfare and employment policies that would raise labor costs and emancipate the Black population. Roosevelt's decision to revert to balanced-budget orthodoxy in 1936–7 may have been a technical mistake, but it was viewed as politically necessary. This, the first case of a 'political business cycle' designed to calm down wage and price developments, was, in the immediate post-war years, exacerbated by conservative attacks on both the social security reform and on the full-employment promise contained in the (strongly formulated) Wagner bill and the (weaker) Taft-Hartley act. The pioneering steps towards a modern advanced welfare state that the New Deal embodied were effectively stopped in the period between 1945 and 1950 (Skocpol, 1987). Price stability was institutionalized as the first-order priority of any government; the chief policy-mix for its attainment became restrictive budgetary policy coupled with anti-inflationary 'political business cycles', especially in response to the inflationary threats of the Korean War. Until the mid-1960s, there were no welfare-state advances, and unemployment levels remained quite high. The relative political independence of the Federal Reserve Bank provided an important institutional means with which to ensure the long-term priority of price stability.

Like the United States, other nations confronted similar dilemmas immediately after the war. The post-war Labour government in Britain presided over a powerful mandate for welfare-state institutionalization along the lines of the Beveridge Plan, and an equally strong consensus for full employment. The successful implementation of both helped fuel strong inflationary pressures. Labour's response was the imposition of an incomes policy with wage and price controls that soon estranged the trade unions. The lack of internal cohesion in the trade unions meant, first of all, that a viable political exchange, or bargain, between wages and future gains was impossible to forge. Secondly, it meant that the trade-union movement was institutionally incapable of sponsoring strategic alternatives either to unacceptable incomes policies or to an endless parade of stop–go policies. As Higgins and Apple (1981) argue in their comparison of Britain and Sweden, the 'positive-sum' solution launched by the Swedish Trade Union Confederation, LO, in the same years and under similar circumstances, could not emerge in Britain – not due to lack of policy creativity, but due to institutional barriers.

Nordic social democracy is often portrayed as a model of balanced full-employment welfare-state growth.[2] The Nordic countries, like Britain and the United States, confronted the dilemma between the promises of redistribution and full employment, and the hard realities of inflationary spirals. In the small, open Nordic economies, too much demand fuels direct and immediate balance-of-payments crises. The problem, therefore, is that competitiveness is jeopardized by too much wage-push. Positioned similarly, Nordic social democracy diverged.

In Denmark, the labor movement was politically side-tracked during the critical years of post-war institution-building. The labor–farmer alliance that carried Denmark through the Depression with a full-employment welfare-state program was curtailed, as the powerful (liberalistic) farmers insisted on budgetary austerity and a price-stablization policy in order to maintain agrarian exports. Hence, welfare-state reforms and full employment in Denmark were not part of the political formula until after the late 1950s. Intermittent wage and price pressures (such as during the Korean War) were, as in the United States and Britain, managed through the 'political business cycle' of stop–go policies.

Within Scandinavia, as well as among all the capitalist democracies, it was therefore only Norway and Sweden that were capable of translating the full-employment commitment into reality. These two nations shared, with Denmark, a social democratic breakthrough that inaugurated active welfare and employment policies in the 1930s. The foundations were similar: strong universalist trade unions, and a labor party capable of dominating the political coalition of farmers and workers that, in the first place, permitted social democratic ascendance.

The decisive institutional contrast to Denmark, however, was that in Norway and Sweden the trade-union movements were far more unified and capable of central coordination of bargaining, while the farmers were both politically and economically more marginal. Unlike in Denmark, the Norwegian and Swedish labor parties were capable of dominating the political terrain because there was no possibility of a unified bourgeois coalition as an alternative. Hence, they presided over a powerful mandate for both full employment and welfare-state reforms. As in Britain, the mandate was implemented over the immediate post-war years, compelling the labor movements to find more permanent and stable solutions to the problem of wage–price pressures.

In Sweden, the issue arose in the late 1940s as the balance-of-payments situation deteriorated. As in Britain, the Social Democratic government saw no alternative but to ask the unions to acquiesce in a wage freeze through incomes policy. The wage controls were naturally most effective among the weaker workers, and least effective among the strongest. This imposed upon the trade unions two problems: first, a future scenario of repeated incomes policies would probably shatter the unity and solidarity of the union movement; second, incomes policies meant that wage restraint would unequally subsidize profits. The active labor-market policy, designed by Gosta Rehn and Rudolf Meidner, and promoted by the trade-union movement as an alternative to incomes policy, became in Sweden the instrument through which an accommodation to full employment was pursued. The instrument was brilliant in its simplicity: across-the-board wage pressure coupled with generous and active labor-market programs to absorb, retrain, and move the workers made redundant in the decaying industries. The policy was, concomitantly, designed to favor dynamic industries with generous profits and an ample supply of highly qualified manpower. Finally, it was assumed that the inevitable wage pressures would be contained through (counter-cyclical) budgetary restraint.

The application of this instrument presumed the presence of two crucial institutional conditions: centralized and solidaristic trade-union organization in political harmony with government policy; and employer confidence and willingness to sustain high investment levels.[3] These institutional preconditions obtained, by and large, until the 1970s, permitting a 'positive-sum' resolution to the problem of full-employment wage pressures.

The Norwegian response was parallel to the Swedish, but with its own institutional peculiarities. First and foremost, post-war Norwegian Labor governments enjoyed absolute parliamentary majorities, and could count on an unusually pervasive political consensus. The bourgeois parties were, in fact, co-signatories of the post-war documents that gave binding commitments to the establishment of the welfare state and full employment. The institutional arrangement was, from the beginning, designed for 'neo-corporatist' interest intermediation. Government boards would, in collaboration with the unions, set wage guidelines in conjunction with economic-growth targets. The most important instrument used to assure compliance with wage guidelines was government's overpowering control over industrial credits and investments. Thus, the trade unions were in a position to trust that wage restraint would be accompanied by investments. In this sense, credit policy became the Norwegian equivalent to Sweden's active labor-market policy. Both are designed to channel labor's full-employment bargaining power into positive-sum directions; both are applicable only in institutional settings where labor and capital command internal organizational consensus, are capable of relatively farsighted political exchanges, and can, in concert with government, translate narrow interests into national interests.

Germany represents a third variant of post-war development. Rapid economic growth with price stability was, in the celebrated 'social market' model, allowed to flow from a combination of laissez-faire market conditions and restrictive fiscal and monetary policy; the public budget was explicitly prohibited from growing faster than GDP. These, however, would probably fail in their application unless supported by favorable institutional conditions. Aside from the unique circumstances of post-war West Germany (foreign occupation, massive devastation, territorial division), the crucial conditions can be summarized in three major factors. First, the autonomy of the German Central Bank, the *Bundesbank*, has been one of the basic institutional means for containing wage and public expenditure growth through restrictive monetary policies. Second, the *de facto* marginalization of both the Social Democratic Party and the trade unions meant that pressures for redistribution remained weak; third, a constant and massive supply of (well-qualified) manpower (from the Eastern territories) long prevented the labor movement from exercising much wage-push. In this respect, the German formula is equivalent to the Italian (with its capacity to draw on Southern labor), and, to an extent also to the American (with its capacity to draw on Hispanic labor).

As long as labor supply outpaced industrial job-expansion, the German 'economic miracle' could proceed without inflationary wage pressures and without effective political claims for major social reform. But the need for institutional realignment presented itself when the labor supply dried up in the early 1960s.

The institutional adaptation to labor's emergent redistributional power began with the formation of the 'Grand Coalition' between the Christian Democrats, CDU, and the social democrats, SPD, in 1966; Ludwig Erhard's neo-liberalist economic orthodoxy was shelved in favor of Schiller's Keynesianism with *Globalsteuerung*. Considerable faith was placed in the capacity of *Konzertierte Aktion* to regulate the unavoidable wage pressures that full employment would entail. 'Concerted Action' was intended to provide unions, employers, and government with an institutional framework within which distributional targets could be coordinated. The realignment of German politics took a second crucial step with the formation of the social democratic–liberal coalition in 1969. This alliance promoted the major policy instruments designed to accommodate the novel matrix of power. Of critical importance were the Swedish-style active manpower program, and substantial improvements in social-benefit programs.

The International Convergence of Full Employment

An international convergence of full employment emerged in the 1960s. In its wake evolved a surprising similarity in the choice of regulatory instruments, even within fundamentally divergent institutional systems. Principally, the welfare state emerged as the favored outlet for distributional stand-offs and threatening wage pressures. With full employment, labor demanded a re-negotiation of the initial post-war 'social contract'.

Unemployment levels declined sharply from the 1950s to the 1960s. For 1950–60, the average in the United States was 4.5 percent, in Germany 4.6, in Denmark, 4.3, and in Norway and Sweden 2.0 and 1.8 percent respectively. Except for the United States, the other nations converged during the 1960s at approximately 1.5–2.0 percent unemployment.[4]

A robust time-series on wage pressures back to World War II is difficult to construct. A fairly comparable measure would be to compute the elasticities of annual change in hourly compensation with respect to annual change in output per hour within manufacturing industries. However, high elasticities in just one year may not necessarily denote wage pressure, only the first effect of negotiated wage increases that are then absorbed the following year. Hence, a solution is to identify the presence of significantly high elasticities over two years or more. Table 7.1 presents an overview of such wage-pressure periods for selected nations. The only cases of significant wage pressure in the 1950s occur in Sweden (where full employment obtained), and in the United States in 1951–2 (when unemployment levels were a record low: 3.2 and 2.9 percent). Otherwise, significant wage pressures in these, as in most other nations, emerged in the 1960s and culminated between 1969 and 1973 (Flanagan *et al.*, 1983; Ulman and Flanagan, 1971; Crouch and Pizzorno, 1978; Sachs, 1979).

TABLE 7.1   The incidence of significant wage pressures in Sweden, the United States, and Germany, 1950–1983

	Years with significant wage pressure	*Years with significant wage moderation*
Sweden	1951–2	1955–7
	1957–8	1959
	1971–2	1963–5
	1975–7	1967–8
		1973–4
		1978–80
		1982–3
Germany	1962–3	1953–4
	1970–1	1959
		1967–8
		1976
United States	1951–2	1962
	1965–7	1968
	1969–70	1971
	1972–4	1976–7
	1978–9	1981–3

Wage pressure is defined as annual rate of change in manufacturing hourly compensation, divided by annual rate of change in per man-hour manufacturing output. 'Significant' wage pressure (or moderation) is identified by taking substantial deviations from the trend-line. Since nations have their own unique trends, the decision-method was fitted to each.
Source: OECD, *National Accounts*, detailed tables; current volumes (Paris, OECD)

The growing wage pressures of the 1960s coincided with declining profitability, inflation, and balance-of-payments difficulties. The new situation gave rise to four major responses. One was deflationary policy in response to acute overheating of the economy. This was attempted in Italy, France, and Denmark (1963), in West Germany (1965), in Great Britain and Sweden (1966) and, if we here include devaluations, also in Great Britain, Denmark, and Norway in 1967. The deflationary measures were primarily in response to sudden balance-of-payment difficulties and, except perhaps for the German case, they were relatively mild. They cannot, at any rate, be interpreted as a return to the logic of the 'political business cycle' in Kalecki's use of the term. They were one-shot crisis measures.

The second response was incomes policy, ranging from explicit and comprehensive deals to vaguer and more indirect efforts to persuade unions to restrain themselves. An early and illustrious forerunner of the former type was the Danish 'package solution' (*Helhedsloesningen*) of 1963, in which government – in consultation with all important interest organizations – pieced together an array of social-welfare benefits for all in return for private-sector restraint on incomes and consumption. This is a pioneering example of how full-employment pressures came to cause welfare-state expansion.

The capacity for workable incomes bargains varied according to class organizational cohesion and capacity for political exchange. France's attempt in 1964 included only public-sector workers, but it was hoped that their wage restraint would trickle down (which it did not). The policy was applied for several years and helped trigger the cataclysmic strike and wage explosions of 1968 (Ulman and Flanagan, 1971; Crouch and Pizzorno, 1978). In Britain, statutory incomes policy was applied in 1966 (with a six-month wage freeze) but, as in France, culminated in strikes and deteriorating relations between the TUC and the Labour Party (Crouch, 1977; 1978). In Germany, the new Grand Coalition's *Konzertierte Aktion*, inaugurated in 1966, sought to include the trade unions in setting wage guidelines. These were followed for the next two years but, due to the lack of 'social symmetry' (i.e. wage restraint was coupled with a profits boom), the result was a proliferation of wildcat strikes and a consequent wage explosion in 1969 (Mueller-Jentsch and Sperling, 1978).

The third response to the new full-employment order was institutional rearrangements to accommodate labor's novel power: the emergence of 'neo-corporatist' structures of interest-intermediation and concertation. The literature on the 'neo-corporatist' phenomenon is very large.[5]

This, as we know, failed in Britain, France, and Italy, and was, at best, a fragile experiment in Germany. In countries where the preconditions were appreciably more fertile, such as in Scandinavia and Austria, the structures of interest concertation were strengthened, especially with regard to the battery of instruments available for distributional bargains. Thus, in Sweden, opportunities for bargains were substantially improved by the development of the (ATP) pension funds, the apparatus for active labor-market policy, and the investment reserve system (Martin, 1981; Esping-Andersen, 1985a), all of which incorporated the trade unions as key decision-makers. In Norway, likewise, the institutional network of public credit and investment agencies was extended, permitting new deals such as redistribution in favor of poorer and less-developed regions. New institutions, with the primary objective of involving labor movements in negotiating distributional priorities, sprang up in nations where they could succeed, as well as in nations where they would remain structurally abortive.

Equally importantly, such attempts at institutional realignment were coupled with frantic searches for distributional outlets. One avenue lay in investment-promotion policies, designed to assure that wage discipline would result in new jobs. The other, increasingly dominant, lay in welfare-state promotion of the 'deferred wage', that is, promises to improve future social benefits in return for present wage restraint. Both led to a tremendous expansion of the public budget.

Finally, the fourth response was to mobilize new manpower reserves. One approach was to invite foreign guestworkers to fill the surplus of vacancies; the other was to encourage greater female labor-force participation. The former response dominated in Germany, Switzerland, and Austria; the latter prevailed in Scandinavia.[6]

The Incompatibilities of Sustained Full Employment

As the 1960s drew to a close, most nations had experienced prolonged full employment; yet, despite major institutional realignments and a variety of policy responses, a new stable equilibrium had not been found. The changed balance of class and organizational power was reflected in growing inflationary pressures (Hirsch and Goldthorpe, 1978), strains within the trade unions as well as between unions and the labor parties (Crouch and Pizzorno, 1978), proliferating strike activity, and diminishing business profitability.[7] Also, as illustrated in table 7.1, wage pressures escalated in the period 1969–73.

The solutions devised by governments and interest organizations to the full-employment pressures of the 1960s permitted, at best, only temporary breathing-room and were, by and large, incapable of longer-term accommodation. First, neither government-induced slumps or the inclusion of new manpower reserves managed to effectively alter the durable full-employment scenario. Second, the trade-offs for wage restraint that were negotiated in the incomes-policy settlements of the 1960s were generally not sufficient to pacify workers' demands, in particular when wage restraint produced profit booms, or when real incomes were affected by inflation. Third, the mix of incomes policies, redistributive wage bargaining, and inflation provoked intense equity conflicts in the labor market. Wage differentials were upset, and the strongest usually managed to compensate with wage drift.

The result was a burst of new distributional bargains. The basic problem that confronted most countries was how to dampen prices and labor costs, strengthen the balance-of-payments situation, and assure sustained investment in the light of declining profitability. In distributional terms, the question was how to formulate alternatives to wage improvements. The political and economic conditions that prevailed during the late 1960s and early 1970s ruled out deflationary policy solutions.

The growing tensions and decaying consensus within the trade unions meant, in addition, that new quid pro quos would have to be more attractive to the rank and file, and that they would have to help restore solidarity. The welfare state became the cornerstone instrument of wage restraint. But, compared to the 1960s, the 'deferred wage' embodied in benefit improvements and new social programs was substantially more costly.

The deferred-social-wage strategy is quantitatively evident in most nations. Weisskopf (1985) has, for example, shown that the (trended) ratio of social wages to private wages leaped from one business cycle to another. The sharpest increases occurred between the business cycle of the late 1960s (roughly 1963–8/9) and its successors in the early 1970s (1968–71 and 1971–4/5). Table 7.2 illustrates the rise of the social wage from 1965–82 in seven countries. The deferred-social-wage strategy found variable expression depending on each nation's institutional profile. In the United States, it took two principal forms: negotiated employee-benefit improvements (such as health care and occupational pensions) within the corporate sector,[8] and social benefit improvements, usually in conjunction with elections. Lacking a firm class or electoral base, the political-exchange model typical of a European social democracy finds its American equivalent in the institutional framework of election maximization.

Hence only one incumbent President (Jimmy Carter, in 1979–80) went to elections on the backdrop of deflationary policies. In the United States, virtually all major improvements in social benefits coincided with either congressional or presidential election years. Tufte (1978) shows

TABLE 7.2   The growth of the 'deferred social wage': the ratio of average annual growth of social transfer payments over average annual growth of wages and salaries, 1962–1982

	1962–5	1965–9	1969–73	1973–8	1978–82
Denmark	1.02	1.07	1.04	1.04	1.07[a]
Norway	1.04	1.06	1.07	1.01	1.05
Sweden	1.07	1.07	1.04	1.16	1.05
Germany	1.00	1.02	0.98	1.08	1.02
Netherlands	1.13	1.13	0.91	1.08	1.06
United Kingdom	1.03	1.06	1.00	1.11	1.10
United States	0.99	1.05	1.10	1.06	1.06

[a] 1978–81.

Source: OECD, *National Accounts*, detailed tables; current volumes (Paris, OECD)

that nine out of 13 legislated social security improvements occurred in election years. However, what is not evident from Tufte's analysis is the role that election maximization policies also play in counteracting wage-push. The social-wage ratio remained firmly constant in the United States during the entire 1950s and up until the mid-1960s. This was a period in which wages generally lagged behind productivity, and in which unemployment levels remained high. The situation was sharply reversed after 1965. From the period 1962–5 to 1965–9, the annual average elasticity of hourly compensation over productivity tripled (Sachs, 1979). It was also in these years that the second American welfare-state expansion occurred (Myles, 1984b).

Besides the War on Poverty (which was principally designed to align the poor and Black electorates to the crumbling Democratic Party coalition), the Johnson administration inaugurated Keynesian stimulus policies (the 1964 tax cut), legislated Medicaid/Medicare, relaxed eligibility requirements, and passed two major raises in social security benefits (1965 and 1967).

It was paradoxically, the Nixon administration that gave the social-wage strategy full prominence. During the years 1969–72, the federal government legislated huge increases in social security benefits, introduced indexation, extended coverage substantially, and passed the guaranteed pension (SSI). Pensions, as a percentage of wages, rose sharply. These improvements coincided with the application of an incomes policy (the wage/price controls) in late 1971. But they were beyond doubt also tailored to winning the 1972 presidential elections. Within the American institutional logic, however, the latter strategy certainly does not preclude the former.

Major social-wage bargains were the order of the day in the late 1960s and early 1970s. Explicit bargains took place in Sweden in 1973, when unions agreed to moderate wage claims in return for a legislated abolition of employee pension contributions. In Denmark, the social wage constituted, since the early 1960s, the only real outlet for wage pressures. Thus, in virtually every case of formal incomes policy, negotiated wage restraint, or devaluation, workers' income restraint was offset with benefit improvements and social reforms. As in most other countries, this pattern climaxed in the early 1970s when pensions were upgraded and major improvements were legislated in unemployment and sickness cash-benefit programs. The result was, in fact, the development of the world's most generous cash-benefit programs.

Turning to Germany, the SPD government's capacity to persuade the trade unions to abide by the wage guidelines within the *Konzertierte Aktion* was intimately connected to its program for upgrading the

German welfare state. Following the Employment Promotion Act, in 1969 the government passed the law on wage continuation during illness – one of the trade unions' top-priority demands over the preceding decade. But the trade unions' wage restraint during the initial years of social recovery was followed by a new wave of militancy and wage push (wages as a share of national income jumped from 61.3 percent in 1968 to 66.3 percent in 1974–5). A second phase of major welfare-state improvements came in 1972, including substantial pension-hikes, a guaranteed minimum pension, and liberalized access to early retirement. Like its 1971 American counterpart, this was a blend of social-wage bargains and election maximization, since the CDU attempted to overbid the SPD's planned-reform for electoral reasons.

The deferred social wage presupposes a willingness among workers to delay a consumption increase that their bargaining power would otherwise permit them to enjoy immediately. It is, however, a complex bargaining item. Broad acquiescence assumes a solidarity not only among the wage-earners themselves, but also between the wage-earners and those most likely to be the immediate beneficiaries, meaning primarily the old. The deferred-social-wage strategy is caught between two simultaneous motives: it is meant to moderate wage claims, but to moderate also inflation. Yet, substantial growth in welfare-state expenditures must invoke higher taxes, and it is possible that rapid public-spending growth under conditions of full employment will add to existing inflationary pressures. Hence the search for alternative, and less costly, instruments for induced moderation.

The major alternative that presented itself in the late 1960s and early 1970s involved various schemes to democratize working life and enhance workers' influence over enterprise decision-making. These were attractive from the point of view of welfare-state finances, and spoke also to the trade unions' internal legitimacy problems. The extension of workers' rights became a major trade-union priority. This was evident in the passage of 'industrial democracy' legislation in Norway, Sweden, and, to a lesser extent, Denmark in the early 1970s; a parallel case is the West German conflict over the extension of *Mittbestimmung* in the mid-1970s. In Sweden, the trade-off was both explicit and of substantial proportions. With a series of laws, workers were given representation on company boards, job-tenure rights, a large degree of control over safety and health conditions, and even over technology decisions.

If social-wage expansion strained government's budgets, industrial democratization led to severe strains and, in reality, to naked conflict as it jeopardized accustomed employer sovereignty. Its introduction meant a *de facto* departure from the 'class consensus' upon which the post-war welfare state and full-employment model has been premised. And it hardly succeeded in dampening workers' lust for wages.

The incompatibilities of either approach soon became evident. Extended worker-control legislation could never provide a positive-sum solution acceptable to employers, and has, since its passage in Sweden, been systematically and powerfully attacked by employer organizations and by conservative parties. It has, undoubtedly, added to the strained circumstances in which collective negotiations have found themselves during the past ten years. And it has also – due to its explicit break with the original 'social contract' – undermined the general conditions for class consensus that, by and large, prevailed over the post-war era in the Scandinavian countries.

The contradictions of the social-wage bargains are considerably more complex. Their weakness does not seem to be that they catalyse rank-and-file rebellions against their labor leaders, as Leninist analyses were ready to predict. Rather, the problem lies in their fiscal consequences. Under conditions of employment and output growth, the revenue requirements that an expanded social wage implies can be met without significant increases in the tax rate. The early and mid-1970s, however, were a period in which growth was modest and inflation rampant. The result was inevitably that taxes on average worker households rose dramatically.[9] Table 7.3 clearly illustrates the problem: workers ended

TABLE 7.3   The tax burden on average worker households, 1965–1980, in Sweden, Germany, and the United States

	1965	1970	1975	1980
Sweden				
average personal tax	22	30[a]	33	33
marginal tax rate	26	45	59	59[b]
Germany				
average personal tax	17	21	26	26
marginal tax rate	20	28	33	34[c]
United States				
average personal tax	13	15	16	19
marginal tax rate	13	20	31	24

Average personal tax includes social contributions. Marginal tax rate is % of worker earnings, assuming a family with one earner and two children.
[a] Estimated.
[b] Figures are for 1982.
[c] Figures are for 1982.
Sources: OECD, *The Tax/Benefit Position of a Typical Worker* (Paris: OECD, 1981); and SSIB data files

up footing much of the bill for the deferred (social) wage.

The combination of inflation and tax growth forced the trade unions into wage-bargaining strategies that were often detrimental to economic stability and continued full employment. In some situations nominal wage increases would have to be in the magnitude of 20–20 percent just to deliver a 2–3 percent real-wage growth. For the trade unions, therefore, tax reductions became a first-order priority and a major item for bargaining against wage restraint. In Sweden, the legislated re-financing of social contributions in 1973 provided a brief respite, but the real issue was marginal taxes. Failure to bring down either taxes or inflation effectively led to the wage explosion in 1975. It was not until 1981 that a major reform helped reduce the marginal tax rate and so, even in the context of an international economic crisis and growing strains of the full-employment commitment, the unions were compelled to continue their wage-maximization bargaining. Wages grew faster than productivity in the years 1975–7, and again in 1981.

In Denmark, the situation was even more dramatic, in part due to the welfare state's almost exclusive reliance on the direct income tax, and in part due to stronger inflation and more rapidly rising marginal tax rates. Thus, by the early 1970s, many households found themselves in the situation that additional labor supply would have directly negative effects on disposable income. The result was the famous tax revolt in 1973, led by Mogens Glistrup's Progress party. From then on, none of the frequently shifting and parliamentarily weak cabinets could impose additional income taxes to offset rapidly rising public expenditures.

In Britain, as Klein (1985) observes, a similar logic operated. Following a period in which the Labour government increased public expenditures in return for wage restraint, it was forced (in 1978) to appease the TUC's demand for considerable tax cuts.

In the United States, as one would predict, the pressure for compensatory tax reductions did not emanate from well-entrenched interest organizations, but instead from (initially) local and (later) national tax revolts. These gave, in 1981, a virtually unchallengeable mandate to the Reagan administration's tax cut, despite a broad expert-consensus regarding its detrimental effects on the economy.

The Re-Emergence of Employment as the Quid Pro Quo for Wage Restraint

The typical advanced OECD country, be it Denmark, the United States, or West Germany, reacted in a contradictory way to the 1973

OPEC price shock, the collapse of the Bretton Woods monetary order, falling industrial profits, and international trade-stagnation. From one side, the strategy of deferring wages and major improvements in social citizenship rights made very large public expenditures necessary; concomitantly, government's capacity to extract additional tax revenue was effectively constrained. The common denominator was an impending fiscal crisis that, over the next decade, could not find resolution in the traditional economic-growth dividend, or in expenditure cuts.

The conditions that came to prevail after 1973 also made the full-employment commitment more difficult to honor. The welfare state found itself saddled with the additional responsibility of upholding full employment or, at least, of averting large-scale unemployment. If the deferred-social-wage strategy, with its ensuing tax constraints, was a convergent national response to the full-employment wage problem before 1973, the post-1973 era gave rise to new fundamental divergences.

The political emphasis on price stabilization versus sustained full employment differed between systems, but a significant divergence also emerged with respect to the means adopted to sustain employment. A cross-national comparison of the situation after 1973, and especially of that after 1979, suggests that none of the prevailing institutional models has been capable of furnishing full employment *and* sustained balanced growth.[10] Counter-inflationary policies based on restrictive monetary and fiscal policies produce unemployment; employment-promotion policies based on a menu of choices ranging from counter-cyclical fiscal or monetary policies to active employment-creation and large-scale production subsidies have proved incapable of delivering balanced growth. The one obvious alternative, namely employment promotion in return for effective and substantial wage restraint, has, so far, been institutionally blocked.

Trade-union organization constitutes one important obstacle to full-employment maintenance during prolonged economic stagnation. Whether employment expansion is to be pursued through massive new investments in the private sector or through public-sector social service growth, it has to be financed with a reduction of disposable wages. Since, however, the representational domain of trade unions is generally confined to employed workers, the solidarity that could be mobilized for a social-wage- or tax-based bargain is likely to be much more difficult to marshall for employment-promotion programs directed at the non-employed – especially since it stipulates actual real-income decline, not merely a declining rate of real-income growth. Due to job-security laws, moreover, the average unionized worker is unlikely to identify strongly with the fate of the unemployed.

The second major obstacle has to do with the fiscal imbalance of the welfare state. Decaying revenue-extraction capacity is matched by rapidly growing social-wage commitments, exacerbated by rising unemployment. Under such conditions, government budget deficits provide one of the few means by which the welfare state is capable of serving the double-barrelled demands for social welfare and full employment.

The third important obstacle lies in the logic of economic rejuvenation that advanced industrialization and heightened international competition impose; namely, that the marginal-employment dividend of new industrial investments is low, and that a restoration of international competitiveness requires either low labor costs or significant redundancies through rationalization. But reduced labor costs and redundancies have become directly connected with welfare-state performance. A cut in the former entails a reduction of employers' social contributions; redundancies assume the presence of welfare-state programs, like early retirement, to absorb laid-off workers. In summary, no matter how the obstacles are perceived, the welfare state emerges as the principal focus of conflict.

Our three welfare-state regimes, exemplified in the differences between the United States, Scandinavia, and West Germany, developed peculiar responses to the post-war full-employment problem. They also retain their distinctiveness with regard to the patterns of political accommodation to post-1973 conditions. In one model (the United States), the dominant characteristic is a mix of political business-cycle management and market regulation; in the second model (Scandinavia), the welfare state becomes the leading force in sustaining full employment, partly as direct employer, and partly through subsidies; and in the third model (Germany), we find a blend of conservative austerity policies and welfare-state promoted dis-employment of older workers. In the two former models, employment continues to grow; in the latter, it contracts. In all, the welfare state is forced to absorb costs for which it is not financially equipped. In none is a return to stable, full-employment-based growth imminent.

As will be recalled, the United States entered the post-1973 era with a substantial rise in social expenditures which, of course, was not matched with tax and social-contribution hikes. The institutionally self-financed social security system faced bankruptcy, especially as unemployment reduced revenues and, together with population ageing, raised outlays. A major source of increased government tax-revenue was the effect that inflation had on escalating incomes into higher tax-brackets. And it was this which provoked broad support for tax reductions.[11]

The Carter administration's ability to counter both inflation and unemployment was severely constrained by its limited financial means and policy options. One approach, the expansion of public-sector jobs, was fiscally (and politically) barred. The liberalized access to early retirement at age 63 helped firms shed some less productive manpower, but further strained social security finances. The hope of introducing an active manpower policy was aborted by concerted business resistance. The CETA (Comprehensive Education and Training Act) program helped absorb large numbers, but was hardly more than a parking lot for labor reserves.

The clear policy priority was anti-inflationary business cycle regulation that produced high unemployment. The increase in employment and growth during 1978 and 1979 was accompanied by a resurgent wage-push (the elasticity of wage growth over productivity growth, 1978–9, was approximately 1.30). Carter's (electorally fatal) response was to introduce deflationary measures in 1979.

The very deep recession that ensued produced the highest unemployment rates since the Depression (with annual averages of 9.5 percent in 1982 and 1983). And, in contrast to previous slumps, the core unionized labor force was severely affected. This spurred the trade unions, especially the larger industrial federations, to sponsor deals both at the level of collective bargaining and in the political arena. The idea was to sacrifice wages in favor of employment security and job-promotion policies. Employment-based trade-offs did occur sporadically through private bargains (in the automobile industry, for example), but did not harmonize well with the new Reagan administration, whose priorities centered on a swift dismantling of CETA, tax reductions, welfare cutbacks, deregulation, and anti-inflationary policies.

Although antithetical to the notion of government employment promotion, the Reagan administration(s) has nevertheless had recourse to stimulation programs. For one thing, the soaring public-budget deficits coupled with large defence purchases stimulated demand. Government net lending as a percentage of GDP grew from 1.4 percent in 1980 to about 5 percent in 1983.[12] Second, the 1981 tax cuts were in effect subsidies to business. Corporate income tax as a percentage of corporate receipts declined from 20 percent to 11.4 percent from 1980 to 1983.[13]

Despite an actual decline in the share of government employment, and despite very high unemployment rates (until 1984), the United States' rate of employment growth has been very strong. This performance, spectacular as it is, cannot be explained by reference to Reagan's reflationary policies, since the trend has been strong throughout the 1970s. It is, however, the case that the employment performance during the early 1980s coincided with a policy-regime that created severe economic imbalances, including extraordinarily large deficits on the public budget and on the external trade accounts. Debt-service payments as a percent of current federal government outlays were more than 11 percent in 1983.

Norway and Sweden are among the very few nations that have been capable of maintaining full employment since 1973. Both nations managed, until the recession of the 1980s, to hold open unemployment under 3 percent. This performance testifies to the strength of the binding full-employment commitment that reigns, and it suggests the possibility that these two countries have produced an institutional system in which the basic economic dilemmas of capitalism are resolvable. A closer scrutiny, however, suggests that this is not the case.

The conditions that pattern Norway's policy-alternatives are naturally unique due to the impact of the oil economy. The oil revenues have afforded Norway a means of simultaneously financing both incomes and employment that few other countries enjoy. Oil incomes were the basis of the extraordinary Keynesian reflation policy after 1973. Borrowing on future revenues, the government-designed income agreement of 1974 increased government spending by 1 billion kroner, and gave major tax reductions to employees. This expansionary incomes policy was repeated in subsequent years, culminating in 1977 with a 2 billion kroner increase in outlays (Esping-Andersen, 1985a, p. 244). These income binges, in the context of full employment, pushed labor costs 25 percent above the OECD average, thus impairing economic competitiveness.

This would have been a ready-made case for heavy unemployment had it not been for government's recourse to production and wage subsidies. It has been estimated that, in the late 1970s, every fifth Norwegian worker's job owed its existence to public subsidies (Haarr, 1982). Moreover, the sheer volume of production subsidies is staggering. As a percentage of GDP, they grew from 5.3 percent in 1972 to 7.7 percent in 1978. By 1983, they had declined to 6.1 percent. This is about 15 times the American rate, three times the West German, and about twice the (high) Danish rate.

The result was, of course, enormous budget deficits (that were eliminated via oil revenues) and, more seriously, a long-term impairment of industrial competitiveness. With the prospect of declining oil revenues in the future, the costs of upholding full employment will become unbearably high. A third, uniquely Scandinavian, response to rising unemployment has also been adopted in Norway, although to a lesser extent than in Denmark and Sweden. This includes expansion of welfare-state jobs (an annual growth rate of about 3.5 percent in the 1970s) and active manpower programs, including retraining and sheltered employment.

The Swedish full-employment performance is the more impressive in that in Sweden there was no manna from heaven – or from the sea either. Moreover, badly orchestrated fiscal policy during the early 1970s placed the Swedish economy in a very unfavorable position. First, in reaction to severe wage-push and overheating, the Social Democratic government manufactured a relatively deep recession in 1971–3. The deflationary measures helped arrest income and consumption growth, but Sweden lost out on the booming international markets that then prevailed, and was forced to absorb considerable unemployment within the active labor-market apparatus. Second, the prolonged income restraint fueled a wage explosion in 1975–7 which, as in Norway, undermined Sweden's economic competitiveness abroad. In 1976, when the Social Democrats were defeated, it was evident that their long-standing 'middle-way' formula had exhausted its capacity to accommodate full employment to balanced growth. Aside from wage-push and sagging competitiveness, investment rates were exceedingly sluggish, inflation high, and real GDP growth low. The social democratic, full-employment hegemony was maintained during the unstable bourgeois cabinets that reigned from 1976 to 1982. Swedish politics, however, remained imprisoned in an institutional system that no longer functioned: wages were difficult to contain; taxes, impossible to raise; public expenditures impossible to cut; and deflationary policies were out of the question.

The remaining option was to accumulate large government deficits to finance employment. Crisis industries were granted colossal subsidies; swelling inventories were subsidized across the board (amounting to 2 percent of GDP in 1977); the labor surpluses absorbed in active labor-market programs mushroomed. The only available option was to escalate welfare-state employment. During the 1970s, average annual growth in public employment was 5 percent. As in the United States, but under welfare-state auspices, Sweden actually expanded total employment in a stagnant economy. The effort to sustain full employment was costly. By 1980, the government deficit was 10.4 percent of GDP, growing to almost 12 percent in 1983. The size of this deficit must be understood in connection with government taxation which, by the 1980s, amounted to 50 percent of GDP.

Sweden's tax-extractive capacity is both unique and intimately related to the solidarity that supports the welfare state and full employment. Additional increases, however, appear blocked. The Social Democratic government that was reinstalled in 1982 was saddled not only with huge deficits, but also with the need to finance major new investments. The government has been able to rely on the unions to sacrifice wages for the sake of the common good since 1982, but the ensuing real-wage decline has also triggered a growing unrest within the labor movement. In 1982, the powerful metal-workers' union broke ranks with the employers. Severe tensions have emerged between private- and public-sector federations.

In the 1970s, Swedish distributional conflicts turned into a zero-sum game that was only precariously patched up by deficit-financed welfare-state intervention. That it was precarious is reflected in the evaporation of the long-standing consensus between capital and labor. In its place developed a remarkable polarization.

Social democracy's way out of the dilemma is premised on the wage-earner funds ('economic democracy') introduced in combination with the devaluation and the economic crisis program in 1982–3. The principle is to make effective wage-discipline acceptable because, in return, workers as a collective receive part of the resulting profits in the form of added revenues to ailing pension funds, and in the form of collective investment capital for future jobs and wages. In a Kaleckian sense, the wage-earner funds constitute a novel attempt at institutional accommodation to full employment; they serve to channel labor's power into positive-sum trade-offs. Their capacity to do so assumes that business is prepared to participate; but in contrast to social democracy's previous institutional innovations, the wage-earner funds signify, from the point of view of business, an additional incursion into the rights of property ownership which is totally unacceptable. Thus, if it can be argued that any form of institutional accommodation to full employment must rest on an underlying social contract, one would have to predict that the wage-earner-funds strategy is likely to ship-wreck.[14]

The specter of a bold new era of social democracy in West Germany was laid to rest only a few years after the SPD came to power. West Germany did not confront the 1973 oil crisis in a particular opportune way. Both private and social wages had grown sharply over the preceding years, profits had declined, inflationary pressures were strong, and Germany's export competitiveness was weakened. With a rise in unemployment after 1973, the SPD naturally opted for expansionary measures. Yet its counter-cyclical budget clashed with the Bundesbank's insistence on restrictive monetary policy to stabilize currency and prices. The Bundesbank prevailed, and the government was forced instead to restrict welfare expenditures and tolerate rising unemployment. Austerity policies designed to bring down inflation persisted until the brief 1978–9 reflation.

The Keynesian breakthrough, coupled to active labor-market policy, was therefore aborted. The trade unions saw, in this context, little reason to maintain an obligation to the kind of neo-corporatist settlements that *Konzertierte Aktion* implied. Yet, due to the tight money policies and rising unemployment levels, they were barred from exerting wage pressures. Wage restraint in the 1970s was therefore a function of the political business cycle; not of negotiated bargains. Indeed, the unions found that there was precious little to bargain about.

In direct contrast to Scandinavia, the German welfare state was not permitted to attempt the double task of social equality and employment promotion. To cover the rising costs of unemployment and pensions, the government was forced in 1977, 1981, and again in 1982, to impose real cuts in social- and manpower-program expenditures and, simultaneously, to raise tax contributions. Most importantly, social democracy's ability to absorb unemployment in active manpower programs was effectively vetoed, as was its freedom to expand welfare-state employment. In spite of general fiscal austerity, government began to run budget deficits. Modest as they were in comparison to either Scandinavia or the United States (5.7 percent of GDP in 1975; 0.3 percent in 1980, and about 1 percent in 1983), they were not politically acceptable.

Two major policies to combat unemployment remained possible in Germany. One was to repatriate foreign workers; the other, to encourage early retirement among older workers in the hope that this would promote both productivity and jobs for younger workers. This approach, typical of most continental European countries, caused a substantial decline in overall employment. In Germany, the participation rate of males, aged 60 to 65, declined from 75 percent in 1970 to 44 percent in 1981.[15] Yet despite the labor-force contraction, unemployment levels continued to rise (to more than 8 percent in 1983). Tight money-supply policies inhibit both consumption and investments.

The dis-employment strategy characteristic of Germany may have produced productivity gains for industry, but it saddled the welfare state with the same kinds of fiscal imbalances found in Scandinavia. The major factor here is that dis-employment escalates transfer payments and diminishes social contributions. Hence, to rebalance the public budget, considerable benefit cuts or tax hikes are necessary.

The narrow scope for alternative policies in Germany, and especially the blocked prospects of bargaining for additional employment, helps explain the trade unions' recourse to a policy of redistributing scarce jobs. Thus, work-time reduction emerged as a major demand, first in

1976 with a demand for a one-hour across-the-board reduction – a proposal which was rejected by the separate union federation. Instead, the Metal Workers' Union demanded a 35-hour week combined with a 5 percent wage compensation. Backed by strikes in 1978, the strategy was defeated. So was its successor in 1984.

The German approach to stabilization policies has imposed three extraordinary costs; 1) fiscal pressures on the welfare state; 2) sub-optimal utilization of manpower; and 3) sluggish investment behaviour.

Conclusions

This chapter has tried to construct a new interpretation of old data. The issues dealt with here have been extensively examined before. There is a huge literature on post-war macroeconomic policies, income policies, the full-employment experience, the welfare state, on trade unions and neo-corporatist concertation, on declining governability and the economic crisis that beset advanced capitalist nations since the early 1970s.

Despite this accumulation of knowledge and wisdom, a new interpretative exercise seems warranted. First, with a few (very important) exceptions, there has been little effort devoted to studying the interconnections between many of the powerful structural changes that took place over the past 40 or so years.[16] This seems to me to be particularly the case with the relationship between full employment, economic-stabilization policies, and the welfare state. Our intellectual forebears saw these as intricately linked in their scenarios of a new and more democratic capitalism. Contemporary scholarship has gone its own specialized ways. The deferred-wage concept, as Myles (1984b) points out, affords us an analytic means by which the welfare state re-enters as an endogenous variable in the study of post-war political economy.

Also, the early 1970s not only created a break in the logic of post-war social, political, and economic evolution, but also gave birth to a new analytical problem for social science: the study of capitalism in crisis. It strikes me that the new, post-1973 'crises-analyses' are largely disconnected from the scholarship and the phenomena that preceded them. The interpretation offered here is one effort to explore the direct links between the politics of the full-employment-growth era, and the politics of the new 'crisis' era.

One of the most central questions of the post-war decades has been how to deliver upon the promises of equality, full employment, and efficiency. The answer that Kalecki provided – namely, through new political and social institutions – will, in itself, hardly stir controversy. On the other hand, if Kalecki had in mind an institutional reordering whereby the right of private entrepreneurship would be seriously weakened, the issue is quite another one.

The success of post-war capitalism lies in its capacity to harmonize democracy with private property. The synthesis of these two institutions was made possible by the 'social contracts' of the 1930s and 1940s, where labor committed itself to respecting the sanctity of entrepreneurial prerogatives in return for the freedom to conduct distributional struggles unhindered.

The stability of post-war decades had a lot to do with the capacity of class and interest organizations to find institutional arrangements within which this fundamental quid pro quo could work. But, if the social contract was a constant, the institutional arrangements came to diverge sharply across nations. This played a vital role in shaping not only the strength and durability of the full-employment experience, but also the capacity for arriving at stable and workable mediations between policy goals and distributional priorities.

Whatever institutional structure came to prevail, a common feature of post-war nations is their rising incapability of managing the altered balance of power which full employment brought about. The basic difficulty lay in finding acceptable outlets for impending zero-sum conflicts. As we have noted, the sanctity of property rights meant that the state came to constitute the realm of the possible. The concept of political exchange therefore connotes two things: the capacity for deferring the fruits of power, and the dependence on the political arena for managing distributional power.

Our cursory overview has, however, shown that the scope for trade-offs in the state can be quite extensive. Political exchanges have involved government credit, investments, nationalizations and subsidies, taxation, employment and welfare policy. The welfare state emerged as the major outlet for full-employment pressures, principally in the shape of the deferred social wage.

But, in whichever form it takes, the viability of a deferred-wage strategy depends ultimately on one's ability to collect on it in the future. This has proven itself the Achilles' heel of the deferred wage. For reasons of bargaining, labor must have to insist against tax increases; for reasons of competitiveness, corporations must similarly refuse. As a consequence, the welfare state found itself in a situation in which it was either compelled to renounce on its original obligations, or to finance the deferred wage by deficits, thereby only delaying the zero-sum confrontation.

The nations' ability to balance distributional demands in a full-employment situation worsened considerably as worldwide trade and growth stagnated. But it clearly also worsened because existing distributional outlets approached exhaustion. Yet empirical evidence suggests that the limits of a deferred-wage strategy are not necessarily strictly financial. That is, a government's capacity to increase taxes to accommodate rising expenditures appears to be positively related to the strength of working-class power mobilization and societal corporatism (Schmitter, 1981). Thus, a nation's capacity for 'solidarity' is closely associated with economic policy options. This is also a key factor in a country's ability to move beyond the conventional policy instruments. The case *par excellence* is Sweden, where the deferred-wage strategy was increasingly exhausted by a combination of forces; 1) internal trade-union problems with cohesion and legitimacy; 2) the incapacity to bargain nominal wages to compensate for both taxes and inflation; 3) the growing disbelief that wage restraint was reciprocated by sustained entrepreneurial investment. These factors led the trade unions to question their traditional adherence to the sanctity of property rights. The trade unions rediscovered a slogan from the 1930s, 'Democracy cannot stop at the factory gates', demanded a re-negotiation of the original contract, and launched, first, worker-control legislation and, subsequently, economic democracy with collective wage-earner funds. These became in the 1970s and early 1980s the core trade-off policies. Their introduction, unlike the trade-off policies of the 1950s and 1960s, was, from the point of view of business, non-negotiable and unacceptable. They were thus the legislative victories of power, not of societal corporatism and interest intermediation. In this way the democratization of property rights became both a novel type of stabilization politics (the Social Democratic government managed to obtain effective wage-restraint against wage-earner funds) and at the same time a source of de-stabilization. Although it may one day become acceptable to business, the politics of workers' control is certainly not so at present. Thus, in Sweden the only possible social democratic formula for a combined action of equality, full employment, and efficiency is precariously upheld by slim parliamentary majorities. It still takes two to tango and, in a world with free capital movements, your partner may choose not to dance.

Notes

1 Between 1950 and 1980, female-labor-force supply doubled in Sweden and the United States (from 23 to 47 percent, and from 22 to 40 percent, respectively). In Germany, female activity rates grew only from 31 to 34 percent (ILO, *Yearbook of Labour Statistics*, 1960, and 1983).

2 A model of post-war political-economic development that is closely parallel to the Scandinavian model is that of the Netherlands. The Netherlands followed quite similar welfare-state policies and strong full-employment commitments; in addition, balanced non-inflationary growth was pursued via an impressively consistent consensus around incomes policies (Ulman and Flanagan, 1971; Braun and Keman, 1986).

3 In fact, the model also assumes that employers are highly organized and cohesive, and that the 'weaker' and decaying capitalists' political sway is marginal. It takes two to make centralized, solidarity-wage bargaining work.

4 The total OECD average for 1960–7 was 3.1 percent and for 1968–73, 3.4 percent. In the United States, unemployment rates began first to decline sharply after 1964 (OECD, *Historical Statistics, 1960–83*, (Paris, OECD,); and Maddison, (1982).

5 For some important and representative treatments, see Schmitter (1981); Schmitter and Lembruch (1979); Lange (1984); Lembruch (1984); Panitch (1980); Cameron (1984); and Regini (1984).

6 The numbers were large. At the peak, foreign workers accounted for more than 9 percent of the labor force (1973) in Germany; in Austria, more than 7 percent (1973); for Sweden, the corresponding percentage is approximately 5 percent, including Finns, and about 3 percent excluding Finns.

7 The profit share (net profit as a percentage of net value added in manufacturing) declined precipitously between 1960–7 and 1968–73 for most countries, including the United States, Germany, Great Britain, Sweden, and Denmark (OECD, *Historical Statistics, 1960–83*, (Paris, OECD, 1985); Flanagan *et al.*, 1983; Glyn and Sutcliffe, 1972; Edgren *et al.*, 1973; Martin, 1985; Nordhaus, 1974).

8 Employer contributions to private pension plans, as a percentage of the total wage bill, grew from 5 percent in 1970 to 7.3 percent in 1975 (OECD, *National Accounts, 1962–79*, vol. 2 (Paris, OECD), 1981).

9 On the employer side the result was parallel. Non-wage labor costs (primarily social contributions) skyrocketed. As a percentage of total, they rose (1965–75) from 17 to 23 percent in the US, from 19 to 32 percent in Sweden, and from 30 to 34 percent in Germany.

10 By sustained balanced growth we here mean economic growth over the medium term which is not bought at the expense of seriously accumulating balance-of-payments deficits or public-sector deficits, disinvestment, or inflation.

11 Note, however, that the first wave of tax revolts focused on the property tax that spiraled in the wake of inflation.

12 Omitting social security funds and including both current and capital accounts, the 1983 deficit was equal to 8.3 percent of GDP.

13 Note, however, that the 1981 tax cuts for business followed a long period in which government tax expenditures implicitly furnished a massive subsidy towards corporations. Break (1980) shows that, in the period 1970–80, tax expenditures in favor of corporations grew almost three times faster than federal government income-tax revenue.

14 The rather rosy picture of economic revitalization that is presented in a recent survey (OECD, 1985) is not necessarily incompatible with the gloomier scenario presented here. Our point is that a *sustained* revitalization is unlikely to occur as long as its institutional framework is under serious dispute.

15 In Germany, total employment declined by an average of −0.7 percent from 1973–83; the figure for Belgium for that period is −1.1 percent; for Austria, −0.5 percent; but, for the OECD as a whole, employment grew by an average of 1.1 percent from 1973 to 1979, and 0.2 percent from 1979 to 1983.

16 One of the most comprehensive synthetic overviews is found in Goldthorpe (1984b)

8

Three Post-Industrial Employment Trajectories

Introduction

The idea of post-industrial society emerged in the 1960s, provoked by contemporary revolutions in technology, management, consumption, and employment. It portrays a new world where technicians, professionals, and managers predominate; where old-fashioned manual labor disappears; where consumers' appetites are driven towards services.

These kinds of 'facts' have been given radically different interpretations. The theorists of social culture believe in the coming of a new majority with post-materialist values focused on the quality of life. The issues of traditional industrial society, such as poverty, scarcity, and social class fade into historical memory (Touraine, 1971; Inglehart, 1977).

For most, however, the burning question concerns the employment consequences of post-industrial change. To economists, the question is whether service jobs will grow enough to permit sustained full employment. Sociologists have been more interested in the quality of jobs and in employment stratification and segmentation.

This chapter is devoted to the study of post-industrial employment. The term itself has rightly been received with some skepticism, in that it too readily suggests the arrival of a society that has surpassed the need for material production. Theories of post-industrialism are also criticized for their frequent recourse to technological determinism.

We use the term 'post-industrial' here, not because we are sworn adherents to the theories that begot the concept, but because it serves to identify the problem we wish to address. First, under the post-industrial label lies a real process of fundamental employment-change: new occupations are emerging; jobs that once were scarce are becoming abundant; physical and manual labor is a dying breed, and mind-labor at various levels of complexity and exaltedness is becoming the norm. Second, we wish to confront the strong undercurrent of theoretical determinism with comparative data. The leading argument in this chapter is that nations are following distinctly different 'post-industrial' trajectories; that, indeed, we confront a variety of future employment-scenarios.

Most theories have stressed the causal importance of technology, modernization, and economic affluence. Following the argument in the preceding chapters, contemporary trends in employment need also to be explained politically. But, aside from general employment performance, this chapter deals more specifically with its structuration and with its influence on social stratification.

A comparison between Germany, Sweden, and the United States serves our purpose well, since they constitute distinct representatives of our respective welfare-state/labor-market regimes. We shall show that post-industrial development generates three qualitatively different employment structures. Prevailing theory offers valuable explanations for some of these differences, but it stops short of explaining the totality. In terms of employment growth, structure, and stratification, we will try to demonstrate that the welfare state is a midwife of post-industrial employment evolution. Different welfare-state/labor-market interactions produce different post-industrial trajectories. They influence not only the rate of growth of services, but also the relative emphasis on social-welfare activities as opposed to personal services; they influence the skill and occupational composition of the labor force; and they influence the distribution of jobs by gender and race/ethnic background.

Theories of Service-Employment Growth

The widespread fears of mass unemployment in the first post-war decade were not just a legacy of the Great Depression, but were also ignited by technological change. Kurt Vonnegut's novel, *Player Piano*, is symptomatic of the era. He describes an imaginary future society in which goods are in abundance, but jobs exceedingly scarce since robots and a few administrators suffice. The fear that high-technology economies can satisfy our wants, but not our need to work, can reach dramatic proportions. It is around this question that most debates revolve.

No one disputes the fact that conventional manufacturing jobs are disappearing; the question is whether they can be offset by new kinds of employment. In principle, new jobs can emerge within the traditional industrial economy, or within the 'new' service sector. In the first case, high technology and complex production-organization may call for more managers, administrators, technicians, professionals, and clerical workers. In the latter case, the demand may shift towards services, and generate growth in the non-industrial sector.

Economists often premise their analysis on Engel's law. As nations become richer, consumption will shift from basic necessities to 'luxury' goods, such as leisure and services (Fisher, 1935; Clark, 1940).

But whether Engel's law will produce compensatory employment-growth is not clear. Some have questioned the assumptions of income elasticity (Kuznets, 1957; Fuchs, 1968), but economists have, generally speaking, been reluctant to venture into a major re-theorization of the problem. In this vacuum of general theory, Baumol's (1967) model stands as the focal point for most hypotheses.

His is a largely pessimistic variation on Engel's law. Starting with the premise that high productivity in manufacturing will release manpower, the service sector's capacity to compensate with job-growth may be limited because of its low productivity-growth. Since it is likely that wages in services will match those in the highly productive manufacturing industries, the result is a 'cost-disease': service-sector labor will tend to out-price itself.

With the emergence of high-technology manufacturing, there is the real prospect of jobless growth (Soete and Freeman, 1985). Bluestone and Harrison (1986) cite projections for the United States, 1982 to 1990, in which computer-programmer jobs will increase by less than 120,000. Service jobs therefore remain the sole hope.

One source of optimism lies in the empirical weakness of the Baumol model. On the basis of cross-national data, for example, Pomerehne and Schneider (1980) conclude that the model fares poorly for the European countries. More importantly, Baumol's assumptions may be relaxed. For one thing, it is possible that consumers are so rich that they willingly will purchase 'over-priced' services. This we could call the Yuppie-effect or, to use Fred Hirsch's (1976) terminology, the propensity to demand positional goods.

In addition, as Baumol himself suggests, government may offset the productivity–wage gap by subsidizing, or directly producing, the services. In this sense, the cost-disease problem finds its solution through politics. A third possibility, of course, is that wages do not behave as Baumol predicted. We cannot exclude the possibility, for example, that workers in services are willing to accept lower wage increases than in manufacturing.

The wage-problem has come to figure prominently in the political debate on employment growth. In Europe, commentators, politicians, and even some economists argue that America's greater wage-flexibility is what accounts for its vastly superior job-performance over the past decade; in Europe, trade unions and labor-market rigidities impose prohibitively high service-sector labor costs. In a recent study, Fritz Sharpf (1985) tries to account for the European malaise by holding together the wage and political dimension of Baumol's model. He argues that, where wages are high, the government's capacity to compensate with public-sector employment depends on its fiscal constraints. For Germany specifically, Sharpf suggests that the combination of high labor costs and an already overburdened transfer-state impede service-employment growth in either the private or public sector.

The fundamental problem with the Baumol model may be not its restrictive assumptions, but its dependence on a questionable definition of productivity. Within the national accounting system, productivity in service work is notoriously difficult to identify; for public services, it is outright impossible. Fred Block (1985) puts his finger on the problem when he argues that services today occupy the role that industry did in the era of the physiocrats: we can fathom the productivity of a metal worker, banging on a sheet of metal, but we instinctively view the day-care assistant as living off the productivity of others.

An alternative argument for why service employment is unlikely to grow is that material goods allow households to engage in self-servicing (Gershuny, 1978; 1983). People will fail to purchase leisure or personal services because of the availability of affordable material alternatives, such as video recorders, food processors, and microwave ovens.

The prospects for employment are less bleak in Gershuny's later work (Gershuny, 1986; 1988). In address to Baumol's model, self-servicing will continue to impede job growth in personal services, but not so in business and producer services where wages are less relevant than expertise and professionalism. He furthermore speculates that households' desire to eliminate unpleasant domestic chores will fuel strong demand for service infra-structures in areas such as shopping (Gershuny, 1988).

Whether his conclusions are warranted or not, Gershuny's analysis confirms the widespread argument that we cannot view services as an undifferentiated mass. The point is obvious with a minimum of history. There is nothing new and revolutionary about services as such. As Fuchs (1968), Bell (1973), and Singelmann (1974) note, many services (such as domestics, shoe-repair, and bartending) are pre-industrial; some emerged in tandem with industrialization (transportation, utilities, and wholesale); and still others exploded with the mass production and mass consumption of 'Fordism' (retail, marketing, consumer finance, and advertising).

In some nations, service employment was already prominent 100 years ago. It accounted for more than a third of all jobs in the 1870s in Australia, the Netherlands, and Britain (Maddison, 1982). What post-industrial theory must unravel is therefore not service-employment growth as such, but its novel forms.

Long-term employment data almost invariably show that growth in the traditional services (transport, utilities, retail, etc.) has stagnated, and that the new vitality is concentrated in social services (health, education, and welfare), in some areas of personal services (leisure and eating places, for example), and in producer services (business services, finance, insurance, and real-estate).

Theories of post-industrial services often imply a dynamic entirely divorced from the functions, requirements, and organization of the manufacturing economy: their growth has a life of its own. Such misconceptions may derive from the appearance that services are directly displacing industry. In the United States, industry accounted for 50 percent of employment in 1950, but accounts for only 20 per cent today. It is services which have taken the place of industry, just as industry once took the place of agriculture. A similar story can be told for many other countries.

But there are many ways of interpreting the story. Cohen and Zysman (1987) make a convincing case for the fallacy of regarding post-industrial services as something divorced from material production. Many, and perhaps a majority, of the services enter as intermediary goods in the manufacturing of final material objects. And when services are produced as final goods, their logic cannot be divorced from the organization of society and economy. Social services speak to the needs of wage-earners and the changes in family and household reproduction that industrial society provoked; many personal services evolve in response to our ways of consuming material goods.

THE CLASSIFICATION OF SERVICE ACTIVITIES

In the past, the service economy was usually defined as the residual economy which is left when you have accounted for agriculture and industry. Alas, we still have no coherent definition of what are services. Sometimes they are defined by the intangible nature of the product, or by the interpersonal character of exchange. A solution to the boundary problem between services and physical goods will depend on whether we focus on branches of the economy (manufacturing versus services), or on jobs and occupations (assembly workers or advertising consultants). Obviously, service occupations are plentifully present in traditional industrial establishments.

To get around the definitional problem, most research offers classifications rather than definitions. The most useful way to classify service industries is a variant of that developed by Singelmann (1974; 1978) and Browning and Singelman (1975). Besides extractive and transformative industries, they distinguish between distributive services, producer services, social services, and personal services.

The Singelmann classification needs some elaboration if our focus is on post-industrial expansion. Retail-store employment may be large and even grow, but it is hard to see anything post-industrial about it. For a classification by 'industries', our approach is to single out as post-industrial activities those most closely associated with novel relations of consumption, production, and human reproduction; to use the terminology of the French regulation-school, we are concerned with the transcendence of 'Fordism'.

What, then, is post-industrial activity? Unfortunately, it is a question without any precise answer. Its theoreticians generally identify it as a preponderance of information and scientific-technical manipulation and processing (Bell, 1973), a definition that is a good starting-point when we turn to occupational analyses. For 'industry' analyses, however, we need criteria linked to the consumption of services.

At the service-industries level, we will highlight those that mainly service advanced modes of: 1) industrial production (producer services; 2) social reproduction (social services); and 3) consumption and leisure (personal services). It is in practice completely impossible to identify virtually any single activity as 'new' – from advertising to nursery homes, there is nothing new under the sun except their enhanced economic prominence. Hence, an empirical treatment, as offered here, can be little more than heuristic.

In the analyses to follow, we shall separate these three post-industrial service-industries from industries related to traditional industrial society (mining, manufacturing, construction, transportation, etc.), and also from those that are in a sense timeless (public administration, distribution, communications, etc.).

A purely industry-based analysis is clearly deceptive unless coupled to occupational analyses. In some cases, manufacturing may be overwhelmingly post-industrial in the sense that scientific and professional manpower dominates the production process. On the other hand, hospitals may operate with a heavy quota of unskilled menial labor.

To develop a useful classification of occupation presents its own problems. In this study we will simply distinguish between occupations that mainly belong to the traditional industrial world (skilled and unskilled production workers, crafts workers, clerical and sales personnel, managers, and administrators); and occupations that epitomize post-industrialism (professionals and para-professionals, scientists, and technicians, but also generally unqualified service-workers engaged in leisure-service production).

The comparison between Germany, Sweden, and the United States is biased in one sense: we have sampled three nations that we already know to be divergent in aggregate and structural employment trends. What is important to note, however, is that these three pretty much epitomize international variations. Hence, broader generalizations may be warranted.

Three Trajectories of Service-Employment Growth

The advanced economies have undergone fundamental changes during the past two decades. New technologies have revolutionized production, the share of manufacturing has declined sharply, services have mushroomed, households have become affluent, and the welfare state has matured. The period is also one of an educational revolution and of women's emancipation from the traditional family role. And, finally, it has brought us one of this century's greatest economic upheavals, with massive rationalization and restructuring among domestic industries, and a decisive reordering of the international division of labor. Many industries traditionally viewed as the core of our economies are disappearing or moving elsewhere.

The aggregate employment-trends have varied sharply from one country to the next. From 1960 to 1985, the labor force grew by almost 50 million in the United States, and by about 20 percent in Sweden. In Germany, it actually declined. These differences serve well to summarize overall international developments.

Labor-force growth may be a demographic effect. Yet, if we instead compare rates of employment participation (men and women, aged 16–65), the conclusion remains the same. Over the same period, the American participation rates rose from 66 to 75 percent; the German declined from 70 to 66 percent; and the Swedish jumped from 74 to a world-record 81 percent.

Sex differences in labor-market participation accentuate the national differences. Male participation has been declining almost everywhere because of early retirement and longer schooling, but, as we have seen, the decline in Germany is exceptionally dramatic. Female-employment growth has been phenomenal in both the United States and Sweden, but negligible in Germany.

Even if employment grows in terms of persons, it may decline in terms of the actual volume of work performed; impressive job-growth may be based on mostly part-time work. Nonetheless, the comparative performance of the three countries changes little if we measure hours worked. The loss of jobs in Germany goes hand in hand with an even sharper decline in the volume of work (a 17 percent decline, 1960–80); in Sweden, there has been no real reduction of hours; and in the United States, there is an overall increase of 24 percent (OECD, 1983; *Bureau of the Census*, 1986, pp. 295 and 322).

The main question is whether part-time work deflates the significance of a nation's employment-performance. If we calculate part-time jobs as a ratio of all net employment growth, 1973–81, we discover a mirror-image of the earlier contrasts. The German ratio is a full 165, compared to 105 in Sweden, and only 17 in the United States. This implies, first, that the spectacular American performance cannot be ascribed at all to part-time work; and second, that for Sweden and especially Germany, part-time jobs have dominated new jobs, but have also replaced erstwhile full-time jobs. As one would expect, the part-time component is heavily associated with women's employment. In Sweden, almost half of all women work in part-time jobs (calculations based on OECD, 1983; and *Bureau of the Census*, 1986). But it is in terms of their structuration that the three countries' employment trajectories really diverge. Table 8.1 presents comparative data on annual average percentage employment growth (or decline) by industrial branches. We employ the rough classification between traditional 'industrial', historically 'neutral', and post-industrial activities.

Table 8.1 displays a number of peculiar national biases that will emerge with added force in subsequent analyses. First, Germany's aggregate job-losses are not solely due to de-industrialization; Sweden experienced the same decline in agriculture and manufacturing, and both regimes have fared similarly with regard to the 'neutral' industries. Germany is peculiar in that its 'post-industrial' employment-growth is sluggish, be it in producer, social, or 'fun' services. Its traditional economy may be in decline, but a new one is hardly emerging.

This is not the case for either Sweden or the United States, yet they represent two very different trajectories. In Sweden, post-industrialism

TABLE 8.1 Employment growth in traditional and post-industrial industries (annual average % growth)

Employment	Germany 1961–84	Sweden 1964–84	United States 1960–84
Industrial			
Agriculture	−2.6	−2.7	−1.5
Manufacturing[a]	−0.6	−0.7	1.0
Neutral			
Distribution[b]	0.0	0.1	2.0
Government[c]	3.8	3.0	0.9
Personal services	0.0	−0.1	2.3
Post-industrial			
Producer services[d]	4.2	5.0	7.9
Health, education and welfare	4.8	8.6	6.2
'Fun' services[e]	1.1	1.6	7.2
Total post-industrial employment	3.5	6.7	6.7
Total employment	−0.1	0.8	2.4

[a] Includes all extractive and transformative industries.
[b] Includes retail and wholesale, transport, and communications.
[c] Includes public administration and non-welfare-related government activities (military, police, sanitation, etc.).
[d] Includes business services, finance, insurance, and real estate.
[e] Includes recreation and leisure, eating, drinking, and lodging.
Source: The data have generously been provided by Thomas Elfring. See also his 'Service Employment in Advanced Economies', Doctoral Dissertation, Rijksuniversitet Groeningen, February, 1988

has a welfare-service bias; in the United States, the business and 'fun' services expand in tandem.

For the United States, specifically, the data contradict two common stereotypes. First, traditional manufacturing does not decline – at least in absolute numbers. Second, the myth that the American employment-machine only produces sub-standard, dead-end, 'junk' jobs does not hold. Indeed, it is in producer services and health care, both highly professionally loaded, that the growth momentum is strongest; the United States also outperforms Germany with regard to welfare services.

Our growth-rates take a fairly long view. If we had concentrated on just the last decade, the post-industrial element would have stood out even more strongly. In the United States, for example, fast growth in the 1960s occurred mainly in education, distribution, and government administration; in the 1970s, mainly in producer services, health, and 'fun' services. The time-dimension is often decisive for one's conclusions. This may be the reason why our rather favorable (long-term) picture of the United States contradicts Bluestone and Harrison's (1986) decidedly pessimistic scenario of a 'junk-job'-dominated growth. Their data were restricted to the Reagan years.

OCCUPATIONAL TRENDS IN EMPLOYMENT GROWTH

Our first portrait of the post-industrial occupational mix will present only broad categories. In table 8.2, we distinguish between occupations identified with conventional industrial society, and those associated with post-industrialism. Both include high-grade jobs (managers/administrators, viz. professional/technical workers) and low-grade jobs (clerical, production workers, viz. general-service workers). For all three countries, the 'post-industrial' occupations dominate the growth profile. In Germany, professional jobs grow more slowly and routine-service jobs not at all. The United States is interesting because traditional 'good' (managerial) and 'bad' (clerical) jobs have both grown strongly, and the same is the case for post-industrial occupations.

When we hold together our industry and occupation data, the outlines of three distinct trajectories emerge. Germany represents stagnation and sluggish service-evolution; Sweden is overwhelmingly biased towards highly professionalized social-welfare employment; and, in the United States, several trends compete: one is the sustained dynamism in the conventional industrial economy; another is a powerful thrust towards professionalism, especially in business-related services; and a third is an explosion of unqualified jobs with an accent on 'fun' services.

TABLE 8.2   Trends in the growth of occupational groups (annual average % growth)

Occupations	Germany 1961–82	Sweden 1965–84	United States 1960–84
Industrial society			
Managers and administrators	1.3	2.5	5.5
Clerical and sales workers	1.7	1.4	4.2
Production workers	−0.8	−1.2	0.5
Post-Industrial society			
Professionals and technicians	4.2	5.5	5.1
Service workers	0.2	2.4	4.7

Sources: For Germany, IAB; Beitrag AB 2.1; for Sweden, AKU raw tables for 1965 and 1984; for the United States, Department of Labor, Supplement to Employment and Earnings (January, 1985)

At this point, three questions deserve attention: 1) why is German post-industrialism so sluggish?; 2) what is government's role in the structuring of employment growth?; and 3) what accounts for the managerial bias in the United States?

THE GERMAN SERVICE-EMPLOYMENT 'GAP'

Germany's feeble approach to a modern service economy may be no more than a statisticsl artefact. It could be that services are internalized within industrial establishments rather than sectorally externalized; if so, Germany's post-industrialization would simply be occurring behind closed doors, so to speak. But there is no reason to believe this. The percentage of service workers engaged in the primary and secondary sectors is almost identical in the three countries: in Germany, 30 percent; in Sweden, 29 percent; and in the United States, 33 percent (OECD, *1984b*).

THE ROLE OF GOVERNMENT

The second question concerns government's role in structuring employment-growth. We have already seen its importance in clearing labor markets of older workers. Here, the main question is its role in the creation of the health, education, and welfare component of post-industrialization, a role of immense importance for female employment. In a pioneering study, Rein (1985) has documented cross-nationally the singular importance of welfare services as an avenue of female employment-entry.

In line with Rein's findings, table 8.3 shows how greatly government's role varies: it is, at best, modest in the United States, overwhelming in Sweden, and somewhere in between in Germany. In the United States, then, post industrialization and women's employment is largely produced in the market; in Sweden, it occurs in the welfare state; and, in Germany, neither state nor market appear capable of new employment development.

At first sight the German government's contribution to female-employment growth appears enormous. The high ratio (149), however, emerges because the government has offset what might otherwise have been a very different significant drop in female employment.

The nexus of government and services has been decisive for women's employment-opportunities over the past two decades. But it differs from country to country. Sweden constitutes one extreme, in which social-welfare services in the public sector dominated everything; in-

TABLE 8.3   The impact of government on employment growth (percentages)

	Germany		Sweden		United States	
	1961	1983	1965	1985	1962	1985
Government employment as % of total	8.0	16.1	18.2	33.0	17.2	15.8
Government share of employed women	7.2	19.8	29.8	55.2	15.5	17.7
Women's share of public employment	39.1	39.4	52.2	67.1	35.6	46.6
	1961–83		*1965–85*		*1962–85*	
Government's share of net total female-job growth	149		106		20	
Government's share of net total service-job growth	65		82		23	

Sources: WEEP data files; and *IAB*; *Beitrag AB 2.1*

deed, women account for 87 percent of total health–education–welfare employment growth in Sweden! The result has been a unique feminization of the welfare state.

In the German nexus the social-welfare component of post-industrialism hardly grew, allowing only a modest level of welfare-state absorption of women workers. Combined with a decline of women's jobs in the private sector, the result is stagnant participation rates for women over the entire period. The German state remains a male domain, and the women stay at home.

In the American nexus, government is a passive force in both women's employment and post-industrial development. The American example suggests that the market is also capable of promoting women's employment. Unlike in Sweden, American women have moved into a much broader menu of employment niches. Besides health and social-service jobs, business services have been the fastest growing sector of female entry.

THE NEW MANAGERIAL REVOLUTION

We now finally arrive at our third question; namely, what accounts for the peculiar managerial bias in the United States? It has often been observed that the American economy is 'overmanaged' (Melman, 1951; Chandler and Deams, 1980; Bowles and Gintis, 1986; Black and Myles, 1986); while corporate management growth seems to stagnate in other countries, it continues unabated in the United States. Many explanations for this phenomenon have been offered, ranging from Parkinson's law and technological imperatives to a Marxist emphasis on workforce control. The problem with all these theories is that bureaucracy, technology, and class struggle should obtain equally in other advanced economies.

One alternative explanation is purely classificatory, in the sense that Americans harbor a unique disposition to grant even low-grade supervisors a managerial label. While this is true, our data presentation has sought to exclude this spurious fact. We propose, instead, an alternative hypothesis.

The starting point is that the United States lacks three features common to European economies. First, its welfare state is under-developed and, as a result, fringe benefits come to figure importantly in collective bargaining and employer obligations. This calls for managers. Second, industrial relations tend to be combative, and American unions cannot, as in 'neo-corporatist' settings, be counted on to police the rank and file. Thus, the American firm is obliged to exercise control with the aid of armies of supervisory staff. And, third, the American labor market is huge, complex, and lacks both a system of labor exchanges and worker-training institutions. Hence, the corporations need talent scouts, educators, and very large personnel departments.

The managerial manpower that a 'welfare-state' vacuum requires in the American firm can be internalized, or it can be purchased in the service sector; in the latter case, we have given it the name of business services. If our hypotheses are correct, we have an explanation for why both managerial work as an occupation, and business services as an industry, grow so explosively in the United States. The same hypotheses would predict that the highly welfare-statist and 'neo-corporativist' Swedish system should require unusually few managers.

Post-Industrial Structures

What are the structural results of the employment trends we have observed? To answer this question, we will continue to examine both 'industries' and occupations, using our rough classification of traditional industrial and post-industrial activities.

POST-INDUSTRIAL STRUCTURE BY INDUSTRIAL BRANCHES

In table 8.4 we find three unique 'industry-based' employment structures. Again, Germany is post-industrially very under-developed, especially with regard to its social-service-related activities. It is an economy

TABLE 8.4 Employment structure in the mid-1980s: % of labor force by industry

Industry groups	Germany 1984	Sweden 1985	United States 1984
Industrial activity			
Industry	41.8	28.8	25.1
Agriculture	5.1	4.9	3.1
Subtotal	46.9	33.7	28.2
Neutral activity			
Distribution	17.6	18.8	21.4
Government	10.0	7.1	8.0
Personal services	3.3	1.7	2.9
Subtotal	30.9	27.6	32.3
Post-industrial activity			
Health, education, and social services	11.5	25.3	17.9
Producer services	6.7	6.4	12.3
'Fun' services	4.1	3.9	7.9
Subtotal	21.3	35.6	38.1

The figures will not add up to 100 due to the omission of marginal groups of activities (domestic service in particular).
Source: SSIB data files

still dominated by traditional industrial work and, indeed, remains more 'industrial' than was either Sweden or the United States 25 years ago.

In Germany, overall employment has declined, but the share of manufacturing employment in relation to the total has remained constant since 1960. Germany's march into 'post-industrial' society seems therefore to lead to mass idleness more than to new kinds of jobs. The growing 'surplus population' is absorbed by the welfare state as pensioners or students, or by the family as housewives. The United States and Sweden are equally de-industrialized, but this is where the parallel stops. Sweden's post-industrialism lies in the welfare-state edifice. The Swedes are great consumers of health care, schools, and day care, but not of food, wine, and 'fun'. The American post-industrial profile is primarily very business-oriented; it is surprisingly stronger than Germany on the social-services dimension; and it is unusually 'fun'-oriented.

Summing up the basic national differences, we can say that Germany's traditional industrial dominance is about twice that of the others; the Swedish social-welfare bias is similarly almost twice that of the others; and in the United States, producer services and 'fun' services are twice as large as elsewhere.

THE POST-INDUSTRIAL OCCUPATIONAL STRUCTURE

In terms of analyzing occupational structure, our approach will differ a little from our earlier one. In table 8.5, we present the relative size of select occupational groups in the economy. Then, in table 8.6, we try to assess the degree to which different industries are dominated by intellectual scientific, and organizational work. For this purpose, we combine managerial and administrative with professional and technological occupations in an overall 'MPT score'. There is a close fit between occupational and industrial structure. In Germany, the traditional industrial blue-collar worker continues to reign supreme; both social-welfare occupations and other service-worker jobs are vastly underdeveloped. As we anticipated, Sweden is the least 'managed' economy. It is, instead, dominated by post-industrial occupations that are heavily welfare-statist and have a surprisingly high professional content. Outside the social-welfare complex, service jobs are underdeveloped. For the United States, table 8.5 reaffirms the over-management phenomenon. In the 'post-industrial' complex, the 'junk-job' occupations (cleaning workers, waiters, kitchen workers, and the like) and other personal-service jobs are extraordinarily large.

TABLE 8.5   The relative size of selected occupational groups (percentage)

Occupations	Germany 1985	Sweden 1984	United States 1986
Managers	5.7	2.4	11.5
Professionals and technicians, less nurses and teachers	9.8	13.4	9.7
Nurses, social service workers, and teachers	7.0	21.9	9.6
'Junk-jobs': food, cleaning, and waiting	5.0	4.4	7.8
Other service-sector workers[a]	3.8	3.8	15.7
Industrial production workers	43.9	29.4	30.5

[a] Excludes domestic servants.
For comparability, we have applied a modified ISCO-based classification system to the occupational titles of each country. The table excludes a number of occupational groups (such as farmers, clerical workers, or transport workers) whose role in this analysis is marginal.
Source: For Germany, *Berufsausbildung und Arbeitsbedingungen der Erwerbstatigen. Fachserie* 1, 1985. For Sweden, *AKU* raw tables for 1984; for the United States, Department of Labor, *Employment and Earnings* (January, 1987)

TABLE 8.6　The dominance of managerial, professional, and technical workers in selected industries, 1980s

Combined managers/ professionals/technicians ratio	Germany	Sweden	United States
Industry	12.0	17.0	14.0
Distribution	8.0	8.0	14.0
Social services	59.0	62.0	39.0
Business services	44.0	44.0	31.0
'Fun' services	N.A.	18.0	11.0
Whole economy	20.2	30.1	28.0

Sources: For Germany, *Berufsausbildung und Arbeitsbedingungen der Erwerbstatigen. Fachserie* 1, 1985. For Sweden, *AKU* raw tables for 1984; for the United States, Department of Labor, *Employment and Earnings* (January, 1987). Note, however, that the item of service workers in industry is based on OECD definitions and is from OECD *Employment Outlook* (1984).

When we turn to table 8.6, we discover that the managerial–professional–technical (MPT) influence is substantially higher in our post-industrial industries. This was to be expected. But, we note sharp national differences. Economy-wide, Germany is a laggard and Sweden a vanguard. The United States has the least professionalized post-industrial economy.

Social Stratification in Three Post-Industrial Economies

In the early post-industrial literature, the future of work was depicted in terms of high-quality jobs. Thus, Bell's (1973) scenario focused on scientific, information-processing, and analytic work. In contrast, many claim that the trend in service employment is consistent with Braverman's (1974) thesis of de-skilling and proletarianization. Kuttner (1983) and Bluestone and Harrison (1986) argue that most new jobs are low-wage, low-skill, and low-quality. Since de-industrialization simultaneously sheds many traditionally well-paid, skilled jobs, the net result is a new class polarization: the middle has shrunk, and a new, numerically small professional managerial elite confronts a mass of 'MacDonalds' workers.

The declining-middle thesis has been questioned. Lawrence (1985) argues, for example, that the facts may be correct, but that the reason is mainly that the large baby-boom generation temporarily flooded the labor market. Myles *et al.* (1988) have recently tested the argument against Canadian data, and suggest that the middle is expanding, not contracting. This fits with Bell's much rosier portrait of post-industrial society.

Comparative analyses of the question have hardly begun. What we have are theoretical generalizations based on, essentially, one case. Also, almost all studies on the 'declining'middle' issue have been based on earnings data. In this chapter, our approach is to examine post-industrial stratification with empolyment data, stressing the importance of the generic quality of jobs. Hence, our focus is on occupations.

THE QUALITY STRUCTURE OF POST-INDUSTRIAL EMPLOYMENT

We can identify a mix of 'good' and 'bad' post-industrial jobs in each of our three trajectories. The good jobs include managerial, professional, scientific, and technical occupations – those with a high content of human capital. The bad jobs, in turn, include menial and routine jobs.

Table 8.7 shows the distribution of good and bad jobs by occupation for the 1980s. We compare professional-technical workers with a middle group of service workers, and with a 'bad' category of food, cleaning, and lodging workers. The middle category consists of non-professional health and social-sector workers (such as nursing assistants) and personal-service workers (such as hairdressers, security personnel, and photographers). Domestic servants have been omitted entirely.

Table 8.7 reveals three distinctive quality-mixes. Germany's is compressed in the middle and the top; Sweden's accentuates the good post-industrial occupations; and the United States's mix emphasizes the middle and bottom, but with a respectable performance also among the good jobs.

TABLE 8.7   The quality-mix among post-industrial occupations

Occupations	Germany	Sweden	United States
Professionals, teachers, and technicians ('good')	14.6	21.0	16.5
Social, health, and personal-service workers ('middle')	6.0	11.3	18.5
Food, cleaning, and lodging workers ('bad')	5.0	4.4	7.8
Good/middle ratio	2.4:1	1.9:1	0.9:1
Good/bad ratio	2.9:1	4.8:1	2.1:1

Sources: For Germany: *Mikrocensus* for 1985, from *IAB, Beruf und Ausbildung*; for Sweden: 1980 Census; for the United States, Department of Labor, *Employment and Earnings* (January, 1987) (data for 1985)

These data are too rough for a real empirical confrontation with the 'declining-middle' debate, but they suggest that national variations are tremendous, and that a generalization from the American experience is unwarranted. If America's large 'junk-job' component supports a proletarianization thesis, other factors point in the opposite direction. First, over the long haul, professional jobs grew faster than bad jobs in the United States. Second, the middle group of service jobs is much weightier than the bottom group. And, finally, the Swedish experience shows that post-industrialization can be very strongly biased in favor of professionals.

What really matters for an assessment of post-industrial stratification is how the good and bad jobs are filled. The question is whether the process of job attainment is more open, meritocratic, and democratic.

Our approach to this question will focus on a limited, yet decisive, facet of openness, namely, the relative opportunities for traditionally disadvantaged labor-market groups to fill the various post-industrial jobs. We will here focus on women in all three nations, and, in addition, on Blacks and Hispanics in the United States.

Occupational mobility in three post-industrial regimes

There is a vast literature on occupational segregation that we cannot review here. The main issue, of course, has been whether disadvantaged groups' opportunities to enter attractive jobs have improved, or whether job segmentation has been sustained.

By and large, the literature finds support for the job-segregation argument (Hakim, 1979; Rosenfeld, 1980; Cromton, 1986; Goldin, 1987; Jacobs and Breiger, forthcoming). And where, for example, sexual equality seems to exist in terms of formal job definitions, micro-level studies at the level of the firm suggest that behind similar occupational labels hides a powerful internal career-segmentation (Bielby and Baron, 1986). Our analyses will focus broadly on those who fill the post-industrial jobs. Our findings are therefore unlikely to be very comparable with those of other studies.

There are numerous ways of studying occupational segregation. We shall first trace changes over time in the over- or under-representation of women, Blacks, and Hispanics among select attractive and unattractive occupations. In order better to identify gender segregation, we extract teachers and nurses from the professional-technical occupations because these are the archetypical traditional female ghettos.

Our subsequent analyses will assess how women and minorities have fared in the distribution of jobs. Here, we will be especially attentive to

TABLE 8.8   Women's over- or under-representation in traditional and in post-industrial occupations, 1960–1985 (percentage points)

Occupations	Germany		Sweden		United States	
	1961	1985	1965	1984	1960	1986
Industrial economy						
Managers	−22	−21	−24	−26	−19	− 8
Clerical workers	+23	+25	+28	+20	+24	+33
Industrial workers	−16	−31	−18	−28	−11	−24
Post-industrial economy						
Professionals/technical workers[a]	−18	−12	−23	−20	−14	− 6
Nurses and teachers	+29	+29	+40	+34	+46	+36
Non-professional service workers	+23	+37	+37	+28	+ 6	+ 7
'Junk-job' workers	+49	+48	+42	+21	+38	+13

[a] Excludes nurses and non-university teachers.
Sources: For Germany, Berufsausbildung und Arbeitsbedingungen der Erwerbstatigen. Fachserie 1, 1985. For Sweden, AKU raw tables for 1984; for the United States, Department of Labor, Employment and Earnings (January, 1987)

the degree to which women, Blacks, or Hispanics have succeeded in penetrating traditional (white) male employment-niches (such as managerial and executive positions), and the extent to which they remain concentrated in unattractive or traditionally female occupations.

In table 8.8, we present an index of women's degree of over- or under-representation within select occupations. A minus-sign indicates under-representation. The index measures the number of deviation points above or below parity, adjusted for the relative proportion of women in employment. With a few exceptions, there is a decline of gender-based occupational segregation. Women have been quite successful in entering privileged 'male' jobs, such as management and the professions; their over-representation in the female-ghetto jobs has lessened, as has their over-representation within the 'junk-jobs'.

The single most dramatic trend is women's departure from industrial-worker jobs. This may be interpreted in two ways: 1) de-industrialization has been especially sweeping within the conventional 'female' industries, such as textiles; 2) having less seniority and weaker job-attachments, women may have been made to bear the brunt of industrial redundancy. Whichever is the case, the net result is that women are much more likely to be found within the post-industrial sector.

The trend towards de-segregation is weakest in Germany, since only in the professional category have women made any significant inroads. German women are exceptionally over-represented in the 'junk-job' group. Swedish women, in turn, have experienced a significant degree of occupational upgrading, but are simultaneously being segregated. They have failed to enter into management, and concentrate heavily in the helping professions of the social-welfare complex. Sweden appears more gender-biased than do the other countries. Sexual de-segregation is strongest in the United States. Women have made great strides in the managerial and professional jobs, and the female bias in the 'junk-job' group has fallen sharply. However, these relative improvements are counterbalanced by a marked increase in clerical work over-representation.

In a sense, the employment fate of ethnic and racial minorities constitutes a more decisive test of post-industrialism's egalitarianism. For Europe and the United States, it has become common wisdom that foreign workers and minority groups, in that order, fill the bottom end of the labor market. In fact, there are two possible scenarios of minority-group job entrapment: one is that they may fill the old unpleasant industrial jobs and thus find themselves barred from the post-industrial economy; the other, that they may constitute the reserve army for the post-industrial 'junk-jobs'.

Detailed data on foreign workers in Sweden and Germany are not available, and we must therefore limit our study to the fate of Blacks and Hispanics in the United States. Due to lack of earlier data, our analysis for the two groups can begin only with 1970. To make the index-measures comparable with previous tables, the indices for Blacks and Hispanics have been weighted to adjust for their share in the labor-force relative to women.

Table 8.9 presents a mixed picture with respect to the reserve-army thesis for minorities. Blacks and Hispanics are vastly over-represented in both the traditional industrial-worker jobs, and in the post-industrial 'junk-jobs'. We notice that, while the 'junk-job' over-representation has declined for Blacks and women, it has risen among Hispanics. The Hispanic population appears to be the new labor-reserve to fill the low-wage jobs in the 'fun' industries.

Despite their clear segregation into both traditional and post-industrial bottom-level jobs, Blacks are nonetheless experiencing a noticeable occupational de-segregation. They have made considerable inroads in the most attractive occupations: in managerial-executive jobs, in post-industrial professions, and most decisively, in the 'welfare para-professions'. Their under-representation in the good jobs has decreased and their over-representation in 'junk-jobs' has declined.

TABLE 8.9   The degree of over- and under-representation of Blacks and Hispanics in selected occupations in the United States (percentage points)

	Blacks		Hispanics	
Occupation	1970	1986	1970	1986
Managers	−27	−21	−17	−19
Clerical workers	−10	+1	−8	+5
Industrial workers	+17	+15	+21	+21
Professionals and technical workers[a]	−20	−14	−15	−19
Nurses and teachers	−3	+12	−18	−18
Non-professional service workers	+10	+20	+1	+11
'Junk-job' workers	+31	+28	+15	+24

The data for Blacks and Hispanics have been weighted to take into account their relative share in the labor market. By adjusting for their share, relative to women, we have sought to make the indices fully comparable between women, Blacks, and Hispanics. The weights used are the following: Blacks (1970): 3.4; Blacks (1986) 4.5; Hispanics (1970): 8.6; Hispanics (1986): 6.7.

[a] Excludes nurses and teachers.

Sources: For Germany, *Berufsausbildung und Arbeitsbedingungen der Erwerbstatigen. Fachserie* 1, 1985. For Sweden, *AKU* raw tables for 1984; for the United States, Department of Labor, *Employment and Earnings* (January, 1987)

Social, and other (non-junk) services are the main avenues for Black upward mobility.

The Hispanic group has fared less well. Its confinement to 'junk-jobs' has increased; its capacity to attain attractive managerial, executive, and professional jobs has actually worsened; its main road to occupational upgrading lies in clerical and non-welfare service occupations.

Still, the passage of time favors Blacks, Hispanics, and especially women. The long-term growth rates suggest that women outpace Blacks and Hispanics in the race for good jobs, but that all three groups are gaining much faster than males in general. The annual percentage of growth into managerial positions is 17 percent for Blacks and Hispanics, 18 percent for women, but only 3 percent for men. Turning to professional jobs (excluding nursing and teaching), the corresponding percentages are 8 percent for Blacks, 9 percent for Hispanics, 13 percent for women, and only 2.5 percent for men.

Our final examination of post-industrial stratification will focus on two issues: first, the extent to which women succeed in overcoming the traditional gender-barriers in the occupational structure; second, how groups are divided between good- and bad-quality jobs. In table 8.10, we present data for the three countries on the change in the percentage of women workers in 'female' and 'male' jobs. Table 8.10 conveys a

TABLE 8.10   The distribution of women workers in typically 'male' and 'female' jobs (percentages)

Women workers	Germany		Sweden		United States	
	1961	1985	1965	1984	1960	1986
In selected 'female' jobs						
Clerical workers	24	28	37	30	38	38
Nurses and teachers	4	8	13	25	9	12
Total	28	36	50	55	47	50
In selected 'male' jobs						
Managers	1.0	4.0	0.7	1.1	3.7	9.6
Professional, technical[a]	2.5	6.7	3.2	7.8	4.4	8.5
Total	3.5	10.7	3.9	8.9	8.1	18.1

[a] Excludes nurses and teachers.
Sources   For Germany, *Berufsausbildung und Arbeitsbedingungen der Erwerbstatigen. Fachserie* 1, 1985. For Sweden, *AKU* raw tables for 1984; for the United States, Department of Labor, *Employment and Earnings* (January, 1987)

double message. Women are, at once, becoming increasingly concentrated in female jobs (clerical, nursing, and teaching) and also gaining ground in the conventional male occupations.

Again, Sweden emerges as the most gender-segregated among the three countries. More than half of the women are locked into typical female jobs, while very few women have penetrated the sanctuaries of male dominance. Post-industrialization in Sweden only augments the sex-segregation problem. Germany, in contrast, may be less segregated, but here we should remember that women are exceptionally concentrated at the lower end of personal and 'junk'-services. And again, the United States proves itself capable of diminished gender-segregation. Although there is a small increase in 'female' job concentration, women are also marching into traditional male jobs. The share of women in privileged 'male' occupations is basically twice that of Germany and Sweden.

In tables 8.11 and 8.12, we complete our analysis with a comparison of the good- and bad-job distribution between groups. If you will, the tables can be read as a rough index of class structuration within labor-market groups. We follow our custom and present comparisons for traditional and post-industrial occupations. For reasons of space, we present the American data separately in table 8.12.

The data leave little doubt that a pervasive occupation upgrading has

TABLE 8.11   The ratio of good/bad occupations for men and women in Germany and Sweden

| | Germany | | | | Sweden | | | |
| | Men | | Women | | Men | | Women | |
	1960	1985	1960	1985	1965	1984	1965	1984
Ratio of clerical and industrial workers to managers	17:1	7:1	44:1	7:1	30:1	18:1	99:1	40:1
Ratio of professional jobs to 'junk-jobs'	10:1	17:1	1:3	1:1	5:1	5:1	1:4	1:1

Sources: For Germany, *Berufsausbildung und Arbeitsbedingungen der Erwerbstatigen. Fachserie* 1, 1985. For Sweden, *AKU* raw tables for 1984; for the United States, Department of Labor, *Employment and Earnings* (January, 1987)

TABLE 8.12   The ratio of good/bad occupations among men, women, Blacks, and Hispanics in the United States

| | All men | | All women | | Blacks | | Hispanics | |
	1960	1986	1960	1986	1970	1986	1970	1986
Managers as % of industrial and clerical workers	22.1	20.5	5.5	12.5	4.8	6.6	7.7	7.6
Professional jobs as % of 'junk-jobs'	565	242	55	126	37	74	63	66

Sources: For Germany, *Berufsausbildung und Arbeitsbedingungen der Erwerbstatigen. Fachserie* 1, 1985. For Sweden, *AKU* raw tables for 1984; for the United States, Department of Labor, *Employment and Earnings* (January, 1987)

occurred over the past decades. In the traditional industrial economy, the managerial-worker/clerical ratio has jumped, especially in Germany and for women in both Germany and Sweden. Here we must of course remember the sharp fall in female industrial-worker employment. Sweden's unimpressive showing has less to do with the decline in manual or clerical workers than with the tiny and stagnant cadre of management. While the post-industrial economy is much more equally distributed between 'good' and 'bad' jobs, its evolution is less favorable for women; in both Germany and Sweden, the ratio of professionals to 'junk-jobs' has deteriorated.

For the United States, shown in table 8.12, the story is fairly similar. Aside from the problem that the American managerial category may be bloated in comparison to that in Europe, the trend is in favor of occupational upgrading. In the manager–worker confrontation, women's position has improved considerably; for Blacks and Hispanics, this is less so. The same goes for the professional/'junk-job' ratio. That there are signficant 'democratizing' forces at play in the American labor market is shown not just by the improvements for minority groups, but also by the radical deterioration in traditional male job-privileges.

We have now waded through mountains of data on the growth, structure, and stratification-profiles of three nations on the road to post-industrial society. Before we draw larger analytic conclusions, it may be worthwhile to briefly summarize the main results.

We are witnessing three divergent paths to post-industrial employment: each country is nested in its own peculiar dynamic of development. There are, to be sure, certain basic parallels: industrial employment is losing its prominence; distributive services are generally stagnant; women's employment chances have improved. Yet, the variations overshadow convergence.

The German trajectory is, perhaps, the oddest. Services and post-industrial occupations are not booming as they are elsewhere. Instead, there is a decline in employment as such, and Germany remains a largely traditional industrial society with a relatively under-developed private- and public-service sector. Neither is the occupational structure being upgraded and professionalized as elsewhere.

The outcome, from the point of view of social stratification, is mixed. Being post-industrially blocked has also meant that Germany barely engenders growth in the new 'junk-jobs'. This results in a less polarized, or dualistic, structure. On the other hand, within the structure that exists, the job distribution is quite gender-segregated. Comparatively speaking, women have not done very well. With a stagnant labor market, women's employment has been unable to grow except for a modest increase in the public sector. Neither has Germany been able to redistribute the stock of jobs much more fairly between the sexes. Hence, with no major growth in the social services, we find that the state remains decidely masculine. German women are more than two or three times over-represented in the 'junk-jobs' relative to their representation elsewhere.

The main prognosis for the German trajectory then, is that Germany will remain predominantly an industrial economy, but with diminishing numbers of people involved in production, and an ever-increasing population of housewives, the young, and the elderly excluded from employment and dependent on the welfare state. Germany approximates Kurt Vonnegut's workless world.

In Sweden, post-industrialization has been paved with social-welfare services. The welfare state has been extraordinarily dynamic, notwithstanding sluggish economic growth. But its bias is a very one-sided female one. The public sector accounted for 80 percent of new jobs; 75 percent of these were female. The welfare-state services have, in turn, marginalized the scope for private-sector services, especially in the area of personal and 'fun' services.

The outcome is an economy with a high degree of professionalism and very few 'junk-jobs'. But again, it is a professionalism weighted by largely para-professional jobs in the health, social, and education establishments. By most conventional criteria, the Swedish women have done exceedingly well, but at the price of an unusually strong sectoral-occupational segregation. In fact, the Swedish employment-structure is evolving towards two economies: one, a heavily male private sector; the other, a female-dominated public sector.

The American trajectory looks like the product of 'unfettered' markets. Overall job expansion has been impressive, even in the traditional economy. A first important conclusion thus presents itself: post-industrial growth may very well go hand in hand with a growth in the conventional economy. The United States has also been capable of job expansion along a very broad front. The American case shows that social services can expand without public provision. Moreover, the dynamic is considerably more benign than most believe: good jobs have clearly outpaced the bad ones in the American 'job machine'.

Nonetheless, the American trajectory harbors its own biased develop-ment. It is at once overpoweringly biased towards business and towards 'fun' services, giving rise to a duality with large quantities of good and bad jobs. The good jobs are heavily managerial, and the 'junk-job' sector is enormous.

The merging stratification-system appears dualistic, with a solid top and a large, precarious bottom. Hence, there is at least a superficial resemblance to the dualisms that marked traditional industrial job-distribution, with women and Blacks confined to the 'junk-jobs', and white males monopolizing the managerial and professional posts. Yet this is where the American post-industrial trajectory surprises.

It is true that women, Blacks, and Hispanics remain heavily over-represented in the less desirable jobs, but it is also true that this is gradually being undone – in some cases, dramatically so. Women have done best, and are today hardly under-represented at all among the managerial and professional occupations – although much greater detail would surely show that within these, women are overwhelmingly relegated to the less desirable and more 'feminine' slots. For minority groups, and especially Blacks, the American trajectory has not been unfavorable. The growth trend for Blacks and Hispanics into good jobs is very favorable. The degree of Black and Hispanic over-representation in the 'junk-jobs' is, today, not greater than it was for women in Germany and Sweden in the 1960s.

The evidence, then, suggests that the American 'market model' of post-industrialization can also be egalitarian in its employment distribution: both the good jobs and the 'junk-jobs' are being assigned more democratically. In spite of some movement into 'good jobs', Hispanics are increasingly filling the unpleasant jobs being vacated by women and Blacks.

It seems implausible that these differences in post-industrial performance are attributable solely to economic or technological forces. Our three countries are more similar than diverse with regard to economic development, national wealth, and the application of high technologies in both the economy and in the household.

There are features in their international position which can provide partial explanations of the trajectories. Sweden, and especially Germany, are exceptionally large importers of some labor-intensive services. Germans and Swedes are probably more likely to be tourists abroad than at home, and this affects negatively the size of their 'fun' industries. For Germany, we must also consider the peculiarity of its industrial dominance: comparatively, its trimmed-down, technologically advanced manufacturing has remained extraordinarily competitive in world markets.

These are ad hoc explanations that highlight structural peculiarities in each of the countries, and they may have a significant bearing on employment trends. Yet they will clearly not suffice as general comparative explanations.

Baumol's model offers one such general theory. The bottom line of the thesis is that services will fail to grow if wages are too high. This argument has considerable immediate appeal. The American job explosion may have something to do with a more flexible wage-structure and very little unionization in the private service economy. Germany, and especially Sweden, are renowned for their strong trade-union penetration in the economy. Sweden's solidarity-based wage-bargaining system would, in fact, preclude service-job growth on the basis of low wages.

However, formulated in this way, the Baumol model runs into difficulties. Beginning with the American experience, it is impossible that more than a margin of the new jobs are caused by low wages. A conservative estimate would put it equal to the 8 percent 'junk-jobs'; a liberal one might include other personal-services jobs, thus arriving at a maximum total of perhaps 17 percent of jobs. A far superior estimation-approach is to compute the employment elasticities of wage-costs by detailed industries over time. For the United States, 1951–84, we find indeed that it is really only among 'junk-jobs' that employment growth depends on low relative wages. The Baumol model obviously cannot explain the huge growth of producer and health services.

The Baumol model also has difficulties with a German–Swedish comparison. In terms of total 'post-industrial' employment growth. Sweden equalled the United States with 6.7 percent per annum, twice the German rate. The explosion of professional and social-welfare jobs in Sweden is not the result of low wages, but rather of high taxes.

The point is that it may be that even the lion's share of post-industrial jobs addresses a demand which is not very price-elastic. Business services, such as engineering and design, management consulting, financial management, and legal advice are sought for their specialized skills; the same goes for most professional and para-professional social services, such as health care.

In other words, we must account for a greater complexity than most theories are equipped for, and it is here that our typology of welfare-states becomes crucial.

Conclusion

Welfare-State Regimes in the Post-Industrial Structure

We have seen how contemporary welfare states cluster into three distinct regime-types, and we have illustrated how different nations' labor markets derive much of their logic from how they are embedded in the institutional framework of social policy. Our study has clearly ignored many crucial policy arenas and institutional aspects of modern industrialized capitalist societies. Yet, on key issues such as social stratification, social rights ('freedom', if you like), the distribution of resources, working life, and the evolution of employment, the evidence seems clear enough to conclude that three models of welfare capitalism have evolved.

In this, the concluding chapter, we shall not tax the reader's patience with a review of the evidence presented earlier. We shall, indeed, concentrate on the argument that welfare-state and employment regimes not only coincide, but that welfare states indeed have a direct causal impact on how employment-structures and, as a result, new axes of social conflict, evolve. We return therefore to a key thesis in this book: the contemporary welfare state is not merely a passive by-product of industrial development. With its institutionalization, it becomes a powerful societal mechanism which decisively shapes the future. We shall therefore explore the degree to which the diversity of 'post-industrial' evolution can be explained by the character of our welfare-state regimes.

It will be clear that our argument is directed against most of the prevailing theoretical paradigms of social science. Be it in Marxism or the developmentalist modernization school, the notion has always been that principally economic forces are what propel societal change. Orthodox and even a good deal of revisionist Marxism is incapable of viewing the state as more than an appended superstructure to the engine of capitalist production. Modernization theory is often captive to the liberal myth that the modern industrial revolution occurred autonomously from state intervention and, indeed, required its absence. Here, it is technology which is the driving force.

Our theoretical heritage emerged in an epoch in which the state was visible primarily in its capacity to conduct war and police the populace. This was also an epoch in which social and economic progress, liberty, and modernity were associated with the dismantling of the absolutist, interventionist, and authoritarian state. It is therefore perfectly reasonable that the leading theoretical paradigms of our discipline saw little relevance of the state in their analyses of economic development.

Ours is an epoch in which it is almost universally agreed that a profound realignment, if not revolution, is underway in our economy and society. The proliferation of labels, such as 'post-modernist', 'post-materialist', 'post-fordist' or 'post-industrial', often substitutes for analysis. But it mirrors the recognition that we are leaving behind us a social order that was pretty much understood, and entering another the contours of which can be only dimly recognized. It is into this mine-field that our analysis now ventures. I do not pretend to offer a theory of the future. The sole ambition is to take the trends that we have empirically delineated in the previous chapters, and suggest that welfare state regime-types offer a fruitful starting point for explaining why we are heading towards divergent trajectories in employment and social stratification and, in the last analysis, towards new conflict-scenarios.

A comparison of 'post-industrial' employment evolution in Sweden, Germany, and the United States is an especially fruitful approach to the identification of welfare-state-regime effects; each country stands as an 'ideal-typical' representative of the socialist, conservative, and liberal regime-type, respectively.

The Welfare State in Post-Industrial Employment

To briefly recall the principal contours of the three employment trajectories, Sweden has produced a social-welfare led post-industrial employment structure; the United States, a dual one of business-services and 'fun', with largely good jobs in the former, and bad jobs in the latter; in Germany, nothing much in the way of 'post-industrial' change has happened.

To account for Sweden, we need to apply little more than a mix of the Baumol model and our knowledge of the Swedish welfare state. As noted, the rigorous application of the solidarity-wage policy over the past decades would have pretty much precluded a growth of 'junk-jobs', except perhaps in the black economy. Swedish de-industrialization, coupled with a rather mediocre rate of economic growth, would then have created severe employment problems had it not been for the welfare state's commitment to three interlocked principles: 1) the improvement and expansion of social, health, and educational services; 2) maximum employment-participation, especially for women; and 3) sustained full employment. The three are united in the welfare-state model of social democracy.

The coincidence of female and social-service employment-growth in the Swedish public sector may appear as a last-ditch effort to meet women's demand for work, and part of the obligation to maintain full employment. Yet this cannot be the case, since the welfare state's service expansion began in the mid-1960s, many years before the fear of unemployment surfaced. Nonetheless, on both the supply and demand side, the logic of the Swedish welfare state is such that it will produce a female-biased social-service explosion. On the supply-side, it provides services, like day care, which women need in order to work and which, coincidentally, provide women's jobs. It also provides flexible working hours and part-time opportunities for working mothers. Moreover, the welfare state's transfers (in particular pensions) and taxes provide irresistible incentives for women to work. Even a part-time job suffices to qualify for earnings-related pensions; high marginal taxes on households mean that two earners are needed to achieve a high living standard.

On the demand side, the Swedish welfare state is one that almost inevitably would produce the peculiar post-industrial outcome we find. As we have noted, its future depends on middle-class support which, in turn, requires expanding and improving the quality and quantity of services. Its financial underpinnings, moreover, depend on maximizing the tax-base, meaning that most people must work and as few as possible depend on benefits. In this nexus, it is obvious that Sweden will refrain from the early-retirement option pursued in Europe, and that, instead, it will optimize employment opportunities even if, as we have seen, the risk is major imbalances in the economy, and serious public indebtedness.

Still, the cost-disease problem cannot be avoided even when the welfare state subsidizes service-employment growth, Expanding public employment to more than 30 percent of total employment, even if much of it is part-time work, will eventually be stalled by tax-ceilings. Hence, government must count on wage restraint. And this, as we have seen, is the Achilles' heel of the Swedish model.

In Germany, too, wage policies (with very high fixed-labor costs) prohibit a low-wage, 'junk-job' trajectory. The German welfare state, however, is institutionally unequipped to act as a compensatory operator of employment. It is, in fact, powerfully biased towards reducing labor supply. On the supply-side, it is a welfare state built on the traditionalist conservative and Catholic principle of subsidiarity, meaning that women and social services (outside health) belong to the domain of the family. Hence, it has been very reluctant to provide the kinds of services which permit women to take employment, and which, in the end, provide them with a job-market. But, it is also a welfare state powerfully dedicated to income maintenance for those who have 'earned' it. However, German eligibility-conditions are comparatively strict, and to earn benefits requires a long work-career, a serious disadvantage for many women. But in response to de-industrialization and slack labor markets, early retirement could serve as the major, and often sole, alternative available to older males in dying industries.

On the demand side, therefore, there has been little will to escalate public services. But, even if a positive policy were to prevail (as it did during the social democratic interlude in the late 1960s and early 1970s), the scope for public-employment growth remains limited. For one thing, the extraordinarily high transfer-burden constrains additional revenue increases (Sharpf, 1985). In addition, the consistently tight fiscal and monetary policy-regime pursued by German authorities precludes expansion in the public as well as in the private sector (Bruno and Sachs, 1985; Blanchard et al., 1986).

In the German regime, then, the decks are stacked against service-employment growth, but in favor of diminished work. And where the Swedish system is dependent on a maximum of participation, the German must put its faith in the capacity of a high-productivity industrial economy to finance the burden of maintaining a growing population of pensioners and non-actives. It is the impending cost-crisis of this economic 'surplus' population which constitutes the Achilles' heel of the German trajectory.

In the United States, there are a number of general conditions that clearly will affect aggregate demand and supply of labor. First, economic policy has been unusually expansionary, mainly in the 1960s and 1980s. Second, being a much more protected domestic market, it was not until recently that the United States had to fear serious foreign competition. Third, America's demography affects both supply and demand; the former mainly through substantial population growth; the latter through a comparatively belated, but nonetheless rapid population-ageing. While such factors will influence aggregate job-growth, they are less likely to explain the peculiar structural features in the American trajectory.

A welfare-state-based explanation would appear at odds with the American market-powered trajectory, yet many of its peculiarities are directly associated with welfare-state residualism. However, to begin sorting out the forces behind the American evolution, we need first to have a clear picture of its components. Of all new jobs created, the 'fun' services account for only 16 percent, compared to 23 percent for business/producer services, and a full 30 percent for social and educational services. If, instead, we count occupations, we find that 'junk-jobs' account for only 12 percent of total growth, compared to 24 percent for professional-technical jobs.

Baumol's cost-disease argument may very well apply to most of the 'fun' sector and all of the 'junk-jobs', and perhaps even a little beyond. This is consistent with the data of Bluestone and Harrison (1986). But, as we have noted, wages cannot explain the even more impressive performance among social and business services. Many of the social services, education in particular, have been spurred by the public sector. Ironically, public-sector social-welfare employment was greater in the United States than in Sweden until the late 1960s (Cusack and Rein, 1987).

The private sector has nurtured an enormous, high-quality job-growth in the social services and in producer services. However, we must seriously question the 'privateness' of the market: it is here that the unique interplay of private and public in the American system becomes important.

Beginning with managerial and business service jobs, we may recall our hypothesis that much of what in Europe forms part of the welfare-state complex is, in the United States, internalized in the business enterprise itself. This affects in particular personnel- and fringe-benefit-management. There are two facets of the American welfare state which propel this kind of managerialism. First, the lacunae of adequate benefits and services means that they become targets of wage bargaining. Second, the tax-expenditure side of the American welfare state encourages companies to offer fringe benefits instead of direct wages. The net result is that American companies are saddled with substantial non-legislated indirect wage-costs.

The employment result ought to be that much of Europe's welfare-state personnel are, in the United States, managers or in business services. There are, for example, more than 1 million people employed in personnel supply services; this alone amounts to 8 percent of total producer service employment. In Sweden, this group would be much smaller and largely employed in the governmental labor-market board.

A similar logic pertains to most of the private-sector social-service employment, be it in health care, education, or elsewhere. The tax structure, in combination with direct subsidies (in large part provided through the private insurance system), constitutes a massive system of service, and therefore also employment subsidization.

The role of the peculiar American welfare state is perhaps best identified with regard to the significant improvements in employment among women and Blacks. Whereas an institutional welfare state, such as that in Sweden, defines itself as directly obliged to furnish equal opportunities and guarantee employment, the American system's inherent preference is to encourage the market to adhere to such lofty ideals; hence the emergence of Affirmative Action and the Equal Opportunity Act, which strove to induce the education system and the job market to improve the chances of minorities.

Our findings suggest that the Equal Opportunity type of approach has worked quite well. Officially, of course, it only applies to companies or organizations with government contracts. Given the proliferation of defence contracts in the United States, this is likely to be a fair number, but probably not large enough to account for the trends we have seen. We can therefore surmise that other companies, as well, have adopted Affirmative Action, perhaps for image-reasons, perhaps because it has proven itself profitable.

In summary, one must interpret the egalitarian results of the American 'market model' with caution. Where government has intervened the least, as in the 'junk-job' sector, the results are not especially attractive; where it has intervened the most, as in the case of Affirmative Action or Equal Opportunity regulation, the egalitarian impulse has been noticeable.

Stratification and Conflict in Post-Industrial Society

To study social stratification is to identify potential conflict-structures. The first generation of post-industrial theorists debated two possible scenarios: one, a general de-skilling and proletarianization; another, a process of professional upgrading with a diminishing bottom of menial jobs. In either case, they believed in convergence.

Our approach to the stratification aspects of post-industrial employment has been little more than tentative, yet it points to the emergence of three unique configurations that are more than likely to produce qualitatively different conflict-structures.

At first glance, Sweden, with its remarkable degree of professionalization and simultaneous reduction of poor jobs, seems to confirm the optimistic scenario. But closer up, the system is severely gender-segmented along the public–private sector axis. It is of course not preordained that such gender-ghettoization will result in a conflict axis, but if we recall the Achilles' heel of the system, the likelihood of a serious gender/sector-based conflict is high.

To sustain and expand welfare-state employment, government is compelled to ask for wage moderation among public employees. In Sweden, the centralized solidarity-wage policy implies that such wage moderation will have to be spread across the entire economy. It is the latter which is proving impossible and, as a result, the most serious conflicts (including major strikes) in the Swedish labor market have, throughout the 1980s, occurred between public- and private-sector trade unions. In this sense, one might easily imagine a war between (largely) male workers in the private sector and (largely) female workers in the welfare state. If this, indeed, is a likely outcome, Swedish social democracy can only hope that the bonds of marriage are strong enough to weather the storm of economic warfare.

German post-industrialism is one with jobless growth. Instead of creating new dimensions of stratification between job-classes or employment sectors, a variant of the 'insider–outsider' phenomenon seems the most likely divide to evolve. In the economic literature, the insider–outsider problem is defined as a situation in which collective negotiations are conducted solely on behalf of those with jobs, pursuing wage maximization at the expense of job expansion for the outsiders. Stretching this definition a little, this is the axis which seems best to fit the German trajectory. As part of an implicit accord between business, trade unions, and government, Germany's response to de-industrialization was to shed manpower through retirement and unemployment programs, and by encouraging guest workers to return. This, of course, resulted in a much slimmer workforce and enhanced productivity. With the additional lack of incentives for female labor-supply, the result is a diminishing yet highly productive workforce supporting a growing but unproductive outsider population. In Germany, the inactive population is 60 percent; in Sweden, only 49 percent, and this is not because Germany has more old people than Sweden.

To support housewives, male earners must rely on high net take-home pay; to support the welfare-state clientele, the employed will have to pay heavy taxes. And this is where the greatest potential for a conflict-axis appears. One side of the insider–outsider problem is that entry into jobs is made inaccessible to the outsiders. As van Parijs (1987) suggests, when jobs become scarce goods, they take on the character of an asset, of which the have-nots will feel deprived.

The other side of the insider–outsider axis is potentially more explosive. When a shrinking active labor force is compelled to shoulder the costs of a swelling human surplus, there is the likelihood of rising tax-resentments, especially since the transfers are so clearly from the productive to the non-productive segment of society. A parallel possibility is a surge in antagonistic and discriminatory behavior towards foreign workers, who will easily be identified as unwelcome welfare scroungers or as job-thieves. The German trajectory risks, therefore, a double-sided conflict where the classes are defined in terms of being job-holders or outsiders.

In the United States, finally, post-industrial conflict-axes are less easily discernible. To be sure, there is a polarization of the service economy around a distinct job-dualism where not only the quality of work but also wages and benefits are highly unequal, much more so than in other countries. A real proletarianization-effect may be the outcome if the 'junk-job' bias of the 1980s becomes a long-run trend. At the low end of the American service economy, wages are close to poverty-level, and fringe benefits almost non-existent.

The question boils down to the allocation mechanism in the employment structure. Clearly, minorities continue to be over-represented at the bottom, yet this is changing rapidly, and there is no question that job distribution has become more equal, both between sexes and among races. Based on our rather limited empirical evidence, we can in fact envisage three entirely different outcomes. The first is that Hispanics, and perhaps other recent immigrant populations, are becoming the new post-industrial proletariat, manning the undesirable end of the labor market. In this case, we would expect an essentially ethnicity-based dualism. This scenario, however, is not very credible. It is evident that Blacks are experiencing substantial upward mobility, but it is also clear that they remain locked into sub-standard jobs.

A second, and more realistic, scenario is that class differences will diminish between the sexes and races, but increase within them. In the traditional industrial economy, it was clear that the American dualism was heavily overlaid with gender and racial segmentation. But the coincidence of being Black, female, and imprisoned in sub-standard jobs is being reversed. As women and Blacks are becoming more fully integrated into the prevailing class structure, the likelihood is that class differences will crystallize more sharply within the various minority groups. As some women become yuppies and some Blacks become bourgeois, the women and Blacks left behind will experience much more keenly the phenomenon of relative deprivation.

The third possibility is clearly the most optimistic for the American post-industrial future. In the first and second version, we more or less assume that the problematic 'junk-job' sector is a dead-end job ghetto from which, having once entered, it is difficult to escape. If, instead, the huge bottom end of the American service economy were mainly a stepping-stone, or way-station, for youth and recent immigrants, our conclusions would have to be different. To verify this hypothesis, we need micro-data with detailed work-histories in order to identify the percentage of persons who remain or escape from poor jobs. It is, nonetheless, indicative that 25 percent of all persons engaged in food-service jobs are between the ages 16 and 20 (Bureau of Labor Statistics, 1987; table D 20).

A final conclusion for the kind of study we have conducted here is clearly not possible. Sweden, Germany, and the United States may very well be heading towards three diverse 'post-industrial' welfare-capitalist models. The conflict-scenarios that we have sketched here may solidify into lasting structural features. But then, it is also possible that events will occur or changes will be introduced that fundamentally alter the course on which these nations now seem to be headed.

This study has been conducted in a period of flux, and its conclusions must accordingly remain open-ended. Hence, it is my hope that this book not be regarded as a more or less failed attempt at forecasting. Its goal was not to theorize the future, but to suggest one way in which we may fruitfully analyze contemporary change.

References

Aaron, H. and Burtless, G. (eds) 1984: *Retirement and Economic Behavior.* Washington, DC: The Brookings Institute.

Alber, J. 1982: *Von Armenhaus zum Wohlfahrsstaat.* Frankfurt: Campus Verlag.

Ashford, D. 1986: *The Emergence of the Welfare State.* Oxford: Basil Blackwell.

Ball, R. 1978: *Social Security.* New York: Columbia University Press.

Baron, J. 1984: Organizational perspectives on stratification. *Annual Review of Sociology,* 10.

Baron, J. and Bielby, W. 1980: Bringing the firm back in: stratification, segmentation and the organization of work. *American Sociological Review,* 45.

Bauer, O. 1919: *Der Weg zum Sozialismus.* Vienna: Volksbuchhandlung.

Baumol, W. 1967: The macroeconomics of unbalanced growth. *American Economic Review,* 57.

Beer, S. 1966: *British Politics in the Collectivist Age.* New York: Knopf.

Bell, D. 1973: *The Coming of Post-Industrial Society.* New York: Basic Books.

Bell, D. 1978: *The Cultural Contradictions of Modern Capitalism.* New York: Basic Books.

Bendix, R. 1964: *Nation-Building and Citizenship.* New York: John Wiley and Sons.

Berg, I (ed.) 1981: *Sociological Perspectives on Labor Markets.* New York: Academic Press.

Bernstein, E. 1961: *Evolutionary Socialism* (1898). New York: Schocken.

Bielby, W. T. and Baron, J. N. 1986: Men and women at work: sex segregation and statistical discrimination. *American Journal of Sociology,* 91, 759–99.

Black, D. and Myles, J. 1986: Dependent industrialization and the Canadian class structure: a comparative analysis of Canada, the United States and Sweden. *Canadian Review of Sociology and Anthropology,* 23 (2).

Blanchard, O., Dornbush, R., and Layard, R. (eds) 1986: *Restoring Europe's Prosperity.* Cambridge, Mass.: MIT Press.

Blau, P. M. and Duncan, O. D. 1967: *The American Occupational Structure*. New York: John Wiley and Sons.

Block, F. 1977: The ruling class does not rule. *Socialist Review*, 7 (May–June).

Block, F. 1985: Postindustrial development and the obsolescence of economic categories. *Politics and Society*, 14 (1).

Bluestone, B. and Harrison, B. 1986: *The Great American Job Machine: The Proliferation of Low Wage Employment in the US Economy*. Study prepared for the Joint Economic Committee, Washington, DC.

Blundell, R. and Walker, I. 1988: The changing structure of the labour force: married women and lone parents. Paper presented at the Symposium on Population Change and European Society, European University Institute, Florence (December).

Bordogna, L. 1981: The political business cycle and the crisis of Keynesian politics. Paper presented at the American Sociological Meetings, Toronto (August).

Boskin, M. and Hurd, M. 1978: The effect of social security on early retirement. *Journal of Political Economy*, 10.

Bower, R. H. 1947: *German Theories of the Corporate State*. New York: Russel and Russel.

Bowles, S. and Gintis, H. 1986: *Democracy and Capitalism*. New York: Basic Books.

Brandes, S. D. 1976: *American Welfare Capitalism 1880–1940*. Chicago, Ill.: University of Chicago Press.

Braun, D. and Keman, H. 1986: Politikstrategien und Konfliktregulierung in den Niederlanden. *Politischen Vierteljahresschrifte*, 27 (1).

Braverman, H. 1974: *Labor and Monopoly Capital: The Degredation of Work in the Twentieth Century*. New York: Monthly Review Press.

Break, G. F. 1980: The role of government: taxes, transfers and spending. In M. Felstein (ed.), *The American Economy in Transition*. Chicago, Ill.: University of Chicago Press.

Briggs, A. 1961: The welfare state in historical perspective. *European Journal of Sociology*, 2, 221–58.

Brown, J. and Small, S. 1985: *Occupational Benefits as Social Security*. London: Policy Studies Institute.

Browning, H. and Singelmann, J. 1975: *The Emergence of a Service Society: Demographic and Sociological Aspects of the Sectoral Transformation of the Labor Force in the USA*. Springfield, Va.: National Technical Information Service.

Bruno, M. and Sachs, J. 1985: *The Economics of Worldwide Stagflation*. Cambridge, Mass.: Harvard University Press.

Bureau of the Census (United States), 1976: *Statistical History of the United States*. New York: Basic Books.

Bureau of the Census (United States), 1986: *Statistical Abstract of the United States*. Washington, DC.: Government Printing Office.

Bureau of Labor Statistics, 1987: *Employment and Earnings*. Washington, DC.: Government Printing Office.

Cameron, D. 1978: The expansion of the public economy: a comparative analysis. *American Political Science Review*, 4.

Cameron, D. 1984: Social democracy, corporatism, labour quiescence and the representation of economic interest in advanced capitalist society. In J. Goldthorpe (ed.), *Order and Conflict in Contemporary Capitalism*, Oxford: Oxford University Press.

Cameron, D. 1987: Politics, public policy and distributional inequalities: a comparative analysis. Paper presented at the Tenth Annual Scientific Meeting of the International Society of Political Psychology, San Francisco, Ca. (July).

Castles, F. 1978: *The Social-Democratic Image of Society*. London: Routledge and Kegan Paul.

Castles, F. 1981: How does politics matter? Structure or agency in the determination of public policy outcomes. *European Journal of Political Research*, 9.

Castles, F. 1986: *Working Class and Welfare: Reflections on the Political Development of the Welfare State in Australia and New Zealand*. London: Allen and Unwin.

Castles, F. (ed.) 1982: *The Impact of Parties*. London: Sage.

Chandler, A. and Deams, D. (eds) 1980: *Managerial Hierarchies: Comparative Perspectives on the Rise of the Modern Industrial Enterprise*. Cambridge, Mass.: Harvard University Press.

Clark, C. 1940: *The Conditions of Economic Progress*. London: Macmillan.

Cohen, S. and Zysman, J. 1987: *Manufacturing Matters: The Myth of the Post-Industrial Economy*. New York: Basic Books.

Colbjornsen, T. 1986: *Dividers in the Labor Market*. Oslo: Norwegian University Press.

Cromton, R. 1986: Women and the 'service class'. In R. Cromton and M. Mann (eds), *Gender and Stratification*, Cambridge: Polity Press.

Crosland, C. A. R. 1967: *The Future of Socialism*. New York: Schocken.

Crouch, C. 1977: *Class Conflict and the Industrial Relations Crisis*. London: Heinemann.

Crouch, C. 1978: The intensification of industrial conflict in the United Kingdom. In C. Crouch and A. Pizzorno (eds), *The Resurgence of Class Conflict in Western Europe since 1968*. 2 vols. New York: Holmes and Meier.

Crouch, C. and Pizzorno, A. (eds) 1978: *The Resurgence of Class Conflict in Western Europe since 1968*. 2 vols. New York: Holmes and Meier.

Cusack, T., Notermans, T., and Rein, M. 1987: *Political and Economic Aspects of Public Employment*. Berlin: WZB Working Papers.

Cusack, T. and Rein, M. 1987: Social policy and service employment. Berlin: WZB Working Papers.

Cutright, P. 1965: Political structure, economic development, and national social security programs. *American Journal of Sociology*, 70: 537–50.

Cutright, P. 1967: Income redistribution: a cross-national analysis. *Social Forces*, 46, 180–90.

Danziger, S., Haveman, R., and Plotnik, R. 1981: How income transfers affect work, savings and income distribution. *Journal of Economic Literature*, 19.

Day, L. 1978: Government pensions for the aged in 19 industrialized countries. In R. Tomasson (ed.), *Comparative Studies in Sociology*, Greenwich, Conn.: JAI Press.

Derthick, M. 1979: *Policymaking for Social Security*. Washington, DC.: The Brookings Institute.

Diamond, P. and Hausman, J. 1984: The retirement and unemployment behavior of older men. In H. Aaron and G. Burtless (eds), *Retirement and Economic Behavior*. Washington, DC: The Brookings Institute.

Dich, J. 1973: *Den Herskende Klasse*. Copenhagen: Borgen.

Dobb, M. 1946: *Studies in the Development of Capitalism*. London: Routledge and Kegan Paul.

Downs, A. 1957: *An Economic Theory of Democracy*. New York: Harper and Row.

Edgren, G., Faxen, K. O., and Odhner, C. E. 1973: *Wage Formation and the Economy*. London: Allen and Unwin.

Elmer, A. 1960: *Folkpensioneringen i Sverige*. Lund, Sweden: Gleerup.

Erikson, R. and Aaberg, R. (eds) 1984: *Vaelfaerd i Foeraendring: Levnadsvillkor i Sverige 1968–1981*. Stockholm: Institutet foer social forskning.

Esping-Andersen, G. 1985a: *Politics against Markets*. Princeton, NJ.: Princeton University Press.

Espind-Andersen. G. 1985b: Power and distributional regimes. *Politics and Society*, 14.

Esping-Andersen, G. 1987a: Institutional accommodation to full employment. In H. Keman and H. Paloheimo (eds), *Coping with the Crisis*. London: Sage.

Esping-Andersen, G. 1987b: Citizenship and socialism: de-commodification and solidarity in the welfare state. In G. Esping-Andersen, M. Rein, and L. Rainwater (eds), *Stagnation and Renewal in Social Policy: The Rise and Fall of Policy Regimes*. Armonk, NY: M. E. Sharpe.

Esping-Andersen, G. and Friedland, R. 1982: Class coalitions in the making of West European economies. *Political Power and Social Theory*, 3.

Esping-Andersen, G. and Kolberg, J. O. 1989: Decommodification and work absence in the welfare state. *European University Institute Working Papers*, no. 367, Florence.

Esping-Andersen, G. and Korpi, W. 1984: Social policy as class politics in postwar capitalism. In J. Goldthorpe (ed.), *Order and Conflict in Contemporary Capitalism*. Oxford: Oxford University Press.

Esping-Andersen, G. and Korpi, W. 1986: From poor relief to institutional welfare states. In R. Erikson, E. J. Hansen, S. Ringen, and H. Uusitalo (eds), *The Scandinavian Model: Welfare States and Welfare Research*. Armonk, NY: M. E. Sharpe.

Esping-Andersen, G., Rein, M., and Rainwater, L. (eds) 1988: *Stagnation and Renewal in Social Policy: the Rise and Fall of Policy Regimes*. Armonk, NY: M. E. Sharpe.

Evans, E. 1978: *Social Policy, 1830–1914*. London: Routledge and Kegan Paul.

Fausto, D. 1978: *Il Sistema Italiano di Sicurezza Sociale*. Bologna: Il Mulino.

234 REFERENCES

Featherman, D. L. and Hauser, R. M. 1978: *Opportunity and Change*. New York: Academic Press.
Feldstein, M. 1974: Social security, induced retirement, and aggregate capital formation. *Journal of Political Economy*, 82.
Fisher, A. 1935: *The Clash of Progress and Security*. London: Macmillan.
Flanagan, R., Soskice, D., and Ulman, L. 1983: *Unionism, Economic Stabilization and Incomes Policies*. Washington, DC: The Brookings Institute.
Flora, P (ed.) 1986: *Growth to Limits: The Western European Welfare States since World War II*. Berlin: De Gruyter.
Flora, P. and Alber, J. 1981: Modernization, democratization and the development of welfare states in Europe. In P. Flora and A. Heidenheimer (eds), *The Development of Welfare States in Europe and America*. London: Transaction Books.
Fuchs, V. 1968: *The Service Economy*. New York: National Bureau of Economic Research.
Gershuny, J. 1978: *After Industrial Society: The Emerging Self-Servicing Economy*. London: Macmillan.
Gershuny, J. 1983: *Social Innovation and the Division of Labour*. Oxford University Press.
Gershuny, J. 1986: Time use, technology and the future of work. *Journal of the Market Research Society*, 28 (4), 335–54.
Gershuny, J. 1988: *The Social Economics of Post-Industrial Societies*. A report to the Joseph Rowntree Memorial Trust, University of Bath.
Giddens, A. 1985: *The Nation State and Violence*. Cambridge: Polity Press.
Gilbert, B. 1966: *The Evolution of National Insurance in Great Britain*. London: Michael Joseph.
Glyn, A. and Sutcliffe, R. 1972: *British Capitalism: Workers and the Profits Squeeze*. London: Penguin.
Goldin, C. 1987: Women's employment and technological change. In H. Hartman (ed.), *Computer Chips and Paper Clips: Technology and Women's Employment*. Washington, DC.: National Academy Press.
Goldthorpe, J. (ed.) 1984a: *Order and Conflict in Contemporary Capitalism*. Oxford: Oxford University Press.
Goldthorpe, J. 1984b: The end of convergence: corporatist and dualist tendencies in modern western societies. In J. Goldthorpe (ed.), *Order and Conflict in Contemporary Capitalism*. Oxford: Oxford University Press.
Goodman, C. 1986: Changing structures of retirement income in Canada. ISSA Meetings, Baltimore (May).
Gough, I. 1979: *The Political Economy of the Welfare State*. London: Macmillan.
Gourevitch, P. 1986: *Politics in Hard Times*. Ithaca, NY: Cornell University Press.
Graebner, W. 1980: *A History of Retirement*. New Haven, Conn.: Yale University Press.
Griffin, L. J., O'Connell, P. J., and McCammon, H. J. 1989: National variations in the context of struggle: post-war class conflict and market distribution in

the capitalist democracies. *Canadian Review of Sociology and Anthropology* (Spring).

Guillebaud, C. W. (1941: *The Social Policy of Nazi Germany*. Cambridge: Cambridge University Press.

Guillemard, A. 1980: *La Vieillesse et l'Etat*. Paris: Presses Universitaires.

Gustavsson, S. 1988: Cohort size and female labour supply. Paper presented at the Symposium on Population Change and European Society, European University Institute, Florence (December).

Haarr, A. 1982: *I Oljens Tegn*. Oslo: Tanum.

Hakim, C. 1979: Occupational segregation. Research paper no. 9. London: UK Department of Employment (November).

Hansen, E. J. 1988: *Generationer og Livsforloeb*. Copenhagen: Hans Reitzel.

Haveman, R., Wolfe, B., and Warlick, J. 1984: Disability transfers, early retirement and retirement. In H. Aaron and G. Burtless (eds), *Retirement and Economic Behavior*. Washington, DC: The Brookings Institute.

Hay, J. R. 1975: *The Origins of Liberal Reforms 1906–1914*. London: Macmillan.

Hedstrom, P. and Ringen, S. 1985: Age and income in contemporary society. Walferdange, Luxembourg: Luxembourg Income Study Working Papers.

Heimann, E. 1929: *Sociale Theorie der Kapitalismus*. Frankfurt: Suhrkamp, rpt 1980.

Hewitt, C. 1977: The effect of political democracy and social democracy on equality in industrial societies. *American Sociological Review*, 42.

Hibbs, D. 1977: Political parties and macroeconomic policy. *American Political Science Review*, 71.

Hicks, A. 1988: Social democratic corporatism and economic growth. *Journal of Politics*, 50, (3), 677–704.

Higgins, W. and Apple, N. 1981: *Class Mobilisation and Economic Policy: Struggles over Full Employment in Britain and Sweden, 1930–80*. Stockholm: Arbetslivcentrum.

Hirsch, F. 1976: *Social Limits to Growth*. Cambridge, Mass.: Harvard University Press.

Hirsch, F. and Goldthorpe, J. (eds) 1978: *The Political Economy of Inflation*. Oxford: Martin Robertson.

Hurd, M. and Boskin, M. 1981: The effect of social security on retirement in the early 1970s. *National Bureau of Economic Research Working Paper*, no. 659.

Ingelhart, R. 1977: *The Silent Revolution*. Princeton, NJ.: Princeton University Press.

Jackson, P. 1977: The philosophical basis of the private pension movement. In D. M. McGill (ed.), *Social Security and Private Pension Plans*. Homewood, Ill.: Irwin Press.

Jacobs, J. A. and Breiger, R. L. forthcoming: Careers, industries and occupations: industrial segmentation reconsidered. In P. England and G. Farkas (eds), *Industries, Firms and Jobs: Sociological and Economic Approaches*. New York: Plenum.

Jantz, K. 1961: Pension reform in the Federal Republic of Germany. *International Labour Review* (February).

Jencks, C. *et al.* 1982: *Inequality*. New York: Basic Books.

Jessop, B. 1982: *The Capitalist State*. Oxford: Martin Robertson.

Kalecki, M. 1943: Political aspects of full employment. *Political Quarterly*, 14.

Katzenstein, P. 1985: *Small States in World Markets*. Ithaca, NY: Cornell University Press.

Kautsky, K. 1971: *The Class Struggle* (1982). New York: Norton.

Kenneth Hansen, F. 1987: Redistribution of income in Denmark. In R. Erikson, E. J. Hansen, S. Ringen, and H. Uusitalo (eds), *The Scandinavian Model: Welfare States and Welfare Research*. Armonk, NY: M. E. Sharpe.

King, F. 1978: The future of private and public employee pensions. In B. R. Herzog (ed.), *Aging and Income*. New York: Human Sciences Press.

Klein, R. 1985: Public expenditure in an inflationary world. In L. Lindberg and C. A. Maier (eds), *The Politics of Inflation and Economic Stagnation*. Washington, DC: The Brookings Institute.

Kocka, J. 1981: Class formation, interest articulation, and public policy: the origins of the German white-collar class in the late nineteenth and early twentieth centuries. In S. Berger (ed.), *Organizing Interests in Western Europe: Pluralism, Corporatism and the Transformation of Politics*. Cambridge: Cambridge University Press.

Korpi, W. 1980: Social policy and distributional conflict in the capitalist democracies. *West European Politics*, 3.

Korpi, W. 1983: *The Democratic Class Struggle*. London: Routledge and Kegan Paul.

Korpi, W. 1987: Class, power and state autonomy in welfare state development. Stockholm: Swedish Institute for Social Research Reprint Series.

Korpi, W. 1988: The politics of employment policy: a comparative study of unemployment insurance, unemployment and active labor market policy in 18 OECD countries. Paper prepared for the workshop of the ISA Research Committee on Poverty, Social Welfare and Social Policy, Stockholm (August).

Kraus, F. 1981: The historical development of income inequality in Western Europe and the United States. In P. Flora and A. Heidenheimer (eds), *The Development of Welfare States in Europe and America*. London: Transaction Books.

Kuhnle, S. and Solheim, L. 1981: Party programs and the welfare state: consensus and conflict in Norway, 1945–1977. Paper presented at the European Consortium for Political Research Joint Sessions, Lancaster.

Kuttner, B. 1983: The declining middle. *Atlantic Monthly* (July), 60–72.

Kuznets, S. 1957: Quantitative aspects of the economic growth of nations II: industrial distribution of national product and labor force. *Economic Development and Cultural Change*, 5 (July), Supplement.

Lange, P. 1984: Unions, workers and wage regulation: the rational bases of consent. In J. Goldthorpe (ed.), *Order and Conflict in Contemporary Capitalism*. Oxford: Oxford University Press.

Lange, P. and Vanicelli, M. 1979: From marginality to centrality: Italian unionism in the 1970s. Paper presented at the Annual APSA Meetings, Washington, DC.

Latimer, M. 1932: *Industrial Pension Systems in the United States and Canada*. New York: Industrial Relations Councelors.

Lawrence, R. 1985: The middle class is alive and well. *The New York Times*, June 23.

Lederer, E. and Marshack, J. 1926: *Arbeiterschutz. Grundriss der Sozialoekonomik*, 9. Tubingen: Mohr.

Le Grand, J. 1982: *The Strategy of Equality: Redistribution and the Social Services*. London: Allen and Unwin.

Lehmbruch, G. 1984: Concertation and the structure of corporatist networks. In J. Goldthorpe (ed.), *Order and Conflict in Contemporary Capitalism*. Oxford: Oxford University Press.

Leo XIII 1891: *Rerum Novarum*. Papal Encyclical. Vatican City.

Lindbeck, A. 1981: *Work Disincentives in the Welfare State*. Stockholm: Institute for International Economic Studies, University of Stockholm Reprint Series no. 176.

Lindbeck, A. and Snower, D. 1984: Involuntary unemployment as an insider–outsider dilemma. Stockholm: Institute for International Economic Studies, Seminar Paper no. 282.

Lindberg, L. and Meier, C. (eds) 1985: *The Politics of Inflation and Economic Stagnation*. Washington, DC: The Brookings Institute.

Lindblom, C. 1977: *Politics and Markets*. New York: Basic Books.

Lipset, S. M. 1960: *Political Man*. New York: Doubleday, Anchor.

Maddison, A. 1982: *Phases of Capitalist Development*. Oxford: Oxford University Press.

Marshall, A. 1920: *Principles of Economics* (1890). 8th edn. London: Macmillan.

Marshall. T. H. 1950: *Citizenship and Social Class*. Cambridge: Cambridge University Press.

Martin, A. 1981: Economic stagnation and social stalemate in Sweden. In US Congress, Joint Economic Committee, *Monetary Policy, Selective Credit Policy, and Industrial Policy in France, Britain, West Germany, and Sweden*. Washington, DC: Government Printing Office.

Martin, A. 1985: Wages, profits and investment in Sweden. In L. Lindberg and C. Maier (eds), *The Politics of Inflation and Economic Stagnation*. Washington, DC: The Brookings Institute.

Marx, K. 1954–6: *Capital*. London: Lawrence and Wishart.

Melman, S. 1951: *The Rise of Administrative Overhead in the Manufacturing Industries of the United States, 1899–1947*. Oxford: Oxford University Press.

Messner, J. 1964: *Die Soziale Frage in Blickfeld der Irrwege von Gestern, die Sozialkaempfe von Heute, die Weltenscheidungen von Morgen*. Innsbruck: Tyrolia Verlag.

Mueller-Jentsch, W. and Sperling, H. J. 1978: Economic development, labour conflicts and the industrial relations system in West Germany. In C. Crouch and A. Pizzorno (eds), *The Resurgence of Class Conflict in Western Europe since 1968*, 2 vols. New York: Holmes and Meier.

Muller, W. and Neussuss, C. 1973: The illusion of state socialism and the contradiction between wage labor and capital. *Telos*, 25 (Fall).

Munnell, A. 1982: *The Economics of Private Pensions*. Washington, DC: The Brookings Institute.

Myles, J. 1984a: *Old Age in the Welfare State*. Boston: Little, Brown.

Myles, J. 1984b: Does class matter? Explaining America's welfare state. Paper presented at the Center for the Study of Industrial Societies, University of Chicago (November).

Myles, J., Picot, G., and Wannell, T. 1988: *Wages and Jobs in the 80s: The Declining Middle in Canada*. Ottawa: Statistics Canada.

Myrdal, A. and Myrdal, G. 1936: *Kris i Befolkningsfraagan*. Stockholm: Tiden.

Neumann, L. and Schapter, K. 1982: *Die Sozialordnung der Bundesrepublik Deutschland*. Frankfurt: Campus Verlag.

Nordhaus, W. 1974: The falling share of profits. In *Brookings Papers on Economic Activity*, 1. Washington, DC: The Brookings Institute.

O'Connor, J. 1973: *The Fiscal Crisis of the State*. New York: St Martin's Press.

OECD 1977: *Old Age Pension Schemes*. Paris: OECD.

OECD 1983: *Employment Outlook*. Paris: OECD.

OECD 1984a: *Tax Expenditures*. Paris: OECD.

OECD 1984b: *Employment Outlook*. Paris: OECD.

OECD 1985: *Sweden – Economic Survey*. Paris: OECD.

Offe, C. 1972: Advanced capitalism and the welfare state. *Politics and Society*, 4.

Offe, C. 1984: *Contradictions of the Welfare State*. London: Hutchinson.

Offe, C. 1985: *Disorganized Capitalism*. Cambridge, Mass.: MIT Press.

Ogus, A. 1979: Social insurance, legal development and legal history. In H. F. Zacher, (ed.), *Bedingungen fur die Entstehung von Sozialversicherung*. Berlin: Duncker und Humboldt.

O'Higgins, M. 1985: Inequality, redistribution and recession: the British experience, 1976–1982. *Journal of Social Policy*, 14 (3).

Okun, A. 1975: *Equality and Efficiency: The Big Trade-Off*. Washington, DC: The Brookings Institute.

Olson, M. 1982: *The Rise and Decline of Nations*. New Haven, Conn.: Yale University Press.

Otruba, G. 1981: Privatbeamten-, Handlungsgehilfen und Angestellten-organisationen. Ihr Betrag zur Entstehung des oesterreichisehen Angestell-tenpensionversicherung-gesetzes 1906. In J. Kocka (ed.), *Angestellte im Europaeischen Vergleich*. Gottingen: Vandenhoeck und Ruprecht.

Pampel, F. and Weiss, I. 1983: Economic development, pension policies, and the labor force participation of aged males. *American Journal of Sociology*, 89.

Pampel, F. C. and Williamson, J. B. 1985: Age structure, politics, and cross-national patterns of public pension expenditures. *American Sociological Review*, 50, 787–98.

Pampel, F. C. and Williamson, J. B. 1988: Welfare spending in advanced democracies, 1950–1980. *American Journal of Sociology*, 93 (6).

Panitch, L. 1980: Recent theorizations of corporatism: reflections on a growth industry. *British Journal of Sociology*, 31.

Parkin, F. 1979: *Marxism and Class Theory: A Bourgeois Critique*. London: Croom Helm.

Parsons, D. 1980: The decline of male labor force participation. *Journal of Political Economy*, 88.

Pelling, H. 1961: *The Origins of the Labour Party*. Oxford: Clarendon Press.

Perrin, G. 1969: Reflections on fifty years of social security. *International Labor Review*, 99.

Pius XI 1931: *Quadragesimo Anno*. Papal Encyclical. Vatican City.

Piven, F. F. and Cloward, R. A. 1971: *Regulating the Poor*. New York: Vintage.

Polanyi, K. 1944: *The Great Transformation*. New York: Rinehart.

Pomerehne, W. and Schneider, F. 1980: Unbalanced growth between public and private sectors. Paper presented at IIPF Conference, Jerusalem (August).

Poulantzas, N. 1973: *Political Power and Social Classes*. London: New Left Books.

Preller, L. 1949: *Socialpolitik in der Weimarer Republik*. Stuttgart: Mittelbach Verlag.

Preller, L. 1970: *Praxis und Probleme der Sozialpolitik*. Tubingen: J. C. Mohr.

Preusser, N. (ed.) 1982: *Armut und Sozialstaat, Vol. 3: Die Entwicklung des Systems der sozialen Sicherung 1870 bis 1945*. Munich, AG SPAK.

Pryor, F. 1969: *Public Expenditures in Communist and Capitalist Nations*. London: Allen and Unwin.

Przeworski A. 1980: Material bases of consent: politics and economics in a hegemonic system. *Political Power and Social Theory*, 1.

Przeworski, A. 1985: *Capitalism and Social Democracy*. Cambridge: Cambridge University Press.

Quadagno, J. 1988: *The Transformation of Old Age Security*. Chicago, Ill.: University of Chicago Press.

Rasmussen, E. 1933: Socialdemokratiets Stilling til det Sociale Sporgsmaal, 1890–1901. In P. Engelsoft and H. Jensen (eds), *Maend og Meninger i Dansk Socialpolitik 1866–1901*. Copenhagen: Nordisk Forlag.

Regini, M. 1984: The conditions for political exchange: how concertation emerged and collapsed in Italy and Great Britain. In J. Goldthorpe (ed.), *Order and Conflict in Contemporary Capitalism*. Oxford: Oxford University Press.

Rein, M. 1982: Pension policies in Europe and the United States. Paper presented at the Conference on Social Welfare and the Delivery of Social Services, Berkeley, Ca. (November).

Rein, M. 1985: *Women in the Social Welfare Labor Market*. Berlin: WZB Working Papers.

Rein, M. and Rainwater, L. (eds) 1986: *Public–private Interplay in Social Protection: a Comparative Study*. Armonk, NY: M. E. Sharpe.

Rein, M. and Rainwater, L. 1987: From welfare state to welfare society. In G. Esping-Andersen, M. Rein, and L. Rainwater (eds), *Stagnation and Renewal in Social Policy: The Rise and Fall of Policy Regimes.* Armonk, NY: M. E. Sharpe.

Richter, E. 1987: Subsidariataet und Neokonservatismus. Die Trennung von politischer Herrschaftsbegruendung und gesellschaftlichem Stufenbau. *Politische Vierteljahresschrift,* 28 (3), 293–314.

Rimlinger, G. 1971: *Welfare Policy and Industrialization in Europe, America and Russia.* New York: John Wiley and Sons.

Rimlinger, G. 1987: Social policy under German Fascism. In G. Esping-Andersen, M. Rein, and L. Rainwater (eds), *Stagnation and Renewal: The Rise and Fall of Policy Regimes.* Armonk, NY: M. E. Sharpe.

Ringen, S. 1987: *The Politics of Possibility: a Study in the Political Economy of the Welfare State.* Oxford: Clarendon Press.

Ringen, S. and Uusitalo, H. forthcoming 1990: Income distribution and redistribution in the Nordic Welfare States. In J. E. Kolberg (ed.), *Comparing Welfare States and Labour Markets: The Scandinavian Model.* Armonk, NY: M. E. Sharpe.

Robbins, L. 1976: *Political Economy Past and Present.* London: Macmillan.

Rokkan, S. 1970: *Citizens, Elections, Parties.* Oslo: Universitetsforlaget.

Rosenfeld, R. A. 1980: Race and sex differences in career dynamics. *American Sociological Review,* 45, 583–609.

Sachs, J. 1979: Wages, profits and macroeconomic adjustment: a comparative study. In *Brookings Papers on Economic Activity,* 2. Washington, DC: The Brookings Institute.

SAF 1976: *Wages and Total Labour Costs for Workers, 1965–75.* Stockholm: SAF.

SAF 1984: *Wages and Total Labour Costs for Workers, 1972–82.* Stockholm: SAF.

Salowski, H. 1980: *Individuelle Fehlzeiten in Westlichen Industrielaendern.* Cologne: DIV.

Salowski, H. 1983: *Fehlzeiten.* Cologne: DIV.

Sawyer, M. 1976: *Income Distribution in OECD Countries.* Paris, OECD.

Sawyer, M. 1982: Income distribution and the welfare state. In A. Boetho (ed.), *The European Economy,* Oxford: Oxford University Press.

Schmidt, M. 1982: The role of parties in shaping macro-economic policies. In F. Castles (ed.), *The Impact of Parties.* London: Sage.

Schmidt, M. 1983: The welfare state and the economy in periods of economic crisis. *European Journal of Political Research,* 11.

Schmidt, M. 1987: The politics of labour market policy. In F. Castles, F, Lehrer, and M. Schmidt (eds), *The Political Management of Mixed Economies.* Berlin: De Gruyter.

Schmitter, P. 1981: Interest intermediation and regime governability in contemporary Western Europe and North America. In S. Berger (ed.), *Organizing Interests in Western Europe.* Cambridge: Cambridge University Press.

Schmitter, P. and Lembruch, G. (eds) 1979: *Trends towards Corporatist Intermediation*. London: Sage.

Schumpeter, J. 1954: *History of Economic Analysis*. New York: Oxford University Press.

Schumpeter, J. 1970: *Capitalism, Socialism and Democracy* (1944). London: Allen and Unwin.

Shalev, M. 1983: The social-democratic model and beyond. *Comparative Social Research*, 6.

Sharpf, F. 1985: Beschaeftigungspolitische Strategien in der Krise. *Leviathan*, 13.

Shonfield, A. 1965: *Modern Capitalism*. Oxford: Oxford University Press.

Shore, J. and Bowles, S. 1984: The cost of labor loss and the incidence of strikes. Unpublished paper, Cambridge, Mass.: Harvard University Department of Economics.

Singelmann, J. 1974: *The Sectoral Transformation of the Labor Force in Seven Industrialized Countries, 1920–1960*. Ph.D. thesis, University of Texas.

Singelmann, J. 1978: The sectoral transformation of the labor force in seven industrialized countries, 1920–1970. *American Journal of Sociology*, 83 (5).

Skocpol, T. 1987: The limits of the American New Deal. In G. Esping-Andersen, M. Rein, and L. Rainwater (eds), *Stagnation and Renewal in Social Policy: The Rise and Fall of Policy Regimes*. Armonk, NY: M. E. Sharpe.

Skocpol, T. and Amenta, E. 1986: States and social policies. *Annual Review of Sociology*, 12.

Skocpol, T. and Ikenberry, J. 1983: The political formation of the American welfare state in historical and comparative perspective. *Comparative Social Research*, 6.

Skolnick, A. 1976: Twenty-five years of employee benefit plans. *Social Security Bulletin*, 39 (3).

Smeeding, T., Torrey, B., and Rein, M. 1988: Patterns of income and poverty: the economic status of children and the elderly in eight countries. In J. Palmer, T. Smeeding, and B. Torrey (eds), *The Vulnerable*. Washington, DC: The Urban Institute Press.

Smith, A. 1961: *The Wealth of Nations* (1776). Ed. E. Cannan. London: Methuen.

Soete, L. and Freeman, C. 1985: New technologies, investment and employment growth. In *Employment Growth and Structural Change*. Paris: OECD.

Statistisches Bundesamt (West Germany) 1972: *Bevoelkerung und Wirtschaft VGR*. Stuttgart: Kohlhammer.

Statistisches Bundesamt (West Germany) 1982: *Statistisches Jahrbuch fuer die Bundesrepublik Deutschland*. Stuttgart: Kohlhammer.

Stephens, J. 1979: *The Transition from Capitalism to Socialism*. London: Macmillan.

Therborn, G. 1978: *What Does the Ruling Class Do When It Rules?* London: New Left Books.

Therborn, G. 1983: When, how and why does a welfare state become a welfare state? Paper presented at the ECPR Workshops, Freiburg (March).

Therborn, G. 1986a: Karl Marx returning: the welfare state and neo-Marxist, corporatist and statist theories. *International Political Science Review*, 7.

Therborn, G. 1986b: *Why Some People are More Unemployed than Others – The Strange Paradox of Growth and Unemployment*. London: Verso.

Titmuss, R. 1958: *Essays on the Welfare State*. London: Allen and Unwin.

Titmuss, R. 1974: *Social Policy*. London: Allen and Unwin.

Touraine, A. 1971: *Post-Industrial Society*. New York: Random House.

Tufte, E. 1978: *Political Control of the Economy*. Princeton, NJ: Princeton University Press.

Ulman, L. and Flanagan, R. 1971: *Wage Restraint: A Study of Incomes Policies in Western Europe*. Berkeley: University of California Press.

United Nations Statistics Office 1949: *United Nations Demographic Yearbook*. New York: United Nations.

Uusitalo, H. 1984: Comparative research on the determinants of the welfare state: the state of the art. *European Journal of Political Research*, 12.

Van Parijs, P. 1987: A revolution in class theory. *Politics and Society*, 15 (4).

Vestero-Jensen, C. 1984: *Det Tve-delte Pensionssystem*. Roskilde: RVC.

Viby Morgensen, G. 1973: *Socialhistorie*. Copenhagen: Akademisk Forlag.

Von Balluseck, H. 1983: Origins and trends of social policy for the aged in the Federal Republic of Germany. In A. Guillemard (ed.), *Old Age and the Welfare State*. London: Sage.

Wagner, A. 1872: *Rede ueber die Soziale Frage*. Berlin: Wiegandt und Grieben.

Wagner, A. 1962: Finanzwissenschaft (1883), reproduced partly in R. A. Musgrave and A. Peacock (eds), *Classics in the Theory of Public Finance*. London: Macmillan.

Weaver, C. 1982: *The Crisis in Social Security*. Durham, NC: Duke University Press.

Weinstein, J. 1972: *The Corporate Ideal in the Liberal State 1900–1918*. Boston, Mass.: Beacon Press.

Weir, M. and Skocpol, T. 1985: State structures and the possibilities for 'Keynesian' responses to the Great Depression in Sweden, Britain, and the United States. In P. Evans, P. Rushemayer, and T. Skocpol (eds), *Bringing the State Back In*. New York: Cambridge University Press.

Weir, M., Orloff, A. S., and Skocpol, T. 1988: *The Politics of Social Policy in the United States*. Princeton, NJ: Princeton University Press.

Weisskopf, T. 1985: Worker security and productivity growth: an international comparative analysis. Unpublished paper, Department of Economics, University of Michigan, (July).

Wilensky, H. 1975: *The Welfare State and Equality*. Berkeley: University of California Press.

Wilensky, H. 1981: Leftism, Catholicism and democratic corporatism. In P. Flora and A. Heidenheimer (eds), *The Development of Welfare States in Europe and America*. London: Transaction Books.

Wilensky, H. 1987: Comparative social policy: theories, methods, findings. In

M. Dierkes and A. Antal (eds), *Comparative Policy Research: Learning from Experience*. Aldershot: Gower.

Wilensky, H. and Lebeaux, C. 1958: *Industrial Society and Social Welfare*. New York: Russel Sage.

Wilensky, H. *et al* 1985: *Comparative Social Policy: Theory, Methods, Findings*. Berkeley, Ca.: International Studies Research Series, 62.

Index